10 THINGS EMPLOYERS WANT YOU TO LEARN IN COLLEGE

10 THINGS EMPLOYERS WANT YOU TO LEARN IN COLLEGE

THE **KNOW-HOW** YOU NEED TO SUCCEED

BILL COPLIN

TEN SPEED PRESS
BERKELEY/TORONTO

Ten Speed Press
P.O. Box 7123
Berkeley, California 94707
www.tenspeed.com

Distributed in Australia by Simon & Schuster Australia, in Canada by Ten Speed Press Canada, in New Zealand by Southern Publishers Group, in South Africa by Real Books, and in the United Kingdom and Europe by Airlift Book Company.

Cover and book design by Ed Anderson, SKOUT
Copyediting by Jean Blomquist

Library of Congress Cataloging-in-Publication Data

Coplin, William D.
  10 things employers want you to learn in college : the know-how you need to succeed / Bill Coplin.
      p. cm.
Includes index.
  ISBN 1-58008-524-5
  1. Career education—United States. 2. College student orientation—United States. 3. Career development—United States. I. Title: Ten things employers want you to learn in college : the know-how you need to succeed. II. Title.
  LC1037.5 .C68 2003
  378'.013—dc21
                                    2003004083

Printed in the United States
First printing, 2003

1 2 3 4 5 6 7 8 9 10 — 07 06 05 04 03

To the memory of

MICHAEL K. O'LEARY

for his support as a friend
and colleague

CONTENTS

X   ACKNOWLEDGMENTS

1   INTRODUCTION

7   **PART ONE: THE TEN KNOW-HOW GROUPS**
(PLUS EXTRA CREDIT)

8   **CHAPTER 1: ESTABLISHING A WORK ETHIC**
10   Kick Yourself in the Butt
13   Be Honest
15   Manage Your Time
17   Manage Your Money

20   **CHAPTER 2: DEVELOPING PHYSICAL SKILLS**
22   Stay Well
24   Look Good
26   Type 35 WPM Error Free
28   Take Legible Notes

30   **CHAPTER 3: COMMUNICATING VERBALLY**
32   Converse One-on-One
34   Present to Groups
37   Use Visual Displays

40   **CHAPTER 4: COMMUNICATING IN WRITING**
42   Write Well
44   Edit and Proof
46   Use Word-Processing Tools
48   Send Information Electronically

52   **CHAPTER 5: WORKING DIRECTLY WITH PEOPLE**
54   Build Good Relationships
55   Work in Teams
58   Teach Others

60   **CHAPTER 6: INFLUENCING PEOPLE**

62   Manage Efficiently

63   Sell Successfully

66   Politick Wisely

69   Lead Effectively

72   **CHAPTER 7: GATHERING INFORMATION**

74   Use Library Holdings

76   Use Commercial Databases

77   Search the Web

79   Conduct Interviews

81   Use Surveys

82   Keep and Use Records

84   **CHAPTER 8: USING QUANTITATIVE TOOLS**

86   Use Numbers

88   Use Graphs and Tables

89   Use Spreadsheet Programs

92   **CHAPTER 9: ASKING AND ANSWERING THE RIGHT QUESTIONS**

94   Detect BS

97   Pay Attention to Detail

99   Apply Knowledge

102   Evaluate Actions and Policies

106   **CHAPTER 10: SOLVING PROBLEMS**

108   Identify Problems

110   Develop Solutions

112   Launch Solutions

116   **CHAPTER 11: EARNING EXTRA CREDIT FOR YOUR KNOW-HOW SCORE**

118   Gain Software Expertise beyond Microsoft Word and Excel

119   Master In-Depth Knowledge of Any Field

120   Accent Foreign Language Skills

121   Emphasize Artistic and Music Knowledge and/or Skill

121   Stress Sports Skills

122   Pursue Pleasure Activities

125 **PART TWO: BOOSTING YOUR KNOW-HOW SCORE**

126 **CHAPTER 12: MAKING KHS-FRIENDLY COLLEGE, PROGRAM, AND COURSE CHOICES**
129 Choose a College
139 Choose a Program
142 Select Courses
147 Find Connections

152 **CHAPTER 13: CREATING YOUR OWN APPRENTICESHIPS**
155 Explore Apprentice-Based Education
157 Build Your Base
164 Land Good Summer Jobs and Internships
169 Make the Most of Your Experiences

174 **CHAPTER 14: EXPLORING OFF-CAMPUS SEMESTERS**
176 Build Your KHS Off Campus
177 Weigh Overseas Experiences versus Experiences in the United States and Canada
181 Earn Credit for Course Work
183 Consider the Negatives
185 Find Programs

188 **CHAPTER 15: DOING WELL BY DOING GOOD DURING YOUR COLLEGE YEARS**
190 Build Your KHS by Volunteering
191 Value Volunteer Activities—Employers Do
191 Explore Careers
193 Cultivate Integrity

194 **CHAPTER 16: THINKING BEYOND COLLEGE**
196 Consider the Graduate Education Alternative
199 Explore the Profitable Alternative
201 Value the Do-Good Alternative
201 Build Your Postgraduate KHS

205 **PART THREE: PLANNING YOUR SUCCESS**

206 **CHAPTER 17: USING YOUR KHS TO EXPLORE PROFESSIONAL FIELDS**
208 Identify Your Professional Interests
209 Begin the Self-Reflection Process
212 Scan the Professions
215 Look at Specific Fields In-Depth to Find Skills
217 Apply What You Have Found to Your KHS

220 **CHAPTER 18: BUILDING YOUR SKILLS AGENDA**
222 Spend Time on Task
228 Plan for a High KHS
235 Develop a Model KHS Learning Plan

238 **CHAPTER 19: MOVING TOWARD A PERFECT KHS RESUME, COVER LETTER, AND INTERVIEW**
240 Select the Skills You Want to Emphasize
242 Present Each of the Ten Know-How Groups
247 Use Extra Credit
249 Capitalize on What You've Learned

253 **ENDNOTES**

255 **INDEX**

ACKNOWLEDGMENTS

This book benefited from the help of many students, alumni, and staff of Syracuse University. Dozens of students, particularly the fifteen in my fall freshman 2002 Honors class 101, reacted to an early draft, and several students provided significant editorial assistance. I deeply appreciate their contributions.

I would like to single out a few students who went beyond the expected. The first is Gina De Rosa, who started this book project with me in June 2002. She worked almost full time on it during the summer and contributed many hours during the fall semester despite her heavy schedule. She also presented herself as a case study in chapter 18. In addition, Cameron Goodman provided detailed critiques and suggestions. Sally Honecker spent her spare time at her summer job with a large financial institution interviewing more than fifteen officials of that company, which generated several quotes for the book and stimulated me to move forward. Susan Crandall and Matt Zarit did extensive research and provided some of the text for chapter 13 on getting and benefiting from internships. Jacob Eastham helped suggest artwork. Patrick and Gregg Hoyle, Zack Denfield, Sandra Derstine, Felicia Feinerman, Kim Gugino, Allison Johnson, Christiane LaBonte, Brian Landau, Stephanie Kessler, Nicole M. Leclaire, Carly Pass, Andrew Shinn, and Frank Shultz provided advice, critiqued the book, or conducted research for specific chapters.

Several alumni helped out their old professor by providing reactions and in several cases text that I quoted. They include Gwyneth Blevins, Sharon Ehm, Rebecca Holmes, Sarah Korf, Matt Marsh, John Mandyck, Lisa Mueller, and Gary Puddles.

Several Syracuse University staff members were very helpful. Mike Pasqualoni, who supported me in training my students to use the library and its electronic services, gave me excellent advice for chapter 7. Sue Shane of the Division of International Programs provided information and advice on overseas programs. Helen Murray, who heads the internship program, provided suggestions on the chapter on internships. Michael Cahill, Karen McGee, and Ann Phelps, who provide career counseling services on campus, introduced me to the latest developments in that field. Over the years, Michelle Walker, Angela Ward, and Carol Dwyer have provided insight into job readiness. Blaine Delancey, recorder for the College of Arts and Science, prepared some written material for chapter 9 and provided perspective on the history of liberal arts. Colonel Mark D. Perodeau of the

Air Force ROTC counseled me on the benefits and costs of the ROTC option. Catherine Smith of the Writing Program provided general comments on the book and specific comments on writing. David Smith, former dean of admissions and now vice president for enrollment management, provided detailed suggestions for the discussion of college selection in chapter 12. Chris Walsh, dean of financial aid, provided information on student debt. John Fiset provided suggestions and advice throughout the process.

Members of my family, especially Britt and Doug, provided advice and encouragement. Terry Simpson, a parent of one of my students, provided support and suggestions for references. Bill Rosenberg, a parent of a very successful alum, made several pointed suggestions for how to make the book more appealing to today's student. More than fifty parents met with me and provided reactions and encouragement. Steve Cohen, a high school principal in Patterson, New Jersey, provided invaluable suggestions.

I want to thank Grace Freedson, my agent, who hooked me up with Ten Speed, the best possible publisher; Brie Mazurek, my editor at Ten Speed, who worked with me in the development of the final manuscript and came up with many bright ideas; and Jean Blomquist, who did a wonderful job copyediting.

Finally, thanks to my wife, Vicki, who shares with me the value of education for a purpose. She provided inspiration for this book, kept me on task for details, and encouraged me to complete the manuscript.

All of these people were helpful, but I take full responsibility for what you are about to read.

"A COLLEGE DEGREE AND A DOLLAR WILL GET YOU FOUR QUARTERS."

—ANONYMOUS

If you are in college or intend to go to college, the single most irritating question that your family and others may ask you is this: "What are you going to do with your college degree?" This book will provide the answer: "I'm not just getting a degree. I'm developing the skills to succeed in whatever career I pursue, and when I finish my degree, I'll be able to prove that to my future employer—and you too!" If you master the skills presented in this book, you can make this statement confidently because you know you will accomplish much more in college than simply completing courses and getting a degree.

Both good news and bad news face all college students, which is why this annoying question is asked so often. In the face of unlimited opportunity (the good news) and a high degree of risk (the bad news), everyone gets anxious. Here's a quick overview of the good and bad news:

THE GOOD NEWS

- Over their work life, college graduates earn an average of $2.1 million dollars compared with $1.2 million dollars for high school graduates.
- Someone with a professional degree (M.D., J.D., or M.B.A., for example) will make $4.4 million.[1]

THE BAD NEWS

- 63 percent of students who begin a four-year college do not finish in four years, and 42 percent do not finish in six years.[2]
- 68 percent of graduating seniors in 2000 borrowed a mean average of $19,785.[3]
- 60 percent of college graduates plan to live with their parents after graduation.[4]

College is not a day on the beach that inevitably leads to a beautiful life. It's a risky business. Like any investment requiring a lot of up-front money, four years of college can have a very big downside. Even if you get a good job, you may have huge debts to pay off. Paying off those debts may take a long time. If that doesn't scare you, think about this possibility: you fail your courses, drop out after two years, and are saddled with $20,000 in debt. That's definitely bad news.

This book will keep you from becoming one of those "bad news" statistics. It will help you avoid those risks and disappointments and take advantage of the big payoffs that a college education can provide. Aside from luck and other uncontrollable factors—such as the state of the economy at the time you graduate or the status of the person you marry—the key to a successful career is what you can *do*. This book will describe the skills you need to acquire in order to convince a job recruiter to hire you, as well as the tools you need to master so employers will find you—and your work—invaluable. Knowing how to do what needs to be done is the key to success in your job and life—and that's what this book is all about.

MAKE THE BEST OF YOUR COLLEGE YEARS

Your college years can be some of the best years of your life. College is a place and time to make your family proud, party, get a credential, find a significant other, or grow up so people will take you seriously. College helps you discover yourself, learn your likes and dislikes, develop your mind and your love of learning, and build an undergraduate record so you can get into a professional school, if that's what you want to do.

But college should also prepare you for finding a good job and a rewarding career. Your college years can be a training period in which you develop your general skills in order to both get a great job right out of college or graduate school and succeed in the workplace. By taking advantage of the opportunities that college offers, you can build the base of skills you need not only to land your first job but also to excel at your first job. Once that happens, you will be on your way to a lifetime of rewarding work.

College can be a truly significant time in your life. That's why it's important to use this time well, including preparing yourself for a good job after you finish. Use your college years to gain and polish the skills necessary for a successful career. You'll be glad you did—and your employer will be too.

You may be thinking, "Well, skills may be nice, but won't prospective employers be looking at my GPA? Prospective employers look at your GPA as a measure of your persistence and your basic intelligence. However, according to the following table, which was published by the National Association of Colleges and Employers (NACE) in 2002 and reports the results of a survey of 457 employers in the United States, your GPA is far from the most important thing employers are looking for. In fact, it ranks seventeenth on a list of twenty. At the top of the list are communication skills, honesty, teamwork, interpersonal skills, and work ethic.

EMPLOYERS RATE THE IMPORTANCE OF CANDIDATE QUALITIES/SKILLS[5]

(based on a 5-point scale in which 1 = not important and 5 = extremely important)

Communication skills (verbal and written)	4.69
Honesty/integrity	4.59
Teamwork skills (works well with others)	4.54
Interpersonal skills (relates well to others)	4.50
Strong work ethic	4.46
Motivation/initiative	4.42
Flexibility/adaptability	4.41
Analytical skills	4.36
Computer skills	4.21
Organizational skills	4.05
Detail oriented	4.00
Leadership skills	3.97
Self-confidence	3.95
Friendly/outgoing personality	3.85
Well mannered/polite	3.82
Tactfulness	3.75
GPA (3.0 or better)	3.68
Creativity	3.59
Sense of humor	3.25
Entrepreneurial skills/risk-taker	3.23

In all fairness, your GPA does count for something—usually as an indicator of the skills it took to acquire it. A respectable GPA reflects some of the skills discussed in this book, especially under work ethic. It also measures how well you play the system by figuring out what your professors want and then delivering the goods. In some ways, meeting the standards of professors is similar to pleasing your boss. Your boss is not likely to ask you to fill up a blue book or take a multiple-choice test, but she or he will expect you to follow directions. For these reasons, you want to have a respectable GPA. A 3.0 is respectable in architecture, the physical sciences, and engineering, but a 3.2 is the bottom line in the social sciences, humanities, and some professional schools. However, while the GPA provides some information to employers, it is not nearly enough for them to make a judgment about your job potential. This was true before the days of grade inflation; it is doubly true today.

Your GPA alone is not a reliable indicator of your potential as an employee because your grades in courses do not reflect the range of skills that today's employers need. A very strong recommendation from your internship supervisor at a respected corporation about your people and problem-solving skills is much more important than a high GPA.

Demonstration of good word-processing and spreadsheet skills will get you your first job faster than a GPA of 3.6 and even a master's degree. Just as college admissions officers look beyond SAT scores when they make their admissions decisions, employers look for qualities beyond your GPA to make hiring decisions. Five years ago, one of my students was hired in the department of education for a northeastern state over several students who had master's degrees. Why? Because she knew how to use spreadsheets. The interviewer, who was looking for the spreadsheet skills, asked about pivot tables. The other applicants had no clue what those were, even though they listed Microsoft Excel on their resumes. They may have taken an introductory course, but they clearly did not have extensive experience using Excel. (Taking a course is like being told where the swimming pool is. It does not mean you know how to swim.) The spreadsheet maven, now high up in the administration doing policy work, directs others to do the spreadsheet work.

The emphasis on skills may seem like common sense to you, but when you get to college you will find that courses rarely focus primarily on skill development. In fact, employers have long complained about the poor preparation of most college students. According to a *New York Times* article, a "1999 report by the Business–Higher Education Forum condemned graduates for lack of skills in problem solving, time management, analytical thinking and basic writing and speaking."[6]

It is not that colleges don't provide opportunities for students to develop problem solving, time management, analytical thinking, and basic written and verbal communication skills. Rather, most college students do not know how to take advantage of those opportunities. This book will show you how to use your courses to build your skills in what I refer to as the ten "Know-How Groups." Let's take a brief look at those Know-How Groups now. (The chapters that follow will take a more detailed look at each group.)

THE TEN BASIC KNOW-HOW GROUPS

On the basis of thirty years of advising experience as well as extensive discussions and interviews with recruiters, successful alumni, and a variety of employers and human resource specialists, I developed ten basic categories of skills that I call the Know-How Groups. The ten basic Know-How Groups are like the six food groups. Just as you need to eat enough from each of the food groups to be healthy, you also need to develop enough of the skills within the Know-How Groups by the time you graduate to be successful.

THE TEN KNOW-HOW GROUPS

1. Establishing a Work Ethic
2. Developing Physical Skills
3. Communicating Verbally
4. Communicating in Writing
5. Working Directly with People
6. Influencing People
7. Gathering Information
8. Using Quantitative Tools
9. Asking and Answering the Right Questions
10. Solving Problems

Although the lists of skills provided by experts and employers may use different terms and groupings, the ten basic Know-How Groups reflect a broad consensus concerning the skills necessary to succeed in today's workplace.

WHAT'S YOUR KNOW-HOW SCORE?

Employers from every sector—big, medium, and small—would love to have a number, a "Know-How Score" (KHS), that tells them how well you perform the skills that make up the ten basic Know-How Groups. Because colleges do not provide a KHS, employers use their interview processes, including written tests, to come up with their own estimate. They do not call it a KHS, but that's really what they are measuring.

Although employers aren't likely to know the term *Know-How Score* (unless they've read this book), they do know what skills they want their employees to have. Show them that you have those skills, and you're on your way to a great future!

This book will help you plan for a high KHS and identify and develop the skills necessary for a successful career. Part one identifies the skills, and part two tells you how to develop those skills. Part three provides tools that will enable you to plan and make the most of your college experience. Used well, these tools will confirm—to yourself, your parents, potential employers, and others—that your college education was a good investment.

A short list of useful resources is provided at the end of each chapter. I have been selective in choosing the books and websites that will help you. If you want more books to read or websites to visit, use Amazon.com and general search engines like Google, as well as the books and links found in the sources I do suggest. Just don't let excessive studying of these materials get in the way of developing your skills.

Blank forms that you can use to plan your strategy for obtaining a high KHS are available at www.tenspeed.com (search for *10 things*). These forms are introduced and explained along with examples in chapter 18. However, you don't need to use these forms to benefit from this book. Just read the chapters, and make a list of all the skill sets. Indicate to yourself what courses you will take or what internships or part-time jobs you will pursue to be able to demonstrate that you do in fact have a high KHS. As you get closer to graduation, test yourself using the criteria provided for each skill set.

Although the book is most useful to those just beginning college, it can also be helpful to high school students and students further along in their college careers. Even if you are a junior or senior, it is never too late to start. Those in part-time learning programs, which extend over a long period of time, can benefit by embracing the philosophy and suggestions provided here.

A high KHS will not only help you achieve a high GPA and get you hired when you graduate college, it will give you the basic tools necessary to continue learning new skills in order to reach the top of your field. College is the place where you lay the fundamental groundwork that provides you with unlimited job options. If you follow the advice in this book, you will earn a high KHS that will wow your job interviewers and put you ahead of the class when you start work.

PART ONE

EXPLORING THE TEN KNOW-HOW GROUPS

(PLUS EXTRA CREDIT)

WE ARE WHAT WE REPEATEDLY DO. EXCELLENCE, THEN, IS NOT AN ACT, BUT A HABIT.

—ARISTOTLE

CHAPTER 1

ESTABLISHING A WORK ETHIC

SKILL SETS

KICK YOURSELF IN THE BUTT • BE HONEST • MANAGE YOUR TIME • MANAGE YOUR MONEY

Why do some people work hard and others just can't seem to get started? You could blame it on genes, family, poor academic preparation, or a first-time boss, but blaming won't do us much good here. Instead, let's just call it a "skills deficiency" and take a look at how that deficiency can be rectified by using your college experience to strengthen your work ethic in a way that will have employers drooling. Work ethic is by far the most essential of the ten basic Know-How Groups, if only because hard and honest work is required to improve your performance in the other nine groups.

The first two skill sets have to do with character, and the last two require precise focus and self-control. Hopefully you're already good at all four skill sets. If not, don't fret—they are usually related to maturity and age. You may have lacked motivation growing up, thought about cheating, or, don't tell me, actually cheated. But let's not dwell on the past. Education is about your future, and you need to move forward.

Just to drive home the point, a study by researcher D. P. Beach in 1982 found that "fully 87 percent of persons losing their jobs or failing to be promoted were found to have improper work habits and attitudes rather than insufficient job skills or knowledge."[1] So one's work ethic really does matter. Let's take a closer look at how you can build yours up.

"We cannot ensure success, but we can deserve it."

—Attributed to George Washington

When things looked dim and many of our leaders were whining about the risks and likelihood of losing the Revolutionary War, George delivered a direct kick in their behinds by making this memorable statement. From the taciturn look on his face in most portraits, one assumes that he had to give himself a kick once and a while as well.

Knowing how not to give up just because it is tough is a skill, just like writing clearly or being a good manager. It is a matter of choosing targets of ambition wisely and then going after them with all you have. This means you have to set priorities and keep a commitment to yourself. Self-motivation keeps you going long after the fear of sanctions by your boss or sweet-talking by your coworker wears off. Just look around at your schoolmates. The truly successful ones are those that do it for themselves.

Too many students I work with need to give themselves a swift kick daily. They need to decide if preparing for the work world is important to them. If so, they need to take action now, not in April of their senior year. A long-term commitment to planing and follow-through has to become a habit if you are going to meet the MSL levels for all ten Know-How Groups.

Learning to defer gratification is part of growing up, and growing up means motivating yourself to get what you want. Where are you on the deferring gratification scale of life-changing goals? Are you at zero (the level of a day-old infant) or at ten (the level of an ambitious and hard-working adult)?

Employers want employees who are self-motivated. A senior VP at one of the leading financial corporations in the world had this to say about self-motivation:

If I had to police everyone in order to get the job done, it'd be faster, for me, to do it myself. I want someone who will get the job done and get it done right. An employee needs to be a self-starter and self-driven. If I have to tell them what to do, they haven't done it.

Unfortunately for employers but fortunately for you, people with a strong will to do what it takes to achieve are in short supply. If you can provide evidence on your resume and in your interview that you are one of the few committed to working hard regardless of rewards and punishments, you will cinch the job. If you deliver on the job, you will be on your way to unimagined success.

A corporate executive with one of the world's largest multinational corporations has another way of saying kick yourself in the butt. He calls it "energy/passion/self-confidence." He writes,

> In the first few minutes of an interview, I can tell if a candidate is ready to play in our company's ballpark. You can have all the skills in the world, but if you aren't excited enough about what you're doing you should re-evaluate the job.

This executive on the move emphasizes self-confidence and says that it is "the only way to make it through a stretch role or some of the tough days." He writes, "There will be a period of time—not necessarily short either—where the job is tough. Self-confidence keeps you on your path, focused on a goal, and able to keep everything in perspective."

One of the most successful books in sales ever published, *How I Raised Myself from Failure to Success in Selling* by Frank Bettger, tells a story that applies to everything you do. He writes:

> Shortly after I started out as a professional baseball player, I got one of the biggest shocks of my life. I was young and ambitious and what happened? I was fired. The manager said he fired me because I was lazy! Well, that was the last thing I expected him to say. You drag yourself around the field like a veteran who has been playing ball for twenty years, he told me. "Why do you act that way if you're not lazy? I said, "I'm so nervous, so scared, that I want to hide my fear from the crowd. Besides I hope that by taking it easy, I'll get rid of my nervousness." He said, "It will never work. That's the thing that is holding you down. Whatever you do after you leave here, for heaven's sake, wake yourself up, and put some life and enthusiasm into your work.

Frank went to a lower minor league and, as his coach suggested, "began to act enthusiastic." He made the majors and may have been a hall-of-famer except for a career-ending injury. He took his enthusiasm to his work and, without a college education, became a wealthy businessman.

Whether you call it enthusiasm, energy, passion or self-confidence, the bottom line is that to succeed you have to get off your butt and do something positive. That is your responsibility and no one else's.

COURSES: There are no courses in sociology or anywhere else on knowing how to work hard, but every course you take is a measure of your capacity for hard work. That is why a high GPA is used as a measure of hard work, although obviously more than hard work is needed to get good grades. Of course, a high GPA is not the only measure of hard work. Non-course learning activities or financial needs may reduce the time you can allocate to getting high grades. Plan carefully so that you will earn at least a C in every course, realizing that you may have to make a tradeoff between higher grades and non-course activities. Set targets ahead of time, knowing how to do the work to get the grade you want. If you do this throughout your courses, you will establish the good work ethic you want to take to your first job.

NON-COURSE ACTIVITY: Whatever internship, part-time, summer, or student activity you undertake, do the same as for your course work. Plan to give it the amount of effort that represents a quality commitment, and then do all of the work required.

MINIMUM SKILL LEVEL BY GRADUATION: Like George Washington, be able to tell yourself that you have worked hard enough to deserve everything you have pursued even if you fail to reach your goal.

"Honesty is the best policy."

—Miguel de Cervantes, author of Don Quixote

Cervantes wrote the novel *Don Quixote de la Mancha,* and in case you have never heard of him, Don Quixote is viewed as an idealist who went through life pretty naïvely. He "tilted at windmills," which is a not-so-nice way of saying he was out of sync with the world.

The reason most people lie is that they think it will save time and maximize interests. Some people are pathological liars because they are bent on self-destruction. If you are one of them, get help. For the rest of you, the key to honesty is knowing how to cope with the pressure to cut corners to the point that it violates others' trust in you and your trust in yourself. The direct way to possess that key is to recognize that dishonesty is wrong.

Honesty is more than telling the truth to others. It is also a matter of telling the truth to your self. In the world of action, this usually means being dependable and taking responsibility for the promises you make. Promising to do a job either within or outside your normal duties and then not delivering as promised is a form of deception that has no place in the behavior of a person destined for success.

Employers want to trust their employees to tell the truth, not just in their travel expenditures but also in their dealings with clients and co-workers. They need to be able to trust their employees to fulfill the commitments they make. Given the business scandals at the beginning of the twenty-first century, companies now demand that students in graduate business programs receive instruction on integrity, which is shorthand for honesty and taking responsibility. Once you have done something to raise concern about your trustfulness, you will face a very hard time gaining back trust. Dishonesty and irresponsibility are the most powerful and quickest ways to lose another's trust in you.

A lobbyist and senior vice president of government affairs/trust services for a university says this about honesty:

As a lobbyist, you are essentially trying to convince legislature to support things that they're not necessarily inclined to do, and for me to be successful I have to be honest and truthful even if it may not benefit my client at that time. If you lose your credibility . . . you can never get it back.

This may sound strange given all the bad publicity about lobbyists, but to influence politicians, they have to trust you. This is true for all careers.

COURSES: To explore concepts of right and wrong, you may want to take courses in philosophy and religion in which rational and metaphysical writing about right and wrong and other moral and ethical questions are explored. If you get philosophy teachers who apply philosophy rather than worship its pristine beauty, such courses can be helpful. But more helpful would be your commitment here and now not to cheat either on tests or through plagiarizing papers.

This recommendation is made for two very important reasons. First, if you can avoid the temptation of cheating in college, you are likely to avoid it in your work life. Cheaters, like alcoholics, usually tell themselves "this is my last cheat." If you cannot resist the pressure of dishonoring yourself in order to move from a B to an A, how can you avoid shredding documents in order to preserve your job or get a raise when you have a family to help support?

Second, if you get caught cheating in college, there are dire consequences for your job search, including losing a possible job reference from a professor or having an F on your transcript. Several students who graduated from the a top university even had their diplomas revoked when it was discovered that they cheated.

Liars and cheaters in the workplace usually get fired or worse. Some actually go to jail, and others have trouble finding another job.

NON-COURSE ACTIVITY: Build trust with everyone in your life— build it where you live, work, and play. This means not promising to do things for others or taking on jobs for a student group that you are not able to complete as promised.

MINIMUM SKILL LEVEL BY GRADUATION: You have not lied or cheated from the moment you read this page. Unfortunately, this is an MSL you only have one shot at.

"Let all your things have their places. Let each part of your business have its time."

—Benjamin Franklin

In most cases, managing your time well is a result of planning and setting priorities. Handing in papers three days late, forgetting assignments, and stressing out over how much you have to do are all symptoms of poor time management. This occasionally happens to the best manager of time, but if it is persistent, you need to do something now.

Don't hide behind the "procrastination defense" because you really do not want to go there. Procrastination for most people is a form of poor time management. Those who say, "I'm a procrastinator!" (like the devil made them do it) are not taking responsibility for poor time management. There is no procrastinator gene as far as I know. "Procrastinators have higher rates of smoking, drinking, postponing seeing a doctor, digestive ailments, insomnia and cold and flu symptoms than the student population at large" according to a study by psychologists at Carleton University.[2] For those who persist in procrastinating, self-loathing and fear of failure may be operating, which if pathological, requires medical attention.

Time management is really pretty simple. You have x number of tasks that must be done at different times and that take different amounts of time to complete. To complicate it a little bit, some tasks have to be done before others. Knowing how to manage your time properly, therefore, simply means listing what has to be done, estimating the time it will take, and in what sequence you will do it. If you can do that, you can figure out when you should not take on more tasks for a while, and you'll have sufficient time to do the tasks you have to do. What it comes down to is learning to plan and follow a schedule that will allow you to complete your tasks with minimum stress and maximum quality.

The ability to handle multiple assignments over a two- or three-week period, as well as to not miss highly routine activities, such as submitting weekly reports, is key to every professional job.

You will frequently hear the term "multi-tasker" to describe a person who juggles several balls in the air and never drops one. With the speed of decision making made possible by computers and the increasing ability of people to deal with a variety of responsibilities, the ability to excel at multiple projects at once can be critical to your success. Employers are not impressed with workers who stay late to finish tasks that should have been completed during regular work hours. Missing more than two important deadlines is usually grounds for immediate dismissal.

COURSES: Some colleges have a study skills course that may help you with time management, but find out before you take it and see if it provides other skills you need. A whole course in time management is not worth the time. Take at least one course each semester in your junior and senior years that requires a major project that must be completed over at least a four-week period. You should be able to do this in most majors, but if not, take a course outside your major that requires a long-term project.

NON-COURSE ACTIVITIES: Treat college as a 9-to-5 job. That will leave you about thirty hours to do homework, which should be more than enough. Use early evening to play and then be in bed no later than 1 A.M. Do not be afraid to have 8:30 A.M. classes in your schedule! Not only will you avoid pulling all-nighters, but you will also be in a class where your regular attendance contrasts sharply with the majority of the class members. That will impress the professor and maybe even lead to a higher grade than you would otherwise get.

A senior who has accomplished a great deal in his college career has this to say:

*Time management is one of those things that I've seen can make or break a student. I laugh when I see a student who is habitually late ask a professor why he got a C on a paper or ask a question that the professor answered five minutes before the student walked in. In college classes, showing up is half the battle. If you're sitting there, you'll get something out of the course even if you don't pay full attention. As for 8:30 A.M. classes, you'll want to get away from them as soon as possible, but **don't**. The real world starts at 9 A.M., not 2 P.M. because that is when you wake up. My best recommendation for time management is to get a planner, because keeping a schedule will greatly improve your time-management skills.*

MINIMUM SKILL LEVEL BY GRADUATION: In your senior year, your assignments are done and ready for final proofing twenty-four hours before they are due.

"Because of frugality, one is generous."

—Lao-tzu, Chinese philosopher living about 2,500 years ago who authored *Tao Te Ching*, a book translated into more languages than any other book except for the Bible

I won't try to convince you that by watching your pennies you will make a better world. But if you are careful about your own cash flow, you will be generous to your future. If you are in constant debt, working extra in order not to fall behind, you will have a very unpleasant future.

Managing money to reach your goals requires careful attention to detail, not only in reading the fine print on a credit card application but also in balancing your checkbook and paying your taxes. Managing money is not just a matter of keeping your expenses in line with your income but also deciding how you will invest your money in the future. Every time you buy something for immediate gratification, you reduce your income to be invested in the future. Money management means thinking through the trade-off and then having the discipline to implement the necessary decisions. Such a trade-off might mean resisting the urge to cash in by selling a textbook for a course you just completed, knowing that you might need it a year later for another course in your major.

Knowing how to manage money well is key to getting and keeping good jobs. First, money problems while in college can hurt both your GPA and your KHS. Taking that extra part-time job or worrying about bills reduces the time you have for studying and maintaining your health. It could mean giving up a great non-paying internship experience. Although many students say they have to work more than twenty hours a week in order to make ends meet, my experience suggests that at least half of them are working for "wants" and not "needs." I find it very strange when students tell me they don't have enough money to buy books in January, and then in April, they tell me about the great time they had in the Bahamas over the spring break.

But some students do need the extra money to pay for tuition, living expenses, and books—not just to have fun. If that's you, careful spending and time management skills are crucial. For example, you may be able to avoid book expenses by taking the time to go to the library to use books on course reserve. You may need to avoid costly activities that serve as entertainment or that save you time, and you may need to take on more debt than you would like. However, careful money management while you are in college can lead to huge payoffs years down the road.

Second, when you graduate, you may be forced to take jobs that you would not otherwise take because you have significant personal debts to pay off. You may be so consumed by the fear of not paying your bills that you take the first job that comes along.

Finally, no matter what job you take as you move up the ladder, you will have increased responsibilities for expenditures. You will soon be faced with projected and actual budgets, and you will learn to make forecasts and monitor expenditures. If you learn good money management techniques for yourself, you will be prepared for the budget exercises you will face on your road to being the CEO of IBM, the executive director of the Boys and Girls Clubs of America, or the secretary of education.

COURSES: Courses in management and consumer studies that introduce you to tax policy and personal financial management are available at most colleges and universities. They can be extremely helpful in preparing you for the work world. You should take at least one of these courses at the introductory level. A really useful course, if your college has one, is one that deals with starting a business or entrepreneurship. Even if you don't plan on having a business career, you can benefit from a course in which you come up with an idea and develop a plan to finance it and keep it going.

NON-COURSE ACTIVITY: Develop a yearly budget of income and planned expenditures that you update monthly. Avoid running up debt on your credit cards. If you do have debt, figure out exactly how much interest you will be paying. If you are lucky enough to have parents that pay your credit card bills, your insurance bills, and everything else, ask them to work out a budget with you. Then, twice a year, have them deposit in your account the amount from which *you* will pay your bills. This is what the parents of one of my students did. She writes:

> *During my first two years, my parents paid all of my school bills, like tuition, housing, all the fees, etc. If I wanted any spending money though, it was up to me. It didn't take long for me to realize that I'd have to get a job on campus if I wanted any money to be left in my bank account by the time the semester ended.*
>
> *When I moved off campus junior year, our deal changed. They still pay my tuition, fees, and rent, but I have to pay for all of my own utilities. I also have to pay for my own*

phone, cable, Internet, and any other household needs.
I'm not given money on a regular basis either. At the
beginning of the semester, my parents give me a check
that covers that semester's rent and the amount of money
they would have spent on a meal plan. I'm responsible for
writing the checks every month. I'm free to spend it how-
ever I want, but if I chose to spend my rent money on a
stereo, I'd have to come up with the rent myself. In this
way, they've taught me to get used to making careful
financial decisions, while still keeping a safety net under
me as I move into the "real world."

If you have someone bankrolling part or all of your college costs, you should ask for a deal like the one described above. It will be a great training device in money management. If you're paying your own way and keeping your debt as low as possible, then you're already getting that training. It may not seem like it now, but one day you will count it as one of the most beneficial experiences of your college career. The payoff will begin with a resume that says, "Financed 100 percent of my college education," and it will carry through to everything you do.

MINIMUM SKILL LEVEL BY GRADUATION: You have no credit card debt, your checkbook has been balanced for twelve consecutive months, you owe no income taxes, and you have a clear idea of how much college debt you will have and how long it will take to pay it off.

USEFUL RESOURCES

The Cheater's Handbook: A Naughty Student's Bible by Bob Corbett (HarperCollins, 1999). A very funny book that will help you cheat—but if you have any character at all, you will realize it is not for you. The book is a vaccination against cheating and all kinds of dishonesty.

College Rules! How to Study, Survive, and Succeed in College by Sherrie Nist and Jodi Patrick Holschuh (Ten Speed Press, 2002). A very helpful little book on how to do well with the academic challenges of college. Each chapter is about ten short and powerful pages. See chapter 7 of *College Rules!* for time management, and chapter 8 for motivation.

How I Raised Myself from Failure to Success in Selling by Frank Bettger (Simon & Schuster, 1977). A quaint and quick read that is all you need to learn about motivation. It's not only about sales—it's also about health, time management, and looking good. Besides, as you will see in chapter 6, every career requires sales.

A SOUND MIND IN A SOUND BODY

IS A SHORT BUT FULL **DESCRIPTION** OF A HAPPY STATE IN THE WORLD.

—JOHN LOCKE, SEVENTEENTH-CENTURY ENGLISH PHILOSOPHER WHOSE IDEAS WERE USED BY THE FOUNDING FATHERS

CHAPTER 2

DEVELOPING PHYSICAL SKILLS

SKILL SETS

**STAY WELL · LOOK GOOD ·
TYPE 35 WPM ERROR FREE · TAKE LEGIBLE NOTES**

Most people don't think of physical skills when considering college unless they are jocks or sports nuts. However, physical skills are very important. First of all, many majors require specialized physical skills. Some are obvious, like the skills required for art and music careers, and some not so obvious, like chemistry where spilling stuff is not really a good idea. There are too many programs and too many physical skills associated with them to provide a discussion of the specific skills for each. If you choose a field that requires physical skills, make sure you add them to your list. We will, however, discuss some general physical skills that are valuable in the world of work—and college too.

I won't discuss the whole range of physical skills necessary for high-paying positions in skilled manual jobs such as plumbing, truck-driving, and electrical work. Most four-year colleges do not offer course work in these kinds of fields even though the starting salaries on average are higher than for many jobs open to new college graduates.

The first two skill sets are obvious and blatantly paternalistic, but need to be said. The last two are as important to you as the speed and accuracy with which bricklayers mix and apply mortar. Fast and accurate typing and legible note taking will raise your chances of success in college and the work world more than you can imagine.

"Eat not to dulness [sic]. Drink not to elevation."

—Benjamin Franklin

Wait until you get mono, strep, and pneumonia all at the same time, only to have those followed by tonsillitis. Avoiding these and other diseases is not just a matter of genes, your general physical makeup, or luck. It also depends on your ability to eat a balanced diet, get enough rest and exercise, and avoid destructive behaviors.

Good health means you'll have the energy and alertness necessary to do a good job. Employers prefer workers who show up on time and are ready to work. "Alertness" is a word frequently used in interviews and published lists of characteristics of a good worker. Good health will also mean higher grades and a more impressive resume while you are at college. Not only is health a blessing money can't buy, it is also a direct path to more money.

An accounting professor I know tells his students that while socializing is part of the job interview, don't drink alcohol even if the interviewer does. He says you need your full faculties to answer the questions well. He has heard plenty of horror stories about reckless talk and behavior resulting from interviewees thinking they are at a keg party. A recent graduate with a great job maintains—on the grounds that it is important to be yourself—that one drink is OK with dinner if you usually have one. No more than one is my recommendation.

COURSES: Courses in nutrition are available on many campuses and may even fulfill liberal arts or general studies core requirements. Courses on self-damaging behaviors in society may be found in psychology and sociology departments. There also may be exercise courses that allow you to work out for credit.

NON-COURSE ACTIVITIES: "Wellness floors," which encourage healthy lifestyles (including no drinking, smoking, and/or drugs), are available in dormitories on many campuses. If you are on a floor with no theme, get your friends to argue for quiet hours after 11 P.M. Make a proposal at the first floor meeting and see who objects. If everyone living near you says "no," try to move right then and there. Floormates are dangerous enough to your health because of the germs they spread. The hours they keep and the pressure they put on you to participate in destructive behavior is an even more serious threat.

One of my serious but fun-loving students has the following advice:

It's not so easy to eat right if you live in the dorms and are given the choice between greasy dining hall food and take-out. Most of the time, though, the fear of gaining that "freshman 15" will keep you from eating too much junk food and will steer you to eating complete meals. The free gym on campus is too tempting to pass up, and you can even take exercise courses. There's nothing more efficient then getting an easy A for a class that helps you stay in shape.

Eating well and exercising—participating in an intercollegiate or intramural sport or a regular exercise program is a great idea—however, are not the keys to staying healthy in college. What's most important is getting enough sleep and avoiding "destructive behavior," such as binge drinking and pulling all-nighters. It's easy to stay up until 4 A.M. hanging out, but get eight hours of sleep as often as possible. If you need to get your stomach pumped because you drank too much, you're not going to get anything done for a while. Be responsible (to yourself and others) when it comes to partying at school.

Likewise, take good care of yourself when it comes to smoking. If you arrive at college as a nonsmoker, don't get addicted. If you are addicted, use your college years to break the habit. Most smokers aren't happy about their habit—I've never met one who was. Smokers get sick more often than nonsmokers, and, by way of secondhand smoke, they jeopardize the health of others. Besides, smoking costs you valuable time and money—time and money that you could be spending on more important things. And on the job front, it's important to know that employers prefer nonsmokers. As an alumnus who works for a big stock brokerage once said to me, "Smokers typically smoke right before attending a meeting so they are stinky, and smokers take more breaks . . . so they are unattractive hires." I have not included nonsmoking as an MSL because smoking is not a major roadblock to a successful career. However, in most cases, it won't do you any good either.

MINIMUM SKILL LEVEL BY GRADUATION: You do not miss or are not late for any classes during your senior year because of sickness or oversleeping.

KNOW HOW TO LOOK GOOD

"Clothes make the man. Naked people have little or no influence in society."

—Mark Twain

On the topic of looking good, Ben Franklin once said:

> *Harvard students learn little more than how to carry themselves handsomely and enter a room genteelly (which might as well be acquired at dancing school) and from whence they return, after an abundance of trouble and charge, as great blockheads as ever, only more proud and self-conceited.*[1]

Ben Franklin was not a big fan of the elitism of higher education. He thought too much of it was "ornamental." But he knew the importance of clothes. When he was the ambassador to France, he did not compete with the fancy clothing of the French but dressed simply to make a statement about the democratic spirit of the American Revolution. Appropriate dress depends on the setting. Franklin did well with eighteenth-century women, if the truth was told, but I don't think he would cut it today. When you decide what to wear for a job interview or to work, just remember you are not a revolutionary.

Let's face it: in the work world, first impressions usually *do* count, unless you are a hypercompetitive brainiac like Bill Gates, for whom looking good is beside the point. People make decisions on physical appearance quickly.

"Looking good" means being well groomed. Not everyone is born looking like Brad Pitt or Cindy Crawford, but the effort that you put into making yourself presentable says a lot about your character. Your appearance communicates who you are, and you must decide what you want it to say about you.

COURSES: Too bad Franklin's description of Harvard doesn't hold up today for Harvard or anywhere else, or that finishing schools are only for spoiled rich girls. Some physical exercise courses might work at least for good posture, but don't count on it. Actually, MIT has a program in how to dress and act like a normal person, but most schools don't.

NON-COURSE ACTIVITIES: Put yourself in situations in which you interact socially or professionally with the kind of people likely to be your future employers. See if you can get yourself appointed to a committee that works with alumni or the board of trustees. Go to local chamber of commerce meetings that are open to the public or to school board and local government meetings. In other words, hang out with the rich and powerful. Watch the way they dress and the way they carry themselves.

My fun-loving student had this to say about looking good:

> Coplin's [comment on looking good] reminds me of a quote from Jerry Seinfeld: "Dating is pressure and tension. What is a date, really, but a job interview that lasts all night? The only difference between a date and a job interview is that in not many job interviews is there a chance you'll end up naked at the end of it." Seinfield is right. Not only do you need to be presentable to get a job, but you also need to be presentable to get dates. So learn to be as thoughtful when you dress for a job interview or work as you would when you dress for a date.

MINIMUM SKILL LEVEL BY GRADUATION: To present yourself well to whomever you're trying to impress.

KNOW HOW TO TYPE 35 WPM ERROR FREE

"Typing 35 words per minute error free is a SET IN STONE necessity—kind of like being able to find the job interview. If you can't even do this, don't bother."

—A senior vice president for a major investment firm

I am truly sorry to bother you with this mundane and manual skill set, but when pursuing education and a job, certain things require a level of competence that can only be achieved through practice. Learning to type at the minimum of 35 words per minute error free is one of the clearest and easiest MSLs to achieve. It just takes commitment—and not looking at your fingers!

Meeting this standard will save you a lot of time during your college career. It will also open many doors for initial jobs and advancement. Good word processors can be hired at between $10 and $20 an hour by "temp" firms, but the minimum level for these firms is 45 WPM. The temp opportunity alone makes having the skill worthwhile. But there is more! Jobs in temp firms frequently lead to permanent jobs. I know several successful, highly paid people who started in a temp position in their company. Chapter 13 provides more information on how temp firms can be important to your KHS education, and chapter 16 shows how a temp job can lead to a permanent career.

Good typing will allow you to be the leader without the embarrassment of asking to be it. If you are at the computer, you are virtually in control of the team because you filter your teammates' ideas as you type. If you learn to not look at your fingers when you are typing and get to 35 words a minute, it could become the difference between a dead-end job and becoming the CEO of a multinational corporation.

Every time I mention the typing skill, people in the audience come up and say something similar to what a special education teacher once said to me: "I never took a typing class, and it takes me four hours to write a four- or five-page report." Don't let that happen to you.

COURSES: Take courses that require typed papers in your freshman year. The practice will help you improve your speed. If your speed doesn't improve, the many extra hours you spend typing these papers will probably provide sufficient incentive for you to take the remedial action suggested below. Type everything you hand in.

NON-COURSE ACTIVITIES: Speedy and accurate typing requires continuous practice, and speed only comes if you do not look at your fingers. If you cannot stop looking at the keys, try a computer-based typing training program like Mavis Beacon, or get an unused keyboard and paint over the keys to practice typing without looking at the letters and numbers. Also, practice your accuracy when doing instant messaging and sending email.

MINIMUM SKILL LEVEL BY GRADUATION: Type 35 errorless words per minute.

"He listens well who takes notes."

—Dante

I had not planned to include legible note taking as an important skill set until I read the following comment from a senior VP at a very large company. He said:

> *Writing clearly and quickly does not seem like it would be important at a first glance, however, in many cases, it makes and breaks success. In many meetings, it is not socially acceptable to be pounding away on your laptop— a simple pen and paper will do fine. Pen and paper allow you to draw diagrams, add side notes, and color-code. Writing clearly is a huge benefit because it allows your notes to be distributed to people who could not attend the meeting, as well as for your future knowledge*

I was opposed to including note taking as a skill because when I take notes, which is rarely, I can't read them ten minutes later. I didn't want to include it because I couldn't face reality: I will never, ever be able to adequately master a part of a Know-How Group in my own book! Upon reflection, I realized that nobody, not even the author, is expected to have a KHS of 100. Unfortunately, this is not the only MSL I can't satisfy. While it is never too late to improve one's skills, it wouldn't be a problem for me at all if I'd just developed better habits in college.

Having good handwriting that enables you to take decipherable notes quickly is a valuable asset. Aside from having a good personal record of what happened at any meeting, taking good notes can be used to influence future meetings and events. You can present what you have recorded faithfully but still organize the information in a way that helps express your point of view.

COURSES: Take clear, careful notes in every class and for all reading you do in your courses. Type the notes a day after you take them, which will both improve your typing skills and help you retain important material for your classes. This habit needs to be developed over time, and the sooner you start practicing, the better off you'll be. Study-skill courses, offered in some colleges, provide help in taking notes.

NON-COURSE ACTIVITIES: Volunteer to keep the minutes for a student group. If you take the job seriously, you will begin to build good note-taking habits. The pressure from your peers to provide good notes will supply you with the discipline you need to be successful.

MINIMUM SKILL LEVEL BY GRADUATION: You never go to a meeting without a pen and paper to take notes.

USEFUL RESOURCES

Mavis Beacon Teaches Typing (www.mavisbeacon.com). This is the most widely used typing tutoring software. It provides a way for the very poor typist to develop speed and accuracy.

SPEAK NOT BUT WHAT MAY BENEFIT OTHERS OR YOURSELF.

—BENJAMIN FRANKLIN

CHAPTER 3

COMMUNICATING VERBALLY

SKILL SETS

CONVERSE ONE-ON-ONE • PRESENT TO GROUPS • USE VISUAL DISPLAYS

Verbal communication is a formal term for talking and listening. Some people are good talkers, and some are good listeners, but you need to be good at both. Good verbal communication leads to mutual understanding. As you will see, talking in an informal conversation is very different from speaking to groups.

This Know-How Group is closely related to working directly with people, the topic of chapter 6. If you are skilled at establishing trust and cooperating with others, you will have an easier time communicating verbally. The two Know-How Groups can enhance each other, but they can also be developed independently.

"Bore, n. A person who talks when you wish him to listen."

—Ambrose Bierce, nineteenth-century writer

Having a conversation with someone, whether in a job setting or not, requires both talking and listening. Communication is a two-way street and can only be effective if your desire and skill at talking is equal to your ability to be a good listener.

Your style of speaking and the clarity with which you speak are just as important as using correct grammar. Equally important is the way you organize your conversation. It's important to stick to the point and not wander all over the place. In short, you need to be strategic about what information you are trying to provide and what information you are trying to get.

Effective one-on-one conversations require a variety of good habits: asking questions to check for mutual understanding, never talking more than thirty seconds at one time, and using terms that both parties understand. Like most skills, reading about how to speak effectively is less important than being reflective about your communication effectiveness in your conversations.

Mutual understanding through good verbal communication in the work world is vital. Misunderstandings can lead to disasters in dealing with customers and coworkers. If you cannot understand what your boss wants you to do, you have the choice of either asking for clarification or doing the wrong thing. The former is better, but getting it the first time is the best. A senior human resource person writes:

> *I think conversing one-on-one is my main skill set. A new-hire must be able to carry a conversation—willing to learn. The training process that all our new-hires must complete can be very confusing, and we expect each new-hire to ask questions in order to grasp a full understanding. If someone cannot hold a decent conversation, I am hesitant to even place them in a lower-end job, even if they have the education and training.*

Solid verbal communication skills are critical for being an effective employee. In the following story, a senior VP for a firm illustrates the importance of listening carefully and thinking about what the other person is saying by his phrase "pushing back the conversation":

An eighty-year-old lady walks into a hardware store and says to you, "I need a ladder, to climb onto my roof." You ask her why she needs to climb onto her roof. She says, "To reach my tree." You realize there might be more to this story and ask her why she wants to reach her tree. She replies, "My cat is stuck up in my tree and is afraid of heights." You offer her a can of tuna fish that will solve the problem of the cat in the tree more effectively and less riskily than the ladder. If you would not have talked with her, she could have gotten hurt and/or never solved her problem. If you were to offer her the can of tuna fish at the start, she wouldn't have understood your reasoning. Pushing back the conversation allows for empathy and builds a trust relationship between you and the client— sometimes they don't always know what they need, but they realize that they want their problem solved.

This story illustrates a pattern found in all jobs. Carefully listening to and questioning clients or coworkers are critical in building good relationships. Your goal is to help others, who in turn will help you do the best job you can.

COURSES: The key to developing good one-on-one communication skills is to constantly reflect on how well you are communicating. Your course work will give you a great deal of practice as you communicate with your instructor and with your classmates. Beyond that, courses that contain the words *human relations* or *interpersonal communication,* whether offered in business, psychology, or speech communications, can be useful. Also, look for courses in mediation and conflict resolution because they put a high premium on effective interpersonal communication. Courses that require fieldwork, direct observation, video playback of classroom presentations, and team activities are most useful.

NON-COURSE ACTIVITIES: Use your experience in your dorm during your freshman year as a place to practice and reflect on your ability to talk and listen as a way of developing mutual understanding. When there is a misunderstanding, reflect on why you think it occurred and talk to the individual with whom you had the misunderstanding. Many universities have programs within residence halls to develop communication and leadership skills. Ask the residence-life staff at your college about these programs; they provide solid experience to develop your one-on-one communication skills.

MINIMUM SKILL LEVEL BY GRADUATION: You will always have to work on your one-on-one communication skills, but by the time you graduate, you should be skilled at spotting miscommunications involving yourself or in conversations you observe.

KNOW HOW TO PRESENT TO GROUPS

"If you can't blow everyone out of the water in the first fifteen seconds of a presentation, you will never be remembered or known as 'the smart one.'"

—Rising corporate star in a big company

Talking to groups means presenting and listening to any number of people, ranging from a few to thousands! The techniques that you use will vary depending on the size and the group setting, but they are essentially different from one-on-one conversations. You will not be able to maintain eye contact with everyone in the group or ask questions about mutual understanding when speaking to a group. Successful group presentations require careful organization and specific ways to find out if you are getting your message across. Learn to ask yourself, "How will I know if my talk to a group has been successful?" before you give the speech. After the speech, take some time to reflect and see if you passed your own test. Did you stay on task and talk at a reasonable pace? Did you make eye contact with different people in the room? Did you receive good questions and give clear answers?

One of the most critical skills you need to develop in order to speak effectively to groups is to not be fearful of a crowd. Some people who do very heroic things get sweaty palms and become speechless when placed in front of a group. The size is not always the determining factor. Some people can handle a couple of hundred strangers well but get nervous in front of a group of ten coworkers.

You also must recognize the short attention span of people, especially in a group setting. Getting an audience's attention in fifteen seconds, as stated in the quote at the beginning of this section, requires real talent, but if you can hook them in sixty—the "golden minute" at the beginning of a speech—you should be safe.

The president of a growing communications business points out a well-known rule about speaking to groups. He writes:

If you want to have people remember something, they must hear it three times: first at the beginning when you summarize your speech, once in the middle when you explain your thesis, and once at the end when you summarize your topic again. Also, the most effective speeches should only make three important points.

Dale Carnegie Training, one of the premier sales and leadership training companies, promoted one of its "high-impact presentation two-day seminars" with these tips:

The end result of giving a powerful presentation should be that your audience comes away with useful information. Here are some guidelines on communicating with greater impact.

- *Have energetic body language and an upbeat tone of voice*
- *Maintain eye contact with your audience*
- *Avoid being tied to a script or lectern*
- *Get your audience involved by using examples and holding a Q&A session*

These may be well-known and obvious points about addressing groups of people, but like many other commonsensical ideas, they are hard to put into practice. Use your college experience to develop good public-speaking habits that you can use when you enter the work world.

You do not have to be an accomplished speaker to reach the MSL. You only need to be able to clearly accomplish limited goals in speaking with a group of people. Decide whether the primary purpose of your speech is to build trust, convey specific information, or motivate future action. You don't have to be entertaining to achieve this purpose.

The ability to talk to groups of people is critical in many workplace situations. Initially, you will probably not be placed in front of a group but will observe how your superiors handle such discussions. A businesswoman who was interviewed for this book said that she does not expect an entry-level person to make presentations to strangers, but by the second year, that person should be able to make presentations to groups of their peers. Over the long run, being able to make good group presentations will catch the eye of people within your organization as well as outside of it.

COURSES: Take at least one speech communications course that focuses on presenting to groups, and take several other courses in which such activities are a requirement. Some colleges have business-presentation courses that are also useful. The best kinds of courses are those in which you are videotaped and then critiqued by the instructor and your peers. Force yourself to raise your hand in class and make a statement so that it becomes second nature.

NON-COURSE ACTIVITIES: Participate in activities in which you are required to make formal and informal presentations to groups. Any organization that you join will have leadership positions that require such presentations. A good place to start in your freshman year is in the residence hall in floor meetings and on councils that you can easily become a member of.

MINIMUM SKILL LEVEL BY GRADUATION: You do not let one classroom experience go by where you wanted to say something but did not.

"To hear is to forget; to see is to remember; to do is to learn."

—Chinese proverb

A visual display does not necessarily mean a fancy PowerPoint presentation. It can be a single sheet of paper handed out to the group that outlines the topics you plan to discuss. However, you do need to become proficient in using PowerPoint as well as creating visual displays on handouts, overheads, or newsprint-like papers that you place on the wall.

Visual displays can be critical even when you are talking one-on-one, but they are always critical when you are speaking to a group. The well-known educational principle quoted at the top of this section is the operating principle when presenting to groups. Visual displays, by definition, help you move from simply telling the audience to showing them. By asking them to react to a chart or a diagram, you involve the audience in the speech, which will naturally keep them more interested.

There are two related tasks that you must perform well in order to use visual displays effectively. First, you need to master and organize your content well enough to integrate a display into your actual talk. Second, you need to produce the display, which ranges from simple layouts on an 8½ by 11 piece of paper to a PowerPoint presentation.

The first skill always precedes and defines the second. As a project manager who is in charge of important clients for a major financial firm said:

I always ask people how they would set up a meeting and prepare a presentation. I remember one girl I interviewed told me she used PowerPoint and set up the meetings two hours apart. Well, that's great, but I wanted to hear that the first thing she would think of is knowing her topic and doing research. I don't want a presentation with no substance and a bunch of pretty flowers.

Although the project manager is correct in saying that substance must precede form, your ability to make pretty displays and use Power-Point to help your boss (who presumably knows the substance) shine can get you a big fat raise. Of course, you will have to understand what your boss is talking about. Most of the people you will be working for will not have the skills—and even if they do, they will not have the time—to take care of displays. Your display skills will make you indispensable. Just be careful to avoid the tag of "A great display maker, but what else can he do?" The best way to avoid such a label is to make substantive suggestions about the content of presentations that will show your superiors you are ready for more responsibility.

COURSES: Some specialized courses in information or educational technology may be available to introduce you to all the possible bells and whistles of display making, but the fancy stuff is not necessary. It makes more sense to select courses that require group presentations, including ones with PowerPoint. They can be found in almost every field.

NON-COURSE ACTIVITIES: In whatever activity you undertake that involves talking to a group, force yourself to use at least paper hand-outs. This will teach you to integrate your talks with visual displays. Volunteer to make flyers and even simple brochures for a student organization or an academic department.

MINIMUM SKILL LEVEL BY GRADUATION: You have created a PowerPoint presentation in at least one class and have used handouts in several small group meetings.

USEFUL RESOURCES

Dale Carnegie Training (www.dalecarnegie.com). Training that is offered all over the world and that provides courses, seminars, and training products in public speaking, management, and personal development. Visit their website to see the kinds of programs offered. Click on site map and try out some of the links. Be sure to click "subscribe to DCT newsletter." You will get a free online newsletter, which will include some information and tips you can use now. Better yet, use the site to locate a Dale Carnegie branch where you live or go to college, and see if you can do an internship with the branch. They will probably include free training in it. This site will help you with the commu- nications skills emphasized in this chapter as well as the skills discussed in chapters 5 (working with people) and 6 (influencing people).

How to Win Friends and Influence People by Dale Carnegie (Pocket Books, 1982). With over fifteen million copies sold since it was first published in 1936, this book can help you establish good personal relationships and speak to groups.

101 Ways to Make More Effective Presentations by Elizabeth P. Tierney (Kogan Page, 1999). A comprehensive and easy-to-read list of tips that will help you in making formal presentations.

PowerPoint 2002 for Dummies by Doug Lowe (Hungry Minds, 2002 or most recent edition). The help information on the PowerPoint software should be all you need, but in case you want to get a comprehensive picture with most of the options, use this book. Make sure you have the 2002 or most recent version of PowerPoint.

"WRITING,
WHEN PROPERLY MANAGED . . .
IS BUT A
DIFFERENT
NAME
FOR CONVERSATION.**"**

—LAURENCE STERNE,
EIGHTEENTH-CENTURY AUTHOR

CHAPTER 4

COMMUNICATING IN WRITING

SKILL SETS

**WRITE WELL • EDIT AND PROOF •
USE WORD-PROCESSING TOOLS •
SEND INFORMATION ELECTRONICALLY**

The purpose of written communication is the same as that of oral communication: promoting mutual understanding between two or more people. No matter what your major, college provides an excellent opportunity to practice and develop your writing skills.

"Writing is easy. All you do is stare at a blank sheet of paper until drops of blood form on your forehead."

—Gene Fowler, twentieth-century writer

Writer's block is OK for starving poets and novelists; it's just part of the process. But for anyone working for a boss, writer's block is a quicker way to get fired than producing poor copy.

At the other end of the spectrum is "writer's diarrhea," where once you start you cannot stop. Clients and fellow workers do not have the time to wade through unnecessary verbiage and figure out what you are trying to say.

Aim to come out of college with the ability to write quickly, effortlessly, and succinctly. In short, learn to write easily and well. A great (and very short) guide to excellent writing is the classic *The Elements of Style* by William Strunk, Jr., and E. B. White. Here's a little Strunk and White wisdom:

> *Vigorous writing is concise. A sentence should contain no unnecessary words, a paragraph no unnecessary sentences, for the same reason that a drawing should have no unnecessary lines and a machine no unnecessary parts. This requires not that the writer make all his sentences short, or that he avoids all detail and treats his subjects only in outline, but that every word tell.[1]*

Writing in the work world usually comes in response to a request for information or a directive to inform others. It almost always takes the form of a memo ranging from a paragraph to no more than two pages, and frequently requires the use of numbered points. Writing for your job will not be like writing for courses, in which the assignment is designed to help you learn something. Instead, the purpose of work writing is generally to brief others about a problem or situation and to possibly propose solutions.

A senior human resources director at a major company says:

> *Being able to write clearly is a must at my company. We have a database that holds problems and potential solutions—imputed by every employee in our implementation field. Our production team uses this database in order to fix problems that the rest of the company encounters. If they can't comprehend what the employee is trying to say, they can't fix it. We also collect writing samples from our potential employees. We ask a number of questions and ask them to respond—quite simple, but we can tell who can write and who cannot.*

As one moves up the ladder, writing becomes even more important. If you have an idea that you can only explain verbally, you are limited to influencing only those you speak to. However, a one-page memo, circulated throughout the organization, can become part of a process that leads to the improvement and implementation of your idea. Also, putting your idea on paper makes it much harder for others to steal it.

COURSES: Most colleges have writing courses, sometimes entitled "technical writing," which attempt to help you write for audiences you are likely to encounter in the world of work. Required lower-level writing courses can be helpful in improving your mechanics and also understanding the importance of writing to an audience other than yourself. In addition, take as many courses as you can that require you to write logs, planning documents, and evaluation reports. These can be found in the social sciences and in many of the professional schools. Those courses in which you write for clients and get feedback from them, or in simulated situations like a legislative hearing, are the most effective. If your school has a communications program, take public relations and news writing classes because they will help you to write more succinctly as well as improve your grammar and punctuation. If you can find a course in grant writing, which actually requires you to write grant proposals, take it.

NON-COURSE ACTIVITIES: Pursue internships, part-time and summer jobs, and student activities in which you will need to write brief reports or plans. Working for a legislator at the state or federal level usually requires you to draft letters responding to constituents. This is excellent training for writing in many job situations.

MINIMUM SKILL LEVEL BY GRADUATION: You can quickly and clearly write a proposal presenting an idea that others have to buy into.

KNOW HOW TO EDIT AND PROOF

"Saint, a dead sinner revised and edited."

—Ambrose Bierce, nineteenth-century poet

Editing and proofing require patience and attention to detail, as well as an ability to understand what the writer is trying to communicate and how the reader will interpret it. Editing refers to revising your first draft—organizing content between and within paragraphs, choosing the right words, and making sure the text is understandable and interesting. Proofreading is the last stage of the revision process, checking for misspellings, omissions, and grammatical mistakes. It should be done with your final draft before you submit it to anyone. Some of the proofing process is simply mechanical and is greatly helped by Microsoft Word with its spell check and grammar-checking features. The editing part, however, is much more hands-on and requires as much practice and skill as writing in the first place.

Most college students develop poor skills in editing and proofing because they write their papers at the last minute. They consider themselves lucky if they have time to run the spell check before they grab their papers out of the printer so they can hand them in on time. If this sounds like you, the most critical step in learning to edit and proof is to reserve time to do just that. This means planning to finish what you consider to be a final draft of your paper well enough in advance to carefully edit and proof it.

It is also a good idea to learn some of the basic symbols of editing, which can be found in most good dictionaries under "proofreading" or "proofreaders' marks." Marks include symbols to delete, begin paragraph, and spell out. Using these symbols will help you revise not only your own work but that of your employers as well. When you get into a job in which your boss wants you to edit and proof something she wrote, you can look professional by using symbols that are well known. See the Useful Resources section at the end of this chapter for a website that provides a full list of symbols.

A misspelling, which would lose you a couple of points on your paper in a course, could spell doom in the workplace. As a senior executive says, "Who wants to buy our multimillion dollar product, when we can't even spell it right? Attention to detail is key in the workforce—without it, don't bother." Sound harsh? That's only because your teachers and professors have misled you with only minor point deductions for misspellings. To put the importance of editing and proofing in proper perspective, leaving a "not" out of a business proposal is about the same as a surgeon taking out your left kidney when your right one is diseased.

On the upside, if your boss knows she can throw a rough draft at you and you can edit and proof it so it is more readable, you will save her time and anguish. As long as you excel in other areas, superiors consider editing and proofing a direct path to higher-level positions.

COURSES: Some basic writing courses will help you develop your writing and editing skills, but you can benefit by more intense course work, such as one that trains you to be a writing consultant and earn credit helping others with their writing. A powerful way to develop your editing and proofing skills is to take courses that generate written products for someone in the community. Your professor will not want to be embarrassed by typos and misspellings and will subject you to a constant review process.

NON-COURSE ACTIVITIES: Try to get a job editing and proofing written manuscripts produced by one of your professors, or seek a job in which you are on a team that is producing a large report. Write or edit for a school publication, even if it is a newsletter with limited distribution. These experiences will help you improve your editing and proofing skills.

MINIMUM SKILL LEVEL BY GRADUATION: When given a rough draft, you can spot lack of subject and verb agreement and a paragraph without a topic sentence as soon as you see them.

> ## *"The real problem is not whether machines think but whether men do."*
>
> —B. F. Skinner, twentieth-century psychologist

Bill Gates is the man behind Microsoft and whether we love or despise him, we all need to thank him for making Microsoft Word, which is the only word-processing tool you need to master. Other word-processing programs, no matter how cheap or quaint, are useless in writing for work. Most of you already know that and have some experience using Word. The rest of you need to get on board.

Even if you use Word, you may not know all of its features, some of which can speed up and clarify the writing process as well as help edit and proof what you write. Check out the menus and toolbar options. How many have you used? It's not necessary for you to use all of them to achieve the MSL, but you should know how to print out readable and attractive copy, to move text around, to save text for future use, and to check for grammar and spelling errors.

My favorite tool, and one that you will find very useful in a job situation, is tracking. Let's say your boss has sent you a business proposal (as a Word document) to review and make necessary suggestions or changes. Open the document on your computer and click TRK at the bottom of your window. Then when you make a change or correction on the document, Word makes the change in red. When you return the document to your boss, she can see both the original version of the proposal and your suggested changes. This speeds up the editing and proofing process immensely. I cite this as one example of the hidden treasures offered by Word. You might find others. Word has terrific timesaving shortcuts that you can easily pick up by watching others or consulting reference books on Word.

Your ability to use Microsoft Word effortlessly and effectively will impress your supervisors, especially those who may not have kept up with the latest innovations. Conversely, if you are not familiar with the time-saving and quality-increasing features of Word, you could be in deep trouble if your colleague, or—even worse—your boss, is watching over your shoulder as you try to figure out the Find and Replace function five minutes before a report is due.

Although word-processing skills don't seem like a big deal, they should not be taken for granted. One of my former students, who is now completing a master's degree at one of the top graduate schools in the world, wrote this to me:

> *I am shocked by how many people in my program don't know how to do a lot of stuff in Word (formatting, tracking, etc.)—things I'm sure I only know because of my undergraduate experience on various projects.*

Hopefully you will master this skill set as soon as possible to avoid "shocking" your future boss or your colleagues in graduate school.

COURSES: No college that I know of gives a course in Microsoft Word. Even if they did, it would not have much impact unless you continue using the skills after the course. Like developing your writing skills, your best bet for learning word processing is to take courses that force you to write and learn the necessary word-processing skills as you write your paper. If you take a course in which you are on a team that produces a paper, watch the person doing the typing and ask questions about some of the procedures he or she performs.

NON-COURSE ACTIVITIES: Find a friend who really knows Word and have him or her coach you on features you don't know. This works particularly while you are actually writing a paper. While working on his or her own project, your friend can be in the same room with you, available to answer your questions when they arise. Another possibility (best done when you don't have a deadline) is to take an hour or two to check out Word's toolbar options and consult Microsoft Help.

MINIMUM SKILL LEVEL BY GRADUATION: You can create a professional-looking resume in a Word document that you can send by email. You can use the following functions: Spelling and Grammar; Cut, Copy, and Paste; Tracking; Bullets and Numbering; Find and Replace; Header and Footer; Styles and Formatting; Insert Table; Borders and Shading; and Word Count.

"The new electronic interdependence recreates the world in the image of a global village."

—Marshall McLuhan, twentieth-century social commentator

Marshall McLuhan made this comment in 1967 before email came into being. He actually was very excited about radio and television. What would he think today, when someone in the United States can communicate with someone in South Africa instantaneously and at no cost, or a buyer in Siberia can transfer funds to a vendor in Chicago?

Electronic delivery of information through email and over the Internet and the electronic support of real-time conversations through Instant Messaging and teleconferencing have revolutionized the world of work. Moreover, as a former student of mine now at a large corporation writes:

> *In many jobs today you might not work directly with anyone or nearly anyone. At some point, you'll be virtual and learning how to be successful when working remotely is a different and important skill from day-to-day management interaction. Global is a reality of today's companies.*

In all careers, communication through email to one individual or a group of individuals is increasingly common. College is a great place to practice the art of virtual interactions. Be familiar with how to use email and the features in Microsoft Outlook or Outlook Express. We have also included basic web design skills in our list. A website can be used as a big filing cabinet of documents that other members of the organization can access. You are likely to be asked to set up websites that can be used as collective filing cabinets or to use some document-sharing system within your company, which is similar.

If you cannot perform these tasks, you will find yourself at a disadvantage with other new-hires. My students have told me horror stories of coworkers who need to be shown how to work the copy machine or the fax machine. These are basic electronic tools that you should have already mastered. When your boss says, "Send me a Word document" or asks you to set up an internal website, you need to say, "No problem."

COURSES: Computer engineering and information technology courses are not the way to learn how to use the tools that most businesses, government entities, and nonprofits now use. They will help you if you want to go into a specialized business, but they are overkill if you want to be up on the existing procedures that will be available to you. However, you can learn a great deal about electronic delivery by taking courses from professors who use the Web and various forms of email to conduct the course or require the use of such technology. Because you need to master these techniques to do the assignments, your time spent on assignments will also help you practice the skills of sending and receiving information electronically. A web design course in which you learn the use of FrontPage could be extremely valuable and might be more useful if offered by the writing program or your college, rather than the various computer or information studies programs.

NON-COURSE ACTIVITIES: Work part time or in the summer in a technologically aware business. The government and the nonprofit worlds are not likely to be helpful because they are usually ten years behind the private sector when it comes to technology.

One of my students who is a computer junkie has some warnings about bad email habits that you should avoid in college because they will be deadly in the job world:

> *First, if you find yourself addicted to AOL's Instant Messenger, it is not useful for developing your KHS. I know of students who will talk to their roommates through AIM. While this may be a way to improve your typing skills and become more global, it is important to realize that the business world does not like AIM. Most businesses look at AIM the same way they look at personal phone calls: neither is going to make you more productive. Sure, AIM will be your sole means of communication your first two years of school, but learning how to talk to*

people in person is a skill that will be better developed by getting away from instant messaging. After all, who is going to do a job interview with you through AIM?

On the flip side, however, email is crucial to the business world. Email moves at the speed of business: fast. Learning how to write properly formatted and easy-to-read emails will help you in the long run. Be careful, however, that you do not let AIM or cell phone text message abbreviations sneak into your emails or your employer will say "C U L8R, U R DONE." Just make sure you know how to use the email program Microsoft Outlook or at least Microsoft Outlook Express: they are both standard in any business. The key to great emails in the business world is to get to the point with numbered or bulleted lists.

Any other applications you might learn are probably proprietary and only apply to specific situations. Don't spend too much time with these, as anything you will need to learn beyond Microsoft Office applications will most likely be taught to you as you begin your job. Knowing the basics will give you a leg up on other applicants.

MINIMUM SKILL LEVEL BY GRADUATION: You know how to use the Web as a storage facility for everything from papers to resumes, and you can use emails to send information (including file attachments). By the time you graduate, you have your resume set to send electronically.

USEFUL RESOURCES

The Elements of Style, 4th edition, by William Strunk, Jr., E. B. White, and Roger Angell (Allyn & Bacon, 1999). This book is short and very inexpensive. The emphasis on few words is right on.

How to Write It: A Complete Guide to Everything You'll Ever Write by Sandra E. Lamb (Ten Speed Press, 1998). Describes the best format for what you write in every situation—from meeting notices and agendas to formal reports, thank you notes to public relations proposals, as well as email and online communications.

The Overnight Resume: The Fastest Way to Your Next Job! by Donald Asher (Ten Speed Press, 1999). This book provides suggestions on how to deliver your resume electronically and have it still look good. It will help you with the last MSL in this chapter.

Rewrite Right! Your Guide to Perfectly Polished Prose, 2nd edition, by Jan Venolia (Ten Speed Press, 2000). This book will help you realize that to write something initially and think that it is complete is a no-no. It also contains the common symbols proofreaders use.

Word 2002 for Dummies by Dan Gookin (John Wiley and Sons, 2001 or most recent edition). If you prefer a book to the Help button in Word, this book is as good as any in helping you master the intricacies of this universal word-processing software.

Write Right! A Desktop Digest of Punctuation, Grammar, and Style, 4th edition, by Jan Venolia (Ten Speed Press, 2001). With over one-half million copies sold, this inexpensive and small guide will help you avoid writing errors.

"NOTHING WE DO, HOWEVER VIRTUOUS, CAN BE ACCOMPLISHED ALONE."

—REINHOLD NIEBUHR

CHAPTER 5

WORKING DIRECTLY WITH PEOPLE

SKILL SETS

BUILD GOOD RELATIONSHIPS • WORK IN TEAMS • TEACH OTHERS

The quote above by Reinhold Niebuhr, one of the most famous theologians of the twentieth century, ended with "therefore we are saved by love." I did not include it because I feared it might make my readers feel uncomfortable. People skills are not just advocated by theologians but also the business people. Dale Carnegie quotes John D. Rockefeller, one of the hardest headed and richest SOBs of the late nineteenth and early twentieth century who said, "The ability to deal with people is as purchasable a commodity as sugar or coffee. And I will pay more for that ability than for any other under the sun."[1]

Knowing how to work with others is critical to your career success, and it also makes life a lot more pleasant. Many human resource directors, employers, and experts rate people skills as the most vital of the ten Know-How Groups. Because they are so important, they constitute two different Know-How Groups—working directly with people, which is this chapter's topic, and influencing people, which we will look at in chapter 6. While there is a fine line between "working with" and "influencing," the skills are different enough to warrant separate chapters. By creating these two Know-How Groups, we give double weight to people skills in the calculation of the KHS. This is justified by the heavy emphasis that all employers place on the ability of their employers to work well together and to influence others both within and outside the organization.

"Smile."

—Dale Carnegie

Building good relationships with others is no easy task because it takes time and requires mutual trust and respect. Learn to take the time necessary to work closely with others. Doing this well requires attention to a broad array of factors including different cultural, ethnic, social, and economic backgrounds. Sensitivity to and understanding of these factors can often prevent struggles over power and authority or conflicts over competing interests, which can badly—and sometimes irreparably—damage relationships. Given the large number of factors, it's important to begin to practice establishing good working relationships while in college.

One of the first tests of your ability to build a good relationship comes when you are interviewed for a job. Very literally, establishing a good relationship with your interviewer will determine whether or not you get the job.

Once you get the job, your success will depend on developing good working relationships with people throughout the organization. Having a good working relationship, one that is built on trust and mutual respect, requires communicating clearly and working to resolve conflict in a positive way. Conflict is part of any relationship, and the challenge is to learn how to work with it effectively. You will deal with customers who may not trust you or your company. Your coworkers, especially if you do your work well, may see you as a threat; perhaps you will see them as a threat as well. Even more prevalent is the tendency for workers in one department to view those in other departments as incompetent or irresponsible. The only way to move past these conflicts is to keep the lines of communication open and to establish good working relationships based on cooperation.

Good working relationships make it possible to work more efficiently and effectively, not to mention more pleasantly. People with whom you have good relationships can also help you learn about or even obtain jobs throughout your career—this is usually called "networking." Whether or not you have people who are willing to help you is a direct result of your ability (or inability) to establish good relationships. If, for example, you've developed a good working relationship with your boss, this could open unexpected possibilities for your future. One of the surest paths to career advancement is when your boss, who thinks you have done a great job, moves to another company and hires you six months later.

COURSES: Some psychology and sociology courses may introduce you to interpersonal and group dynamics that shape relationships. The more these courses require fieldwork and role playing, the more helpful they will be. Your college may have courses in mediation and/or conflict resolution, which will be based more on experience than traditional courses in the social sciences. Social work courses may also be helpful, but they may not be open to you unless you are registered in a social work program. Other professional schools or programs like nursing and human development have courses that will prepare you to deal with future clients in those fields.

NON-COURSE ACTIVITIES: Fortunately you will find opportunities to develop trusting and respectful relationships with others every day. Working things out with your roommate is a good sign that you are building interpersonal skills. A particularly useful non-course activity is to join a group that provides services to others, like Habitat for Humanity or a service fraternity. The internal cooperation between members as they seek to serve the outside world is very similar to what you will face in a job situation. Try to get an internship with a local Dale Carnegie Training, which is described in the Useful Resources section of chapter 3. They offer training in communication skills and other work-related people skills.

MINIMUM SKILL LEVEL BY GRADUATION: You consciously seek to develop good relationships with your professors, landlord, teammates, or associates in student organizations as well as with the full range of people you meet in part-time jobs and internships.

KNOW HOW TO WORK IN TEAMS

"You can't spell team without an 'I.'"

—David A. Goldsmith, management consultant

You probably got a taste of working in teams in high school classes and, if you are like the majority of students I've interviewed, you didn't like it. The dislike of working in teams is natural since we live in a society that praises individualism and competition. If you are very competitive and want high grades, you do not want to depend on others. You want the control. If you are relaxed, you do not want the hyper people on the team bugging you.

Teamwork in high school classes, however, is not the same as teamwork in the world of work. You will have stronger common interests with your fellow workers than with your classmates, and the measure of success is not just what grade your teacher or professor gives you. Several of the skill sets already discussed are critical to your ability to work well in a team. They include time management, honesty, good verbal communications, the ability to proof and edit, and the capacity to form good relationships. Email skills will be important because email facilitates communication prior to and following meetings. Many businesses set up virtual teams in which the team members rarely meet face to face, if at all. There are also specific skills for working in a team, including reaching agreements with others, understanding the importance of concurring on how decisions will be made, running productive meetings, and designating roles like recorder. Accepting responsibilities assigned to you by the team and helping others to do the same is also critical.

Perhaps the most important skill set you need for teamwork is patience and tolerance for the process. Teams rarely perform as well as team members think they should perform. The work of teams can take more time than expected and produce compromises that frequently lead directly to failure. Learning to be tolerant and to carefully pick your battles is essential to being a good team member.

Having said what you usually hear about teamwork, I direct your attention to the quote at the beginning of the chapter. David Goldsmith was a student of mine who turned a T-shirt business in college into a business that was eventually purchased by a conglomerate. He consults all over the world now and writes a monthly newsletter. His point is that each member of the team is an "I," and if each member does not accept the responsibility for failure and success, the team will fail. He writes:

> *I, I, I is the building block of teams just like there are four building blocks of a DNA strand. Any one link that is damaged cannot fulfill the organism's need, will cause a weakness in its ability to survive.*[2]

College is the place to practice balancing your individual pursuit of excellence with the need to have a common goal and set of strategies. Don't make the mistake that many students do of seeing teamwork as one gigantic pebble in their shoe. See it as a challenge that you need to meet and a setting in which you can enjoy the success of the team by doing your very best.

Expressing dislike or even a little uneasiness about working in a team will result in a short and unproductive job interview. Once you are in a job, failure to work well in teams leads to poor job reviews. Conversely, working well in teams gains you positive points throughout the organization and may lead to promotions that you would not otherwise get. You can whine about your team to your significant other, but always be positive about it at work in word and in deed. It's frustrating, but good teamwork is the law of most high-functioning organizations.

COURSES: Teamwork experiences can be found in every college program, especially in upper division undergraduate courses. Look for professors who create team projects, especially those evaluated by someone other than them. Courses that prepare you for team mock trial competitions, teach you to set up a public relations campaign for the local Boys and Girls Club, or instruct you how to create a business plan for a start-up company provide excellent opportunities to develop teamwork skills.

NON-COURSE ACTIVITIES: The most powerful experience outside the classroom is probably in a fraternity or sorority or in another tight-knit student organization that has to meet a budget projection or put on an event. Learning teamwork occurs best when failure has serious consequences. You can also gain valuable experience working on a college committee. These committees might involve faculty members who give awards for teaching or select a speaker for commencement. They might be advisory groups to important programs like peer advising or residence life.

MINIMUM SKILL LEVEL BY GRADUATION: You are able to work cooperatively in a variety of team settings.

"A teacher affects eternity."

—Henry Adams, nineteenth-century author

Henry Adams, like most of us, may have been thinking of teaching as a situation of academic tutoring or one that involves a person lecturing at the chalkboard in a classroom. However, teaching occurs all of the time in informal settings. It is as important in the world of work as it is in your everyday life with family and friends.

Teaching is a process in which one person—the teacher—takes action to improve what another person—the learner—does. Within that definition, knowing how to teach is essential in every aspect of your life, whether it be teaching your little brother how to get dates or your room-mate to stop throwing trash on your side of the room. You may even find yourself in a more formal setting, such as teaching CPR to a group of college students or training residence advisers on how to deal with out-of-control students.

The skills of a good teacher grow out of many of the skills discussed in this book. Verbal communication is critical, but so is asking and answering the right questions. Beyond that, teaching requires a consciousness about where the learner is and the ability to implement strategies that get the learner to move to where they want to be. The best approach according to a president of a growing and successful company is to promote learning by doing. He writes:

> *I have often taught my trainers that if you want to teach someone something, show him or her how to do it and then get out of their way and let them do it. If they get it wrong, well, at least they tried. Using this method has also helped me delegate better because teaching by doing requires the teacher to remember that everyone will do things differently.*

This quote not only provides good advice on how you can be a better teacher but also illustrates that even the president of a company has to be a teacher on a regular basis. The best companies are committed to encouraging or even requiring senior staff to guide and educate junior staff. You will need to become a teacher within your organization soon after you arrive; your capacity to "train" others to do your job will also help you move into other positions. Sometimes the word "mentor" or "coach" is used, but it still means teaching and mostly teaching by example.

COURSES: Courses to develop your informal teaching skills are not necessarily offered in education departments or programs. The best kinds of courses for your development as a teacher are those in which you practice teaching. It might be an adult literacy course in which part of the requirement is to tutor adults, or it might be a course in social work or psychology in which part of the credit is earned by tutoring at a community center. Jump at the chance to be an undergraduate teaching assistant if given the opportunity.

NON-COURSE ACTIVITIES: In many community service activities, you can find opportunities for doing one-on-one tutoring. In addition, your work in any student organization will eventually involve teaching new members about the organization or training your replacement to do your job if you are an officer. Part-time jobs in a fast-food restaurant or at Kinko's will require you to train new employees even if you remain in the job for a short period of time. This practice will improve your teaching skills. Peer advising for you college can also improve these skills.

MINIMUM SKILL LEVEL BY GRADUATION: You have had at least three teaching opportunities in which you were successful in helping others develop key skills.

USEFUL RESOURCES

How to Win Friends and Influence People by Dale Carnegie (Pocket Books, 1982). Already mentioned in chapter 3 with respect to verbal communications, this book is the best way to gain a perspective on how to build trust with other people. Also, see chapter 3 for information on Dale Carnegie Training and www.dalecarnegie.com, where you can sign up for free tips about working with others.

The 17 Indisputable Laws of Teamwork: Embrace them and Empower Your Team by John C. Maxwell (Thomas Nelson, 2001). This book is reader friendly and will help you see how important and effective good teamwork can be and what you can do about it.

BEGIN WITH PRAISE AND HONEST APPRECIATION.

—DALE CARNEGIE

CHAPTER 6

INFLUENCING PEOPLE

SKILL SETS

**MANAGE EFFICIENTLY · SELL SUCCESSFULLY ·
POLITICK WISELY · LEAD EFFECTIVELY**

Oftentimes, working with your colleagues and others outside the organization requires you to treat them as objects of influence. This may sound a little harsh, but it is reality. This chapter will introduce you to four different and relatively distinct roles that you may play when you try to influence others in the world of work.

Keep in mind that there are many styles of managing, selling, politicking, and leading. You will need to develop the style that is both effective and comfortable for you. Practicing these skills during your college years is important because it will give you the opportunity to find your style through a process of trial and error.

Another theme in this chapter is the role of honesty and character in the actions you take as a manager, salesperson, politician, and leader. All of these roles require you to convince others to do something that they would not otherwise do. Deceit and the arbitrary or unjust use of power are tempting, especially if you are faced with a roadblock. Learn how to control that temptation in college, because in the long run, such control will serve you well in your professional career.

"The best managers think of themselves as playing coaches."

—Robert Townsend, author of best-selling book *Up the Organization*

In chapter 2, we discussed managing your time and managing your money as a key to the work ethic Know-How Group. To manage time and money, you make decisions over allocating your own resources.

Managing people is a whole different thing. Your task is to convince people to do their assigned jobs competently. In other words, managing people is using human resources assigned to you over which you have some influence but little control. For this reason, management is always stressful, and effective managers are in short supply.

Efficient managers usually come up through the ranks. They have performed well in their entry-level jobs and convinced those who managed them that they would be able to manage their former peers. To get the most from their people, managers need to build on many of the skills already discussed, especially those described in the previous chapter. They must also know how to use the tools their organization gives them, including salaries, benefits, and training programs, to motivate those they manage.

Good managers have to maintain the respect of those they manage while still encouraging them and listening to their feedback. As noted at the onset of this chapter, you need to find a comfortable management style. Situations that allow you to practice these skills in college can help prepare you to manage in the work world.

Management potential is a key consideration, especially in higher paying entry-level jobs, and it may be part of the interviewer's agenda when meeting with you as a prospective employee. In order for organizations to grow, they need to recruit people who can eventually take over the jobs of the top leaders, thus allowing the top leaders to move on to new fields. These leaders want you to do your job in a way that makes their task as your manager less burdensome. Moreover, advancement within the company will ultimately lead to a management position.

COURSES: Courses that will introduce you to the art and science of management are usually found in schools of management and public administration. Although more likely to be found at the graduate level, some upper division undergraduate courses may be offered. In any case, take those courses that include roleplaying and simulation or, better yet, observation and participation in the real world. For example, serving as an intern or assistant to a mid-level manager in a business or nonprofit organization will give you an opportunity to see how the manager interacts with subordinates and superiors.

NON-COURSE ACTIVITIES: The single most powerful way to develop management skills and demonstrate them to potential employers is to work your way up in an organization from an entry-level to a management position. On-campus jobs, such as one in food service, can allow you to move from server to a manager of servers. Off campus, working your way up in a fast-food restaurant to shift supervisor or assistant manager will impress any job interviewer. Another valuable management experience is to run a fund-raising event or start a program by recruiting college students to offer tutoring at a local Boys and Girls Club.

MINIMUM SKILL LEVEL BY GRADUATION: You have efficiently managed at least three other workers in a job or community service experience.

KNOW HOW TO SELL SUCCESSFULLY

"The main problem in the sale is to find the basic need, or the main point of interest, and then stick to it."

—Frank Bettger, author of a best-selling book on sales

You probably think selling is about selling jeans at the GAP or about cold calling to peddle charities, family portraits, or new phone companies. If you are literary at all, you may be familiar with the play *Death of a Salesman* and do not want to end up like the main character, Willie Loman, who is considered an out-of-date, terrible salesman. He has an affair with a woman he meets on a sales trip and then ends up committing suicide so that his sons do not become failures like himself. It is part of our culture to see sales as a difficult and dirty business.

The traits of a good salesperson are dependent on almost every single skill set mentioned in this book. You have to work hard, stay well, have excellent communication and people skills, and be good at problem solving as well as finding and analyzing information. Several characteristics critical to being an effective salesperson are being able to handle sustained and continuous rejection, keeping pressure on yourself to work hard, and having solid product knowledge.

Get rid of negative thoughts about sales before you enter the workforce because those who make it to the top of every field are always good at selling themselves, their products, and their ideas. Sales skills are important to your future for the following reasons:

- Good salespeople are in very short supply. Sales positions are easy to land and are monetarily rewarding. When it comes to pharmaceuticals or financial products, we are talking about six figures in less than five years.
- Successful salespeople have a fast track to the top of the company— sales representatives become sales managers, who become marketing managers, who become VPs for marketing, who become senior VPs, who become CEOs.
- Selling is a very good training ground for all other professions because it involves synthesizing information and persuading people.
- Regardless of which career you pursue, you will ultimately be a salesperson if you are successful. The most successful lawyers are those who bring in new clients. The most successful government workers are those who sell themselves and their departments to others. Even teaching incorporates a sales component; selling your students on the importance of a subject may be more critical than giving good lectures. The highest position in academia, chancellor of a university, entails fund-raising, the most difficult form of sales. And, if you want to make the world better, you will be selling "change" to others.
- If you are a successful salesperson, by the time you are forty you will have lots of free time and excellent contacts to be a mover and a shaker.

I am not suggesting that you take a sales job; although for reasons stated previously, sales can be a very good career choice. Instead, I'm urging you to develop your sales tools in college because they will be handy during your job interviews and in every job you take.

COURSES: Management schools offer courses in marketing, of which direct selling is a component. A marketing course might be helpful in alerting you to the dynamics of selling. Speech communication courses that focus on methods of persuasion can also help. Courses in negotiation and mediation might also contribute to your ability to close the deal. Those courses that have simulations or fieldwork integrated into the course should be selected over those that do not.

NON-COURSE ACTIVITIES: There are enormous opportunities to learn sales in both internship and job activities. You can receive great basic training in sales by working for a political candidate during a campaign or in door-to-door solicitation campaigns of Public Interest Research Groups (PIRGs), which can be found in many colleges. Telephone sales skills can be practiced through a job with the alumni fund at your college. Cold calling alumni provides you with plenty of rejection, an experience that employers love to learn you can handle. Summer and part-time telephone sales jobs or assisting those making the calls and visits can be important experiences in learning how to persuade people and how to think on your feet.

MINIMUM SKILL LEVEL BY GRADUATION: You have had at least two different positions in which you have successfully convinced others to buy a product, donate money, or sign a petition.

"One of the penalties for refusing to participate in politics is that you end up being governed by your inferiors."

—Plato

Plato was a little harsh and elitist here, but there is much to be said for this quote. Politics has a bad name whether we are talking professional politicians or the political types in corporations and organizations. You will find that playing politics is the price of career success, especially as you move up the career ladder. It you don't want to be political, then you cannot really complain about those who are. You could face much worse than being ruled by inferiors, as Plato says, you could actually end up being fired.

The skills discussed in this section have very little to do with running for office. Instead, they require understanding the role of power, authority, and self-interest. In short, the reality is that people, not reason, control decisions, and politics is the art of getting people on your side. As a human resource director from a large corporation said:

> *Don't step on people's toes. Know when to speak up, but do it with respect; play nice with everyone, but disagree with people politely. If you know when to speak up, this can lead to not only a promotion for you, but success for the company.*

Wherever you work, you will face a long history of relationships and power structures. The easiest and perhaps least risky path to follow is to do what you are told and refrain from calling for substantial change. While this path makes sense for the first year of your tenure, be ready to offer suggestions about policies and procedures that would improve the company and your job performance after that period. As we will see in chapter 10, effective problem solving requires a good grasp of politics.

Playing politics well requires that you avoid whining and complaining in the workplace. If you need to vent, wait until you get off work. You may be driven crazy by the fact that your boss is too slow to respond to a changing business environment or a policy that is outmoded. Don't complain to your colleagues, and never go over the head of your immediate supervisor unless you are prepared for the worst. Instead, realize that the political forces within the organization are generally averse to change, and you must always be planning as though it were a political campaign. Your job will be to build a coalition for change.

Moving up the organizational scale requires that you develop the very difficult skill of balancing interests. One of the primary reasons that all politicians are viewed with suspicion is that their job is to balance different interests. This guarantees that anything they do will result in many of their constituents being disappointed. The first thing you need to learn from this is that people in those kinds of positions deserve a break, and the second is to realize is that you will be in that position sooner than you think. Politics is very frustrating, but there is no alternative.

From this discussion, it should be clear that developing strategies and techniques to convince your superiors to make the decisions you want—whether it's giving you a bigger salary or altering an existing policy—are skills necessary for your career. From the day you start work, you will see and hear things that will push you to react. Reacting out of emotion or even out of clear evidence should be avoided until you know the political forces that lie behind what you see or hear. If you don't, you may find yourself looking for another job very quickly or languishing in a dead-end position.

You are likely to see corruption at various levels in the workplace. Your first experience might be a coworker padding an expense account. Given the corporate fraud and corruption making the headlines in the United States these past few years, you should be aware that various kinds of tax evasion, incorrect reporting, and downright stealing occur on occasion. It may not occur more than 5 percent of the time, but eventually you will be confronted by it. The question then becomes, "What are you going to do about it?" Your political knowledge and skill will help you develop a strategy, but ultimately it is your character that will be most important.

In your college years, you will be confronted with many forms of corruption—dorm residents breaking dorm rules, resident advisers looking the other way, student organizations leaders acting immaturely, classmates cheating, and faculty acting irresponsibly. Learn how to recognize these forms of corruption, how to avoid being corrupted, and how to politick wisely to work for change.

COURSES: Political science courses would be an obvious choice for learning about the politics of the workplace. However, these courses usually deal with public affairs–type politics and frequently are very heavy on theory. Those courses that use simulation exercises or fieldwork experiences could be very instructive since they will confront you with the reality of politics with a small "p." There may be courses in public administration and sociology available to undergraduates that deal with theories on how organizations behave. They will be most helpful if there are some hands-on experiences associated with them.

NON-COURSE ACTIVITIES: You can learn a great deal by getting involved in student or residence-life organizations. The dynamics of power and authority will be very instructive. Equally valuable, will be your appointment to a decision-making committee of a department or the college. You can become a member of the college or university body that represents faculty and usually involves students and administrators. Try to get appointed as the student representative to the board of trustees for the college or to a tenure and promotion committee. This will give you a picture of how the day-to-day flow of events is shaped by the rules and structures of the institution. Finally, some job and internship experiences may give you a glimpse into the politics of that particular organization. You might even find yourself playing a direct role by being asked to do something you think is wrong or being treated unethically. If so, try to learn as much as you can from the experience.

MINIMUM SKILL LEVEL BY GRADUATION: You have participated in one student organization activity and one college-level activity in which you were involved in some sort of decision making.

"A leader is like a shepherd. . . . He stays behind the flock, letting the most nimble go out ahead, whereupon the others follow, not realizing that all along they are being directed from behind."

—Nelson Mandela

Leadership is one of those words that conjures up all kinds of things from being president of the United States or the CEO of General Electric to the captain of a team. It is a positive term. Most students want to have leadership experiences if only because they think it will look good on their resume or grad school application. It has to do with the American emphasis on individualism on the one hand and the natural drive for money and power on the other. Ironically, effective leadership is about limiting individualism and avoiding a preoccupation with money and power.

Leaders, by definition, have followers. Leaders are able to take the initiative based on a vision of making things better and then to motivate supporters to follow their vision. All this requires special talents in problem solving, which we will discuss in chapter 10, and in the people skills discussed in this and the previous chapter.

Like managing, selling, and politicking, leadership styles vary greatly, so your goal in college should be to explore the kind of leader you might like to be. Do you prefer the autocratic and heavy-handed approach of someone like Lyndon Johnson or the "lead from behind as a shepherd" approach of Nelson Mandela? Style is important, but so is the situation. One of the things you will need to learn is when one style is more effective than another. You may have one comfortable leadership style, but if that does not work, then you may be required to adopt one you find less comfortable.

Employers frequently say they want to recruit potential leaders just as they want potential managers. In both cases, the top leadership of an organization wants to expand and needs solid candidates to manage things and lead in new directions. Employers value leaders who are good at stimulating their colleagues to take reasonable initiatives. They appreciate a little movement outside of the box, but not too much. Leadership that is revolutionary is rarely encouraged.

COURSES: Many universities have credit-bearing courses in leadership. Some may be offered in traditional departments like political science and sociology, but others may be offered in what they call interdisciplinary centers or programs. Courses in entrepreneurial skills, which are associated with leadership, are frequently offered in management programs and schools. As in many of the other skills we have discussed, those courses that are project based and involve experiences outside of the classroom, or at least simulations, are preferred.

NON-COURSE ACTIVITIES: Becoming a member of the executive board of an established group can provide great opportunities to feel comfortable in a leadership role and to develop leadership skills. If the position is elected, it will mean that you gained the confidence of the members of the organization. Establishing a new organization can be a great leadership development experience even if the organization fails. All these kinds of activities require you to exercise the skills of motivation and vision that will get people to take responsibility for the organization. Many colleges have non-credit leadership development programs run by student affairs or resident life departments.

MINIMUM SKILL LEVEL BY GRADUATION: You have held at least a minor leadership position in an existing organization or in a team project.

USEFUL RESOURCES

Common Sense Leadership by Roger Fulton (Ten Speed Press, 1995). This inexpensive book summarizes a lot of good ideas about leadership in one-page sections. If you can master them, you will have achieved your MSL for leadership.

How I Raised Myself from Failure to Success in Selling by Frank Bettger (Simon & Schuster, 1977). Even if you are not going to be a salesperson by profession, this book will help you be the salesperson you will need to be to succeed in whatever you do.

How to Win Friends and Influence People by Dale Carnegie (Pocket Books, 1982). Why not use the bible of how to get people to do what you want? This book will help you manage, sell, politick, and lead effectively. Also, see chapter 3 for information on Dale Carnegie Training and www.dalecarnegie.com, where you can sign up for free tips about working with others.

Leadership by Rudolph W. Giuliani (Hyperion, 2002). The former mayor of New York City provides his experience in the form of rules, one for each chapter. Some people don't like some of the things that happened under Giuliani's government, but few would argue that he was not a master of leadership.

Long Walk to Freedom by Nelson Mandela (Little, Brown and Company, 1995). Any book you read by or about a great leader will be useful, but this one is about someone who did the impossible. He was able to keep his own supporters on his team while gaining the trust of those who opposed him. Meta-Matrix Consulting Group (www.metamatrixconsulting.com). David A. Goldsmith's discussion of the importance of I in teamwork was discussed in the previous chapter. His monthly newsletter is available to you free, so sign up for it at this website. The focus is on business management, but most of the lessons about management and leadership can be applied to any field.

One Day, All Children: The Unlikely Triumph of Teach for America and What I Learned Along the Way by Wendy Kopp (PublicAffairs, 2001). This book describes how Ms. Kopp came up with the idea of Teach for America (TFA) in her senior thesis at Princeton. For all readers, whether interested in making the world better or making money, the lessons provided by the book will make you a better manager, salesperson, politician, and leader.

100+ Tactics for Office Politics by Casey Fitts Hawley (Barron's Educational Series, 2001). Although this book deals with the business world, it will help you understand the role of politics in any career. You will also find parallels with your on-campus experiences while in college.

The One Minute Manager by Kenneth H. Blanchard and Spencer Johnson (Berkley Books, 1982). This book made quite a stir when it came out two decades ago. A short, inexpensive, and to-the-point presentation that will help you manage not only others in your job but also your roommates and your parents.

"SEEK
AND YOU SHALL
FIND."

—JESUS CHRIST

CHAPTER 7

GATHERING INFORMATION

SKILL SETS

USE LIBRARY HOLDINGS • USE COMMERCIAL DATABASES • SEARCH THE WEB • CONDUCT INTERVIEWS • USE SURVEYS • KEEP AND USE RECORDS

I know that this great religious leader was not talking about the Web or sample surveys when he made this inspirational statement. He was talking about something much bigger. However, he was talking about focus in the world of chaos where meaninglessness can overpower the meaningful. On a less cosmic and spiritual scale, focus in your gathering information is as important to your career success as focus is to the rest of your life.

Knowing how to collect information is critical to any job. Without the necessary information, you cannot perform your job. As our up-and-coming corporate type suggests below, information is an important key to advancement. He writes:

Hunt or be hunted. The majority of my accomplishments have come as a result of having information that someone else needed. The first step is to know what someone needs and why. The second step is being resourceful enough to know where to get the data and quickly. I can't stress the quickness enough. Organizations need speed, and when you're gathering information you have to be organized.

Getting information is more than a high-speed scavenger hunt in which you are given a list of things to find. It requires focus in the face of chaos. It is like going to the mall to shop for a family member without knowing what to buy. As you acquire information about more stuff, you start thinking about what to buy. You will be successful only if you keep in mind the tastes and interests of the family member. You are searching for something, but you are not always sure what it is, and it is very easy to just pick up a gift that does not fit.

Not being sure what you are looking for creates substantial difficulties. If you have ever written a large paper, you know that you start with basic information to understand the questions you want answered, and then you need to find more information to answer the questions, which leads to more questions and more information. As you analyze your information, you will need to ask better questions. To make the whole activity even more aggravating, as you start to write your paper, you realize that your information base is weak and that you need to search for more specific information. Moreover, even after you have written the first draft of the paper, reactions from others may require you to go back and do more research. Collecting information is an unlimited, open-ended process.

But we have to start somewhere. This chapter features six skill sets that will provide you with the know-how to collect different kinds of information essential to most jobs.

KNOW HOW TO USE LIBRARY HOLDINGS

"Libraries are not made, they grow."

—Augustine Birrell, a nineteenth-century writer

The library used to be a place where you simply found information. Today it is a place that houses some of that information but also provides electronic access to an unlimited amount of information. You need to know how to locate information in a large library by using its computer-based catalogue system, as well as its hard copy and electronic publications.

Your job may not require going to a large public library, but it will require you to search for information. In addition, you may find yourself required to use the holdings of a corporate or other private archive to locate information, or perhaps even consult a government library, including federal, state, and local records. Efficiently and effectively using library research tools and actual holdings will prepare you to use those and other tools to research relevant topics such as mailing lists, government programs, available products, and the work of relevant professional associations for future employers.

COURSES: Lower-division courses in library science or information studies are available at many colleges and universities, big and small. These courses help you understand the available tools, but they may be too general to give you focused experience. Courses in the social sciences and humanities that emphasize research will give you some additional skills in using the library. In every field of study, journals, magazines, newsletters, and a growing number of electronic services are used in upper-level courses. Look for courses that require you to do research. Because whatever job you go into will have very specialized information needs, the purpose of this activity is to become familiar with the library search tools and not the specific sources.

NON-COURSE ACTIVITIES: Spend some time in the library just learning what information sources are available. Some colleges offer library research skill education through self-paced online tutorials, videos, taped walking tours, or briefings by librarians. Librarians will be very glad to give you general and specific briefings if you approach them before the last minute.

Our fun-loving undergraduate, who is always looking for an angle, has this to say:

> *For the most part, the research you do in college is going to be computer-based because it is faster and easier than going to the actual library. This presents a problem for most students because when it comes to a project or a paper where their professor demands that a hard copy of a book be used, it's easy to become lost in the library. The best solution is to get a job at a library because you get paid to learn how to use its resources, and when there is downtime, you basically get paid to study.*

MINIMUM SKILL LEVEL BY GRADUATION: Use library catalogues and databases in a variety of fields.

"There is no better ballast for keeping the mind steady on its keel, and saving it from all risks of crankiness than business."

—James Russell Lowell, a nineteenth-century writer

The term *database* has two very different meanings. It can mean a piece of computer software where information is recorded, like Microsoft Access, which we will discuss in chapter 11. Database also means a large set of information available electronically. In this section, we will talk about the growing number of specialized bodies of highly organized information available in libraries and for purchase.

Because of the explosion of information in print and on the Web, people or businesses who need to find relevant and accurate information quickly are willing to pay for it. As a result, databases that charge to be used are usually more focused and more reliable than those found on the Web. The largest journalistic and legal general source can be found on Lexis-Nexis, which also has good coverage of statistical sources. ProQuest also has a wide variety of financial, academic, and background information. There is one exception to this rule; the free government websites are usually very reliable. You need to be aware of these databases, how to find appropriate ones, and how to search them using the sophisticated search engines developed by commercial services.

Very specialized databases exist on every conceivable topic. These databases can be accessed through the Web at a fee. Businesses frequently pay for them, but you can't. However, your library will purchase and make them available to you as a student. Whatever job you enter, several databases are likely to be used by the organization that hires you regardless of whether you are in marketing, research, or production. Having some experience in any one of these databases will give you a leg up on your competition.

COURSES: General commercial databases like Lexis-Nexis are likely to be a valuable source of information for you in many of your courses. More specialized databases may be used in upper-division courses in the social sciences, management, and communications. Look for mention of these databases in course syllabi.

NON-COURSE ACTIVITY: Research jobs at business or government organizations may require you to work with databases they purchase. This is not usually the case with nonprofits, which rarely can afford such services. However, a nonprofit could have access to databases created by government agencies, larger and wealthier nonprofit organizations, or the complex search engines of research institutes. So spend some time as a research gofer for the research, marketing, or public relations department of a business.

Frank, who knows a lot about electronic sources, writes:

> *Sometimes I think it's a bad thing to have access to these databases because it makes it possible to do almost anything without even setting foot in the library! Depending on which databases your library subscribes to, you'll be able to search newspapers and magazines across the country, sometimes up to fifty years in the past. These commercial databases are a great place to get historical data or even cutting-edge ideas and studies, as some are updated several times a day. Regardless, my advice is to get into a few of the main databases like FirstSearch, Lexis-Nexis, and Dialog@Carl and play around with them because it'll pay off when you need sources for a paper or project.*

MINIMUM SKILL LEVEL BY GRADUATION: Use at least these commercial databases before you graduate: Lexis-Nexis, ProQuest Direct, FirstSearch, and Dialog@Carl.

KNOW HOW TO SEARCH THE WEB

"There's no such thing as a free lunch."

—Attributed to Milton Friedman, a twentieth-century Nobel laureate economist and defender of the free market

Finding information you need *and* can trust on the Web is time-consuming unless you have web-search skills. The key is to know search strategies and to also assess the organization providing the information. When you are able to find the 5 percent of material that can be trusted, you will have achieved a great deal. Learn about the strengths and weaknesses of various search engines and how to use them.

The Web contains an infinite amount of information that can answer many questions in very specific detail. Think of the Web as a pile of newspapers that would probably reach the moon if placed in a single stack. Given the sheer volume of stuff on the Web, finding the right information sucks up as much time as looking for a needle in a haystack. If you can get critical information to your boss at the near speed of light, you will become indispensable and reach the stars.

You can also find sites on the Web that will do things for you. For example, the site recommended at the end of this chapter can produce correct APA- or MLA-style work cited entries. There are sites that allow you to tabulate survey results or translate into English a report written in French and many other languages. The Web is primarily an information source, but it is also a potential workhorse.

Not only will being an expert at searching the Web help your GPA and make you a star at work, it will help you find jobs throughout your working life. According to Richard N. Bolles, whose book *What Color is Your Parachute?* is the best book for career and job searching by far (eight million copies printed and counting), the Internet is an essential tool for exploring careers, finding out about companies, and, most important, getting jobs. Bolles describes a case in which someone in New Mexico looking for a job in San Francisco posted her resume at 10 P.M. on a Monday night and had seventy responses from employers by Wednesday morning.[1]

COURSES: Any course that requires research will provide experiences in web research. Especially valuable are courses that require you to use government websites, like the one created by the U.S. Census Bureau, because the government is a major source of information for all businesses. These courses can be found in political science, economics, public policy, and history. To get a better feel for the power and limitations of the Web, you may want to take a course in which you design websites.

NON-COURSE ACTIVITY: Get experience through part-time work, an internship, or summer job doing research. Businesses are often hungry for assistance with web-related projects and rarely have staff that has the time to devote to these projects. On-campus research jobs may also give you some experience in searching the Web for useful and reliable information.

An undergraduate who was a top student and a web junky, weighs in on the Web:

> *Learning how to search the Web AND get relevant information will make or break you in many career paths today. I do Internet research all the time, even when trying to find bargains on clothes at online stores. Odds are, someday an employer is going to say to you, "Find out what services our competitors are offering . . ." and you're going to be wondering where to start. If you're not an experienced web searcher, you're going to spend 80 percent of your time sifting through garbage and personal pages, and the remaining 20 percent will be actually finding what you want.*

MINIMUM SKILL LEVEL BY GRADUATION: You can find the telephone number and address of someone you know, and you can use at least three different search engines. You can locate desirable internships and jobs through web searches.

KNOW HOW TO CONDUCT INTERVIEWS

"An expert is one who knows more and more about less and less."

—Nicholas Murray Butler, early twentieth-century president of Columbia University

Getting information is like being a detective, and the best initial source of information is people who are working in the field or studying the field. The skill to find the right people, establish a basis for their help, ask the right questions, and probe for accuracy is, therefore, essential.

You probably already know how to do this if you are like Gina, my research assistant, who is both personable and confident. She writes:

> *Granted you can get scores of questions answered on the Internet, but you can get information you trust from actual people, and you can get it fast. For example, asking a neighbor or a friend's parents about the best place in town to buy a car is a lot easier and more dependable*

*than searching through tons of automobile websites. To
get the information you want, you need to figure out **who**
are the best people to ask and **what** are the best questions to ask that will get you what you need. Start small,
first asking your close contacts for information or for
names of people who can better help you, and then you'll
be able to work your way toward the experts.*

The single most important reason for conducting effective interviews
is to save time. With little background, you can get more basic information
and leads in less time than going to the library or searching databases and
websites. Even if you only ask someone who knows something about the
subject questions like what is the best book, article, website, or database,
you will be way ahead of the game. If you are good at interviewing, you
will be able to help your boss when he says, "Find out about x and brief me
on it." This principle applies to any kind of information search. To illustrate, the most important part of a job search is getting information from
career counselors, from future employers at job fairs, and in "informational" interview situations.

COURSES: Courses in sociology, psychology, political science, speech
communications, journalism, and writing sometimes provide training in
conducting good interviews. Any research course could provide you with
opportunities to interview experts as you educate yourself about your
topic.

NON-COURSE ACTIVITY: You can obtain excellent experience in
developing your interviewing skills merely by spending time figuring out
what major fits you best or what courses are good to take. Figuring out the
best person to ask and the questions that will provide you with the most
useful information are critical to making good program and course choices.
Moving from there, get yourself involved in a student group that is trying
to get something from the administration or from the student government.
As both groups give you the run around, you will develop your ability to
find good information sources and ask the right questions.

MINIMUM SKILL LEVEL BY GRADUATION: Before you are a
senior in college, you have conducted at least two interviews about careers
you may want to pursue.

"If one or two people tell you that you're an ass, you can ignore them. But if three or four people tell you you're an ass, you might think about putting on a saddle."

—Yiddish saying

There are many different kinds of surveys, ranging from customer surveys and focus groups to market research and public opinion polls. Learn how to appreciate the limitations of all surveys and how to adjust for those limitations in using them. Everyone who graduates from college does not need to know how to conduct a survey, but they certainly need to know how to interpret survey findings.

Any job you take will be in an organization that works with a large number of people either within the organization or as customers or both. Having information about the characteristics and attitudes of these people will be crucial. Surveys are frequently used to acquire that information. In some cases, you may even participate in designing and implementing a survey. At a bare minimum, you need to be a skeptical consumer of the surveys that come your way by asking the right questions about the quality of the sample and the biases in the surveys.

COURSES: Although you do not have to become a professional designer of surveys, the only way to develop the skills necessary to be a skeptical consumer is to participate in the design, implementation, and analysis of a survey through a course. Courses that require students to conduct their own survey can be offered anywhere in the social sciences and professional schools. They are usually more work than other courses, but the benefits are enormous.

NON-COURSE ACTIVITY: Volunteer to help a student organization do a survey or sign up with a political campaign to help conduct surveys. Professors and think tanks around the university frequently hire students to do the mundane work of conducting a survey, which you should do at least once.

MINIMUM SKILL LEVEL BY GRADUATION: You have a reflex reaction whenever you get survey results to ask critical questions about the sample and the nature of the questions.

KNOW HOW TO KEEP AND USE RECORDS

"Without records, we have no way of knowing what we are doing."

—Frank Bettger, author of a best-selling book on sales

Record keeping may sound like the ultimate mindless activity, but unfortunately, keeping and checking records is a critical skill. You should use college to learn how organizations keep records and how you can assess their accuracy. Develop habits of good record keeping for what you do yourself.

Frank Bettger, who is quoted at the beginning of this section and identified as a useful resource in chapter 1 and 6, found that keeping detailed records was a key to his success as a salesman. By keeping records, for example, he saw that 70 percent of his sales were made on his first call, 23 percent on his second, and only 7 percent on his third call. His conclusion was that he should make more first-time calls and fewer third-time calls. This doubled the amount of money he made for each phone call he made.[2]

Whether you have a job in business, government, or the nonprofit sector, records of expenses and services are critical. Lawyers charge clients by fifteen-minute intervals on phone calls. Keeping good records is related to money, and money is what makes the world go round. This is true for not only businesses in which accounting procedures are the ultimate in record keeping but also for nonprofits that must show the government funders what they are doing with government money.

At a personal level, you will need to put in requests for travel reimbursements. Develop a capacity to keep good records for what you do. Even more important, learn how to use and assess the quality of the records that are important for making decisions in your job. Just in case you are not convinced, think about how important it is for your grades that your professors accurately record your test and paper scores or how the fraudulent accounting practices contributed to the stock market decline in 2002.

COURSES: Record keeping is at the heart of the physical sciences, so a lab course will help you develop your capacity to make detailed and legible records. Many management courses will introduce you to different methods of record keeping. In several social sciences, you may find a course that requires you to collect data using code sheets.

The key is to find hands-on courses in which you collect and record data or use data recording by existing organizations. Courses in which a log is required for an internship or fieldwork will also help you develop this skill set.

NON-COURSE ACTIVITY: The most powerful way to develop this skill is to do a good job in managing your time, which requires careful and detailed planning. If you can record when and where you want to complete a task and then check off when you have done it, you will be on your way to becoming a good record keeper. Become the treasurer or secretary of a student organization that requires good record keeping. You will review the work of the predecessor and learn how to assess accuracy while you are learning the principles of good record keeping yourself. A sure-fire way to develop the capacity to keep good records is to use a computer-based tool such as Microsoft Money or Quicken on your own finances.

MINIMUM SKILL LEVEL BY GRADUATION: You can keep a log of your daily activities that can document to someone else what you have done.

USEFUL RESOURCES

A Foot in the Door by Katherine Hansen (Ten Speed Press, 2000). This book's main purpose is to help you establish contacts for job hunting. It contains a useful section on informational interviewing, and it will prepare you to meet the MSL for interviewing.

Landmarks for Schools (www.landmark-project.com). This site, which was designed for high school teachers, has all kinds of great things that will help you with finding resources. The "citation machine" is particularly handy. It queries you for the necessary information and then types it out in the right MLA or APA format.

Power Reporting (www.powerreporting.com). To improve your web-searching skills, go to this excellent all-purpose website that is maintained for use by journalists. Click on "Search Tools" and look for a tutorial on web searching: strategy and syntax. If you go through the activities on the site, you will be more efficient at web searching. Another source of help may be your college library, if it offers a short training program or handout to help increase your efficiency in web searching.

"EVERY TOOL CARRIES WITH IT THE SPIRIT BY WHICH IT HAS BEEN CREATED."

—WERNER KARL HEISENBERG,
TWENTIETH-CENTURY PHYSICIST

CHAPTER 8

USING QUANTITATIVE TOOLS

USE NUMBERS • USE GRAPHS AND TABLES • USE SPREADSHEET PROGRAMS

This chapter introduces you to the three most basic quantitative tools you need to develop while in college. These tools are necessary for any job that you will take. Usually you will use them immediately. Please note that the Minimum Skill Levels for all three are set at a very low level, so if you are not a numbers person, don't get scared. Take a deep breath and read this chapter. Hopefully you'll see that anybody can achieve the levels called for.

If you're a numbers person, heed this word of warning: Getting 800 on your quantitative SAT, being a whiz at calculus, and knowing how to calculate the most exotic statistic are not the same as using quantitative tools. You may consider the skill sets in this chapter trivial, but unless you've used numbers and spreadsheets to make or recommend decisions, you will need to practice these skills during your college years.

*"That is the news from Lake Wobegon,
where all the women are strong,
the men are good-looking, and
all the children are above average."*

—Garrison Keillor, radio personality

If you did not immediately figure out what is wrong with the above quote, you have a lot of work to do in developing a minimum competence in the use of numbers. Don't leave college without having the ability to (1) calculate and interpret percentages, (2) use simple statistical terms like average, range, and correlation, (3) put together a budget, and above all, (4) have a healthy skepticism when numbers are thrown at you. If you are one of those number-phobic people, learn to love numbers as much as you want money. It never ceases to amaze me how number-phobic people can calculate, in a flash, the amount saved from a 40 percent sale.

No matter what your job is, you need to calculate in your head what it means when your boss tells you that you are getting a 5 percent raise next year. Your performance will be measured in numbers just as the performance of your company or agency is measured in the number of sales, the amount of income, or the number of people served. For most jobs, you don't have to be a mathematical whiz, but you do need to grasp the basics of sixth-grade arithmetic and apply them to help you make decisions.

COURSES: Some mathematics courses may help you develop the basic number-crunching skills that you will need on the job, but don't count on it. Mathematics courses taught in college are usually taught as a science or art form in which you master mathematical reasoning. A better alternative is to take courses on how to use statistics in a specific field like management, political science, economics, or sociology. Even in these courses, the level presented is usually way beyond what will be used in most jobs. Engineering, some areas of business, and many research jobs require the use of higher forms of statistics and math. The rest only require the ability to use and understand percentages and add, subtract, divide, and multiply. Try to find a research course in which you conduct a study for a real-world client like a business or nonprofit agency. They will want the results to be in simple charts, just like most of your potential employers. Any course requiring you to look at budgets—real or projected—would be the best way to develop your applied number-crunching skills.

NON-COURSE ACTIVITY: The best training here would be to become a comptroller or treasurer of an organization with a real budget. If you can get on the finance committee of your student government, you will get a lot of practice in calculating and interpreting numbers.

There are many activities that you might enjoy doing that would improve your number skills. Shopping is one, especially if you start figuring how out much your use of credit will cost you or if you are purchasing a car and need a loan. Sports statistics is an enjoyable way to gain practice with numbers for sports fanatics. Stock market or business simulation computer games can also make exercising math skills fun.

MINIMUM SKILL LEVEL BY GRADUATION TIME: You can determine the percent change between your GPA in the fall semester and your GPA in the spring semester. If you can do this, you will be able to do just about any general calculating function you will face in the job world, including creating and adjusting projected budgets.

"A picture is worth a thousand words."

—Anonymous

You probably already know how to use simple graphs like those with bars and pie charts, and simple tables that show how numbers are related to each other. We include it as a skill set because while the mechanics are easy, many people are not used to thinking with or are not good at using graphs and charts to make a point about a problem or decision that they face.

Whatever job you take will require you to analyze numbers and present them. Graphs and tables are important because you cannot just read lists of numbers to people. After the third number you give them, they'll either be asleep or thinking of something else. They're busy and want to know the bottom line—*now*. A carefully constructed graph or table clearly illustrating a problem facing the organization (or better yet, a possible solution) will gain you considerable credit as you move to the top.

COURSES: Math and statistics courses rarely get into making tables and graphs. Besides, you probably already have the mechanics. You need practice in creating graphs and tables that help you make a point. For that reason, your best bet are research courses in any social science or professional-school field in which you present quantitative information in the papers you write.

NON-COURSE ACTIVITIES: Work in a part-time position, an internship, or in student organizations in which you make charts and tables. Use such situations as a learning opportunity.

MINIMUM SKILL LEVEL BY GRADUATION: Whenever you see a group of numbers, you can display them by use of a graph or a table and make the point you want to make.

"Order and simplification are the first steps toward the mastery of a subject."

—Thomas Mann, nineteenth-century novelist

One of the best-kept secrets for those not in the workforce is the revolutionary impact of spreadsheets for both analysis and action in a professional job. Spreadsheets are as important to the analysis of information as a map is to getting to Grandma's house. Spreadsheets bring order and simplify huge amounts of complex information so that you can make decisions.

If you don't even know what spreadsheet programs are, don't worry because you can easily understand the basics. A spreadsheet program helps you order information into lists and charts and conduct statistical analyses and make graphs. It is only slightly more difficult to learn than Microsoft Word.

The only spreadsheet software you will need to know at the MSL is Microsoft Excel, the spreadsheet of choice for most business, government, and nonprofit organizations. Once you have mastered that, you may want to learn a database like Microsoft Access and other advanced statistical analysis packages. However, the minimum standard for any college graduate who wants any kind of real world job is Excel. Spreadsheets can be used to organize numerous pieces of information, such as that contained in a mailing list. That information can then grouped in new ways for analytic or practical purposes. In the case of the mailing list, after you've entered the information into the spreadsheet program, you could then print out different lists by zip code, gender, or alphabetical order. As mentioned above, spreadsheets can also be used to generate the statistics, tables, and graphs.

Organizing information in lists and tables as well as compiling and presenting statistics is becoming an increasingly important part of any job, particularly at the entry level. Solid Excel skills will get you in the door and make your boss forever grateful. Because spreadsheet programs are so widely used, temp firms are constantly looking for individuals to enter data for their clients. This means you can get a higher paying part-time job from a temp firm—much more than you would get parking cars or serving punch for the faculty. As we noted earlier, typing well can give you a chance for a temp job, which can easily lead to full-time employment. That goes triple for Excel!

Although Excel is presented here as a type of software, it is much more than that. Thinking in terms of spreadsheets means you can organize information in a systematic way, which is a key to problem solving. If both you and your boss can think in spreadsheet terms, you will be speaking the same language. If the rest of the staff is spreadsheet-challenged, you will leave them in the dust as you move on to bigger and better things.

One of my recent graduates, who now works at a large corporation and who is about as far from a computer nerd as anyone can be, wrote me the following:

> *I will deny this if you repeat it, but I totally underestimated your emphasis on Excel. It is slowly becoming my best friend. Lately I've had dreams about how to improve my pivot tables and use V lookups.*

COURSES: College courses rarely focus directly on spreadsheet training, except perhaps in the management field. However, courses that require the collection and analysis of quantitative data are likely to give you an opportunity to exercise your Excel skills once you have learned them. Take statistics courses in the social sciences or the professional schools that require you to use spreadsheets as part of the course.

NON-COURSE ACTIVITY: If you have the basic skills in using a spreadsheet program, you should be able to find part-time and summer jobs within and outside the university that will give you additional experience. These jobs may become mundane and routine after awhile, but you will be getting higher pay than if you were putting mashed potatoes and gravy on the plates of your dormmates—and practice does make perfect.

Some colleges have on-site testing centers. By signing up at these centers, you can complete a self-study course in a Microsoft application. Once you are confident in your abilities, you can take an exam and become certified in that program. These programs are called MOUS (Microsoft Office User Specialization) certification programs. It never hurts to have on your resume that you are certified by Microsoft in Word, Excel, or Access. These certifications may not earn you college credit toward a degree, but it does not hurt to ask.

I've recommended one book for learning Excel at the end of this chapter, but the best way to learn the program is by using it. The program's tutorials can get you started, but getting help from someone who already knows the software is usually quicker and more effective than reading a manual.

MINIMUM SKILL LEVEL BY GRADUATION: You can visual-
ize how to use a spreadsheet when you see a large amount of data that
needs to be analyzed, and you can set up the spreadsheet and generate
tables and graphs.

USEFUL RESOURCES

Excel 2000 for Windows for Dummies by Greg Harvey (Hungry Minds, 1999 or
most recent edition). The self-help sections of the Excel program will not be
enough. A book like this will help you master the basics of Excel. Make sure
you get a book that corresponds to the version you have.

How to Lie with Statistics by Darrell Huff and Irving Geis (W. W. Norton, 1982).
Unlike most statistics books, which include a lot of formulas and try to teach
concepts too complicated for everyday use, this book provides a thorough
grounding in sampling and the use of percentages—tools you'll need no matter what field you enter.

"EVERY MAN IS FULLY SATISFIED THAT THERE IS SUCH A THING AS TRUTH, OR HE WOULD NOT ASK ANY QUESTION."

—CHARLES SANDERS PEIRCE,
A NINETEENTH-/TWENTIETH-CENTURY
PHILOSOPHER, PHYSICIST, MATHEMATICIAN,
AND LOGICIAN

CHAPTER 9

ASKING AND ANSWERING THE RIGHT QUESTIONS

DETECT BS • PAY ATTENTION TO DETAIL •
APPLY KNOWLEDGE • EVALUATE ACTIONS AND POLICIES

Let's take Mr. Peirce's quote at face value and assume that it makes sense to search for truthful information even if we can never be 100 percent certain that we've discovered it. What you really need to do is develop the skill to discover information that is as accurate *and* useful as possible, which means asking and answering the right questions.

All four skill sets are open-ended in the sense that you cannot do any of them well enough all of the time to avoid making mistakes in your decisions. You will get better at these skills over your lifetime but only if you see them as your "critical-thinking skills."

While we are on the subject of critical-thinking skills, I should point out to you that the term is frequently used by employers and by college faculty as the most important of all "skills." However, the term is so general that it needs to be to defined more specifically. The four skill sets listed above as well as the topic of the next chapter, problem solving, constitute what those in the work world view as critical-thinking skills.

To illustrate the four skill sets discussed in this chapter, think about a medical doctor. When doctors meet with their patients, they need to listen carefully to what the patients say to determine whether the patients are blowing smoke (detect BS). If you ever tried to tell a doctor you had a fever but answered "No" when asked, "Did you take your temperature?", you were blowing smoke and likely to be rebuked by the doctor. Doctors need to piece each item of information together and pay close attention to detail. The difference between a temperature of 100.3°F and 103°F is very big. Doctors are inundated with studies about diseases and medication. They have to not only look past the BS with the help of the FDA and various medical journals but also decide what information applies (apply knowledge). Finally, medical doctors must always evaluate to see if their medicine is working (evaluate actions and policies). These four skills provide the base from which doctors problem solve, which we will discuss in the next chapter.

Whatever job you take, you will need these four skills. Your ability to use these skills may not be a matter of life and death as they can be for a physician, but they will affect the future of your job and your organization. Unfortunately, you will not have the precise tools and systems for generating knowledge that medical doctors have. However, you can think and make decisions like a skilled physician whatever field you work in.

KNOW HOW TO DETECT BS

"Two-thirds of the things that are taught in college, even when they are well taught, are not worth knowing. The main thing is to learn the differences between appearances and reality."

—H. L. Mencken, twentieth-century journalist and commentator

College is really a place to learn how to determine the accuracy of information, and how perceptions and values bias much of the information you receive. H. L. Mencken's quote is right on.

You need to understand something about H. L. Mencken to see how insidiously appearance eats away at reality even for the "Baltimore Sage," as he was called. Mencken is considered one of the greatest journalists and intellectuals of the first half of the twentieth century. His anti-BS style combined with a great sense of humor made him a darling of the reading public. To give you an idea of how funny he could be, the quote below should suffice:

Philosophy consists very largely of one philosopher arguing that all others are jackasses. He usually proves it, and I should add that he also usually proves that he is one himself.

Mencken specialized in debunking politicians for their hypocrisy. This brilliant and anti-BS writer, however, expressed anti-Semitic views. It took Mencken many years after Adolf Hitler came to power to see how dangerous he was, and even then, he never gave Hitler the vicious treatment he gave F.D.R. Having a German heritage, Mencken could not believe that his homeland could follow such a monster.

If you learn nothing else in college, learn how to see through what people say by looking at why they say it. Is it self-delusional as it was in Mencken's case, or is it aimed at making a sale or garnering support? Even more critical, compare what people say with what they do.

BS detection is critical to your job success. Whatever job you take will require getting the correct information about the tasks you need to perform and the conditions affecting your performance. This information comes from written sources as well as from statements by your boss, coworkers, those you serve, and others. Unfortunately, the information is always generated for a purpose, and that purpose often gets in the way of the truth. Consequently you need to develop a very strong "BS detector."

Having a broad range of background knowledge can help you detect BS. Even though I said "Skill beats the knowledge you can obtain in college" in the first chapter, having lots of solid knowledge can greatly improve your BS detector skills. As Blaine DeLancey, a long-time college recorder/academic adviser at Syracuse University and a champion of liberal arts wrote:

> *The more one knows about various subjects, the more easily one can recognize and can challenge "BS" on various subjects. In my experience, individuals who BS on one topic tend to make a habit of BSing on every topic. If I can recognize, due to independent knowledge, that my blowhard coworker is uninformed about one topic— baseball, Mozart, epistemology, fill in the blank—then I am forewarned that my coworker is also likely to BS on other topics about which I know nothing—even work topics. Conversely, if I know that a colleague tends to speak only on topics about which she is well informed, then I need be less suspicious of her potential to "BS" about any topic.*

DeLancey makes a lot of sense. I will discuss the value of knowledge further in chapter 11.

COURSES: Every course you take in college will provide an opportunity to improve your ability to distinguish appearance from reality. First, examine carefully what professors say and do. Ask yourself questions about how accurately the course is depicted in the syllabus and how professionally a professor responds to questions from students. Second, most courses present different interpretations of the same events and patterns. Listening to different opinions about the causes of the Civil War or the meaning of a piece of literature gives you the opportunity to make judgments about conflicting ideas yourself. The ability to weigh different viewpoints is critical to getting beyond appearances and moving toward reality.

Specific courses that could perfect your BS detector are more likely to be found in the fields of psychology, which looks at the mechanisms of the mind that generate self-flattering statements, and history, which focuses on how to resolve conflicting interpretations of fact and explanation. Beyond these two fields, most courses in the humanities and the social sciences are about getting beyond appearances to discover reality.

NON-COURSE ACTIVITY: Any piece of information you get, from whatever source, gives you an opportunity to strengthen your BS detector, but you will need to turn it on in order to develop it. Whether you are a part of the pep band, a member of a fraternity or sorority, or a representative in the student government, you can learn a lot by watching your peers spin their webs. If you want an unlimited opportunity to distinguish appearance from reality, rush a fraternity or sorority and compare what was said to you before and after you pledge, especially about fees. If you decided not to pledge, ask a friend who did. This is only one of many sales situations you will face in your life with hidden and unanticipated costs.

While you are at it, don't forget to turn the BS detector on yourself, especially when you excuse your poor grades by saying, "My grade sucked because the class was so incredibly boring. If I am truly interested in a course, I will learn a lot and do well."

MINIMUM SKILL LEVEL BY GRADUATION: Whenever you read or hear something, you immediately ask yourself what motivated the information and what you can do to check its accuracy.

"To generalize is to be an idiot.
To particularize is the alone distinction
of merit."

—William Blake, eighteenth/nineteenth-century poet

Blake must have been irritated with the science of the day. His quote is a little over the top because, as we see in the next section, applying general knowledge is a key skill set. However, paying attention to detail is more important than generalizing because the effective use of generalizations depends on the mastery of detail.

In whatever task you undertake, you must get as many details as possible. You need to be like a medical doctor and piece the sequence of events together and create a pattern in your mind that helps you understand the motivation of those involved. Can you, in effect, create a story that makes sense to explain why a patient is ill, a client did not buy your services, a student failed a course, or a person you supervise did the wrong thing?

Paying attention to detail will help you answer critical questions that could catapult you to the top of your career. Ignoring the details and the questions could result in a pink slip. Why does the boss keep criticizing you? What accounts for the sale of one item instead of another? Why does an individual praise or attack your organization? Answering these questions often demands a strong focus on details.

If you cannot draw meaning from what happens day to day on your job, you will be in a continual state of surprise and unable to respond to changing conditions. Adaptability, a quality that shows up on many lists of important skills, will bring incredible success in whatever job you pursue.

One of the most important things you can do to develop your capacity to pay attention to detail is to learn how to "read" a document. As a professor of writing, Catherine Smith suggests:

Documents inform in more ways than through words on the page. They convey context such as:

1. *Human—does the document sound friendly, hostile, neutral?*
2. *Social—where does the document fit into the situation, to simulate action or to be filed?*
3. *Organization—who is the sender; who is copied; are you the principal receiver?*

Just because it is in print doesn't make it true, real, or useful. Don't leave college without the ability to read around/between the lines of text in a document.[1]

COURSES: All your course work can be viewed as training in paying attention to detail. You will discover that success comes in mastering the detail consistently and carefully. Whether you are doing a lab experiment in science, completing an accounting exercise, criticizing a piece of literature, or presenting an analysis of a historic event, paying attention to detail is the difference between passing and failing. How many points have you lost in your academic career for an incorrect citation format, a decimal place in the wrong place, or just misreading a multiple-choice question? Using every course as an occasion to sharpen your habit of paying attention to detail is a good idea for your future, not to mention your GPA.

Courses that use a lot of case studies are best. They can be found in history most often, but also in anthropology, economics, geography, political science, and sociology. Case studies are frequently used in business and social work but also in undergraduate professional programs. The humanities, especially literature courses, develop the capacity to think about the causes and implications of things that happen. Courses that require fieldwork or community service along with weekly logs are especially powerful in developing your capacity to make sense out of what happens.

NON-COURSE ACTIVITY: Participate in student groups in which collective decisions have to be made. The never-ending discussion of what to do and what happens as a result of specific events can provide skill in getting to the bottom of things. To draw meaning from specific events, stop and reflect after the events occur to see if you can figure out their causes and implications. An enjoyable activity to develop your ability to look at detailed cases is to watch a TV show like *Law and Order* in which the details about both behavior and the law are required to follow the show. Reading fiction and nonfiction that analyze events and behaviors is also helpful.

MINIMUM SKILL LEVEL BY GRADUATION: You are able to "read between the lines" of documents you come across and determine the causes and implications of events.

KNOW HOW TO APPLY KNOWLEDGE

"Knowledge is power."

—Francis Bacon, sixteenth/seventeenth-century scientist

Bacon's quote is not quite correct. Knowledge is a source of power, but for it to translate into actual power, you need to use it effectively. The usefulness of the knowledge you find or develop requires that you continually ask, "What does this mean for my job and my organization?"

The ability to get key statistics, find people who have the knowledge you need, and be alert to current literature in your field can help you in whatever job you have. Outstanding employees always look for the "best practices" that they can apply to their problems. You also need to be aware of "bad" and "mediocre practices" so you can avoid the mistakes others have made. Look at what other organizations do so you can bring up new ideas to your colleagues.

Whatever job you have will require you to do what medical doctors do with respect to continuous learning of new knowledge. You'll need to keep up with publications, go to professional meetings, and translate the general knowledge that is relevant to your specific job. If studies related to your job exist, you will need to apply the principles of the scientific method to make judgments about how much faith you can put in those studies. You will also need to learn how to decide which sources can be trusted. An eagerness to learn and a curiosity about all aspects of your job field is the holy grail of success.

A successful insurance underwriter speaks about the importance of continuously searching for new knowledge in the following statement:

I've found throughout my career in insurance that I've been able to move up through organizations more quickly, and possibly higher than others (even those with advanced degrees), because of my commitment to search for knowledge during all waking hours. I'm always looking for new knowledge as it relates to my field. This may include the sources already discussed, but also includes searching the Net or watching the news for information. I'm also continually aware of my "market value." What are my skills, experience, and knowledge worth in my industry locally, regionally, and nationally? This skill allows ME to be in control of the success or failure of my career. It also puts me at a competitive advantage personally, as I become a more valued "asset" of my organization, rather than another face in the crowd.

You must also be able to decide what knowledge applies, does not apply, or at least needs serious adjustment. Although Blake's argument in the previous section that "to generalize is to be an idiot" is extreme, the uniqueness of each decision you face requires you to be very careful about applying generalizations from previous experience or existing studies.

Like physicians, an appreciation of scientific methods and research design is critical. You need to think like a scientist in two very important ways. First, scientists are meticulous about describing things. The use of quantitative data is preferred but not always possible. Second, a scientific approach seeks to figure out causation. The key question scientists ask all the time when they think they have formed a hypothesis that x caused y is "What else could have caused y?" If you think sales are slipping because the economy is weak, for example, ask what else might be causing sales to slip.

Despite the great advances in the physical sciences over the past five centuries, controversy over measurement and causation persists. In the application of knowledge to your job, the limitations of scientific techniques are even greater. You can never be sure if you are measuring reality, and you can only make educated guesses at cause and effect. However, having a scientific approach to understanding things is an important part of knowledge application.

Employers frequently cite the ability to adjust to changing circumstances and continuous learning as highly valued qualities they want in their employees. They want their employees to exchange views among members of their profession (without giving away company secrets, of course). They want them to ask questions about the data and about factors affecting their organization.

However, employers also want their employees to be clear-headed about the knowledge they find. They do not want them bringing in irrelevant knowledge or chasing fringe ideas that have little factual backup. If the studies related to your job exist, apply the principles of the scientific method to make judgments about how much faith you can put in them. You will also need to learn how to decide which sources can be trusted. Finally, you may have to design and conduct a research project yourself to answer a specific question. If so, understanding scientific methods will give you more accurate results, even if you cannot get the precise and representative information required by such methods.

COURSES: Applied research courses are difficult to find at the undergraduate level in most colleges and universities. They are usually reserved for graduate students. However, some professors, especially in the professional schools, incorporate applied research in their curricula. Try to get into a course that supports that research or, better yet, offer to take an independent study for professors on one of their client-based projects.

To develop skills in the scientific method, start by taking courses in the physical sciences. The goal of these courses is to help students understand the scientific way of thinking. Those that have labs integrated into the course are better than those that have no lab or fail to make a connection between the lab and the content of the lectures and class discussions.

Science courses are only a beginning. Almost every course you take in college can provide you with a way of searching for patterns that can allow for generalizations about causes and forecasts about the future. Courses in all of the social sciences and many professional schools can give you additional practice with the scientific methods as well as the limitation of those methods. The best courses to take are those that require fieldwork and real-world application because they are more likely to help you see both the value and limitations of the scientific method.

NON-COURSE ACTIVITY: Participation in student activities such as residence hall councils or student government will give you an opportunity to look at the big picture and develop tentative ideas about why things are the way they are. This experience will develop your faculty to generate hypotheses and then look for evidence to support, reject, or revise the hypotheses. The most powerful learning experience in applying knowledge will come from doing applied research work in part-time jobs, summer jobs, and internships both within and outside the university.

MINIMUM SKILL LEVEL BY GRADUATION: You are able to develop and test explanations and use them as a base for making forecasts in your own life.

KNOW HOW TO EVALUATE ACTIONS AND POLICIES

"If you don't measure results, you can't tell success from failure."

—David Osborne and Ted Gaebler,
authors of a best-selling book on improving government

You are reading this book because you want to have a successful career and therefore cannot avoid the challenge of evaluating your own performance and the performance of others. Unfortunately, the task of evaluation is anxiety producing. Most students do not like tests and get sweaty palms before receiving a paper grade. The anxiety comes from the combination of the excitement of winning and the fear of losing.

For that reason, the natural inclination is to avoid evaluation or to see it as a win-or-lose proposition. People develop many clever ways to avoid evaluation. They may blame others or take actions that are "safe," a practice also known as C-YA. They may procrastinate. If they are confronted with a failure, they go into a depression and blame themselves or, in the terms of our current jargon, "lose self-esteem." If they decide they have been successful, they may conclude that they are a winner and can do no wrong.

These behaviors need to be avoided if you are going to develop a capacity to evaluate your own actions and the actions of others. To put it in the proper perspective, take the advice of Louis Blair, the director of the Truman Foundation, which provides graduate scholarships to future government and nonprofit leaders:

The main difference between a successful person and an unsuccessful person is that the successful person has had a lot more failures.

Success belongs to those who take risks and have some way of recognizing success and failure. Three steps are required to evaluate your behavior or the behavior of others:

1. Identify goals. Sometimes goals are not clearly stated or even shared by everyone in your organization.
2. Measure goals. You have to have information organized in such a way that you know when you or your company has reached its goals.
3. Determine success and failure. You need to develop an idea of what success or failure is in order to decide whether or not you want to make a change.

This process is critical for the world of work. By continually asking yourself "How am I doing?", you will be improving your job performance. By asking how your unit is doing or company as a whole is doing, you will be contributing to a team effort to do the best.

To drive the point home, realize that your employer will conduct performance reviews periodically, and those reviews will determine whether or not and how much of a raise you receive as well as whether or not you will advance in your career.

The way to have a successful performance review, which might occur a couple of months into your job and then at least annually, is to say, "My goals have been *x, y,* and *z,* and I have met *x* and *y* and made progress on *z.*" You will be in a much better position for a good review. It will also help your boss fill out the required human resources form and work with you to advance your career.

Evaluation skills are essential for improving the performance of your organization. You will be a better employee if you can help your organization focus on clear goals, measure performance according to those goals, and draw conclusions that will lead to future improvement.

I may seem to be stating the obvious here, but, as already noted, words like "evaluation," "assessment," and "performance," are threatening to the majority of people in the world of work. More often than not, people play evaluation games that require your BS detector to be fully operational. The evaluation game can be played by setting goals that are too low, by using poor information, by selectively reporting information, and, in some cases, by not even reporting the information at all.

To be successful in the work world, you need to distinguish between two types of evaluation. The first is evaluation to improve performance, and the second is to punish or reward you or others. The former is the most important over the long run and is part of what businesses call "continuous improvement." The latter can cause a lot of trouble, but it is used in most organizations as a major tool of promoting excellence. An organization that uses evaluation only as a reward or punishment is not a good place to work.

COURSES: Courses that provide direct training in evaluation are usually offered at the graduate school level, but you can probably find some upper-level courses in the social sciences, management, and other professional schools that introduce you to the skills of evaluation. You can practice evaluation on your own performance in every course that you take by setting both goals for learning and grades, and then making judgments as to whether you have achieved them or not. You can also learn a lot about evaluation if you study how your instructors evaluate their courses. Ask yourself whether or not instructors are using end-of-semester surveys only because they are forced to and will be rewarded or punished on the basis of them? Or do they seem to really be interested in the results so they can improve the course? As a student, you would prefer the latter use.

NON-COURSE ACTIVITY: You can practice evaluation every time you do something, especially, as suggested above, in every course you take. Get into the practice of making a list of goals for every major new activity you undertake in student activities or in jobs, and then reflect on whether or not you achieved your goals.

MINIMUM SKILL LEVEL BY GRADUATION: You set clear goals with specific measurements that will help you evaluate how well you performed your job search.

USEFUL RESOURCES

I hesitate to recommend books and other activities for the skill sets described in this chapter because there are many ways to improve these skills. Whether examining the sciences, humanities, and social sciences or the various professions like management, public communications, or social work, serious study will improve your skill in all four areas. So will playing games, especially chess, bridge, and poker. Arguing with others about sports, movies, or just about anything will also help if you try to use evidence and logic rather than argue for the sake of arguing. How you choose to practice your evaluation skills depends on your interests, background, and the way your brain is wired. Just follow the guidelines presented in this chapter when you evaluate yourself or anything else. Despite my hesitance in recommending a book for this chapter, take a look at the following:

Citizen Muckraking: How to Investigate and Right Wrongs in Your Community by the Center for Public Integrity (Common Courage Media, 2000). Written primarily by Charles Lewis, who heads the center and was once a producer for *60 Minutes,* this book helps you see how ordinary people can see through the BS and apply technical knowledge to make a change.

"YOU SEE THINGS; AND YOU SAY, 'WHY?' BUT I DREAM THINGS THAT NEVER WERE; AND SAY, 'WHY NOT?'"

—GEORGE BERNARD SHAW

CHAPTER 10

SOLVING PROBLEMS

IDENTIFY PROBLEMS • DEVELOP SOLUTIONS • LAUNCH SOLUTIONS

Effective problem solving starts with an attitude that asks "why not?" Why can't we do a better job? Problem solvers are into continuous improvement. Problem solving is much more than just pushing around a lot of information. It requires you to use information to form a plan of action and then to make decisions and take action, or talk to others who can help you implement the solution.

The three problem-solving skill sets build on all nine Know-How Groups previously discussed. They require character, good communication skills, excellent people skills, and good research and analysis skills. The skill set in the previous chapter—detecting BS, paying attention to detail, applying knowledge, evaluating actions and policies—is as critical as it is rare. In addition, a problem solver must be willing to take risks and to think about the big picture. The willingness to see problems and do something about them is critical to success in a career. A senior VP writes:

> *While anger and fear are typical responses to change, optimism is the more appropriate one. Ironically, when people are worried about keeping their jobs, they are most resistant to change. They adopt the exact opposite behavior of what companies are looking for in their employees.*

If you embrace problem solving as a part of your work strategy, you will be able to deal with the kinds of crises and negative information that people face as they move up the ladder of success. I am not just talking about the problems your organization faces, like how to improve services, but those you face every day. An employee who has to check with the supervisor every time there is the slightest new wrinkle is not a problem solver and in fact is a very big problem to the organization.

Employers rarely explicitly list problem solving as a key skill, but they do frequently mention critical thinking, initiative, adaptability, and leadership. These terms are frequently associated with the employees' willingness to improve themselves and their organization. Employers want workers who are optimistic about change. They want to hire employees who, in the words of one employer, "know how big the problem is, the frequency, and how long it will take to solve." Willingness to recognize and provide evidence of problems helps your boss quickly understand what needs to be addressed and makes him or her ready to listen to your suggestions. Your interviewer may not use the term problem solving, but it will be the key to your career success.

KNOW HOW TO IDENTIFY PROBLEMS

"People tend to process solutions, rather than identify the problem."

—Senior VP for a large investment corporation

Each unit in an organization is responsible for a specific function that, taken together, hopefully accomplishes the goals of the organization. So you will need to know the mission or goals of your unit and see the degree to which those goals are being achieved. The first and most critical step in problem solving is to see where what is happening is not in line with the goals of an organization. If you are in marketing, the problem could be not enough sales in some geographic area, or that goods are not being shipped fast enough.

Identifying a problem is more than just saying one exists. It also requires evidence that demonstrates the problem is real. You may use statistical evidence showing the increase in time it takes between the ordering and the shipping of the goods on a trend-line graph. You may use a survey to show the frequency of customer complaints. You may simply decide to show that everyone in your unit agrees that there is a problem. The key is substantiating in concrete terms that a problem exists.

One of the keys to good problem identification is making sure you have a problem before you even start to discuss solutions. Say the executive committee of a senior citizen's center decides that more publicity is needed to attract more people to their facilities. The committee will get into arguments about how best to publicize their center. They will do this without first understanding the real problem, which in this case, is the lack of participation. If they look at lack of participation as the problem, maybe they would realize that the real cause is the lack of attractive programs and not the lack of PR. People always tend to come up with solutions without adequately defining and measuring the problem. A problem-solving orientation will help you avoid this trap.

This example suggests that many of the skills presented in this book are needed to solve problems effectively. To identify the problem in such a way that the definition of it is clear and some evidence is available that it actually exists, requires people, information-gathering, verbal and written communication, and quantitative analysis skills.

COURSES: Identifying problems can occur in any field. Helpful courses can range from mathematics and science classes in which the problem can only be answered through logic or research to social science and professional school courses in which the answers come from working closely with those who have a stake in the problem. Literature courses, in which novels and plays, more often than not, pose a set of problems for the main characters, can also be useful. Research of similar problems through interviews and reading case studies can also be helpful in social science and professional school courses. Identifying problems in a measurable way could be practiced in research methods courses.

NON-COURSE ACTIVITIES: Whether working in a student group, a committee with faculty and administrators, or an internship or job setting, looking for and clearly measuring problems can be practiced. Force yourself to observe how problems are identified and measured by a group trying to make a decision. Ask frequently and with forcefulness, "Now what problem are we trying to solve?"

MINIMUM SKILL LEVEL BY GRADUATION: In at least three different group sessions in which an event is being planned or an action is under consideration, you are able to get the group to be clear about the problem and how to measure it.

KNOW HOW TO DEVELOP SOLUTIONS

"For every complex problem, there is a simple solution that is elegant, easy to understand, and wrong."

—H. L. Mencken

Once you have identified a problem, the next step is to come up with possible solutions. If we acknowledge the quote at the top of this section, "solutions" is too strong a word in many cases. Difficult and persistent problems are never solved. Problem solving is frequently about reducing the negative effects and not necessarily eliminating the causes of the problem.

In medicine, you treat a cough of unknown origins with cough syrup to reduce its severity. In the business world, your competitors' products and advertising are frequently the primary underlying cause of your poor sales. You cannot eliminate the competitors, but you can improve your product or advertising to win back sales. A preferred solution would be to put your competitors out of business, but that rarely happens.

I have purposely used the verb "develop" because solutions may be found by looking at what others have done in similar situations as well as creating new solutions. When it comes to solving problems, research and creativity are both required. Research into what has been done means searching for the best, or most effective, practices, as well as those that have failed. Applying those best practices to your problems requires creating an action plan that adapts the idea to a new situation. If your research does not yield a relevant best practice, you need to think up an idea on your own. When car sales were slumping for Chrysler under Lee Iacocca, he came up with the idea of the minivan, which helped to revitalize a company that was on the ropes. This was a creative idea that worked much better than trying to build better cars and use better advertising gimmicks than the competitors.

Employers want you to always be thinking about ways of solving problems that you, your department, and your organization face. They recognize that problem solvers sometimes are at risk if their ideas clash with their immediate superiors, which is why many use the suggestion box to get ideas from their employees. Many bosses not only want you to bring problems to them, but when you do, they also want you to propose a solution. If you just bring the problem, you may be perceived as whining. If you bring a solution with clear evidence of the problem, it shows that you are into continuous improvement, which is every boss's dream.

COURSES: Policy courses in the social sciences and all of the professional schools provide examples of solutions to problems in the profession or society in general. They are usually offered in the junior and senior year. A particularly valuable experience, no matter what job you take, is a course, increasingly offered in management programs, in which you propose a new business and develop a business plan to make the business profitable. This kind of exercise requires you to come up with solutions to problems you would face when starting a new enterprise.

NON-COURSE ACTIVITIES: Student organizations and committees working within the college are frequently focused on developing and implementing actions to deal with problems. Problems range from what kind of entertainment to bring to the university to how to allocate funds among student groups and how to build membership for existing organizations. The key to these activities is seriously considering multiple solutions and then implementing the best one. When you are in a situation in which there are consequences to your actions, you will learn much more about problem solving than in hypothetical or simulated learning experiences.

MINIMUM SKILL LEVEL BY GRADUATION: You have helped one student or administration organization implement a decision that deals with some clearly definable problem.

"There is nothing more difficult to carry out, nor more doubtful of success, nor more dangerous to handle, than to initiate a new order of things."

—Niccolò Machiavelli

As an HR person for a large corporation states, "You need to be able to make a decision and not be afraid of making a mistake. . . . I'd be more worried if someone couldn't make a decision rather than if they made the wrong one." Solutions can be discussed for only so long. Some kind of test, even if it is a pilot program, needs to be attempted after the research and discussion have been completed.

Your chances of successfully launching a solution will be greatly enhanced if you solicit the opinions of others in creating solutions. Part of the creative process is soliciting others' reactions to your initial ideas and then adjusting those ideas in response to legitimate criticism. Creating a solution alone is never as effective as creating a solution through mutual exchange with those who have influence over the action. You may have thought of the idea, but you should be happy to give ownership to those around you.

After you have clearly identified the problem and settled on a solution you think will work (at least partially), you face the most difficult and frustrating part of problem solving: either implementing the solution yourself or getting your organization to do it. The solution may be a collective idea, but you need to develop skills in getting solutions accepted.

"Solutions," by definition, create change in the way things are done. People resist change primarily because they fear the unknown and are afraid they will personally lose something (like their job or a promised raise). The first and most important skill in launching solutions is to be tolerant of the resistance to change.

For changes that you do not completely control yourself, you will need a second skill: getting the problem and the solution on the agenda of those who have the power. Those who have power are usually very busy, and although they say they want solutions, they usually want them at no cost to themselves or their organization. Moreover, to get your solution on the table, you need to convince those above you that there is a very serious problem. To do this, while not offending those who are responsible for the problem is no easy task. As Eldridge Cleaver, a famous black radical in the 1960s, said, "You're either part of the solution or part of the problem." Nobody likes to be told they are a part of the problem.

Finally, you need to be able to build support so that your solution is seriously considered. Building support requires getting others to buy into the idea: the more powerful, the better. Your people, communication, and analysis skills will be critical.

Being a problem solver within your job responsibilities is not as difficult as launching a solution that eventually will need backing from above. When you start out, be satisfied with problem solving in your own job. Solving your own job problems will give you legitimacy; it will lead to raises and promotions as your boss realizes that you are improving the performance of the department he or she manages. After a few years of successful problem solving within your job, you may be ready to venture outside of it.

As you gain more experience, coming up with solutions will increase your worth to the company and make you more appealing if you decide to look for another position. A typical interview question is "What decision or action are you most proud of?" If you can tell how you built support within the organization for a solution, you will impress the interviewer.

Many people in the highest management positions see themselves as problem solvers or as creators of teams of people who can solve tough problems faced by the organization. Even entry-level interviews may touch on your capacity to improve yourself and others. Because launching solutions is such a difficult and complex task, practicing it in your college years will get you started on a road to fame and fortune.

COURSES: History courses that focus on specific decisions, such as U.S. action during the Cuban Missile Crisis, are valuable in learning about the processes surrounding decisions that lead to solutions. Political science courses that help you look at specific cases of political decisions and policy-making processes may also help. Those courses that use simulations and fieldwork are likely to be more powerful than those that rely only on lectures, discussions, and readings.

NON-COURSE ACTIVITIES: The only way to really learn about launching a solution is to launch one yourself. Within a student organization or acting alone, try to get something changed for the better while in your college years. The best way to do this is to get a leadership position such as treasurer, vice president, or president. You will be faced with plenty of problems and have the opportunity to come up with and implement solutions. This is less likely to happen at an internship or part-time job, but keep your eyes open for the opportunity. After you gain your supervisor's trust, you may be able to suggest solutions to problems you know your supervisor is concerned about. Look for small and specific problems that can be easily solved.

MINIMUM SKILL LEVEL BY GRADUATION: You can write a chronological outline of how you developed and tried to implement a solution to a specific problem.

USEFUL RESOURCES

All of the books related to leadership that were recommended in chapter 7 provide examples of outstanding problem solvers or suggest ways to solve problems. Leaders organize people to solve problems. Here are a couple of other books.

American Self-Help Group Clearinghouse (www.mentalhelp.net/selfhelp). More than one thousand groups are described, ranging from those dealing with physical disease to all types of family problems. Self-help groups are a result of actions that are taken to ameliorate problems. You can also order the directory *The Self-Help Sourcebook: Your Guide to Community and Online Support Groups* by Barbara J. White and Edward J. Madara.

How You Can Help: An Easy Guide to Doing Good Deeds in Your Everyday Life by William D. Coplin (Routledge, 2000). I wrote this book to help people see that they can improve the world through limited and competent actions. Part four of the book presents a problem-solving framework that can be applied to any problem.

Rules for Radicals: A Pragmatic Primer for Realistic Radicals by Saul Alinsky (Vintage Books, 1989). A famous 1960s radical, Alinsky writes how to get those in power to solve the problems those out of power face.

LEARNING IS NOT ATTAINED BY CHANCE, IT MUST BE SOUGHT FOR WITH ARDOR, AND ATTENDED TO WITH DILIGENCE.

—ABIGAIL ADAMS, WIFE OF PRESIDENT
JOHN ADAMS AND ALSO HIS PRINCIPAL ADVISER

CHAPTER 11

EARNING EXTRA CREDIT FOR YOUR KNOW-HOW SCORE

SKILL SETS

GAIN SOFTWARE EXPERTISE BEYOND MICROSOFT WORD AND EXCEL • MASTER IN-DEPTH KNOWLEDGE OF ANY FIELD • ACCENT FOREIGN LANGUAGE SKILLS • EMPHASIZE ARTISTIC AND MUSIC KNOWLEDGE AND/OR SKILL • STRESS SPORTS SKILLS • PURSUE PLEASURE ACTIVITIES

The use of extra credit is controversial, especially in college. Most professors believe that extra credit leads to grade inflation, which is viewed as part of the "dumbing down" of education in the United States and therefore very bad. Since your KHS is more important than your GPA, grade inflation is not such a terrible thing for those of you seeing college as a path to a successful career. As a professor, I use extra credit as a way to entice students to learn something relevant to the course but beyond the basic requirements. The additional points a student earns are always small, perhaps no more than 5 percent of the grade, but the reward is earned because students, if they take it seriously, learn more.

The same logic applies for adding extra credit in the calculation of your KHS. As you must realize by now, getting a perfect KHS of 100 is very difficult because you are likely to have weaknesses in some of the areas. If you can't meet the MSL for each of the skill sets described in the previous ten chapters, the extra credit items discussed in this chapter can make up for some of those weaknesses.

The items identified in this chapter represent only a beginning list. You may think of others, but the ones described here are the most likely to be helpful. I have included these extra credit opportunities because you could be introduced to them in college or develop them from the base you already have when you begin college.

The opportunities discussed in this chapter are not essential requirements for the world of work. They are extras that could make a difference in your career, but more than that, some may simply help you live a more enjoyable life because of their own intrinsic worth. This leads to me a very important point about extra credit. When instructors offer extra credit, too many times students will only see the points and fail to learn anything. Those students have really missed the opportunity. The same goes for the extra credit on the KHS. If you take an art course just to raise your KHS, don't count it in your KHS. If you take one because you are interested in the subject and genuinely learn from it, then add it to your KHS. You can only add to your KHS if you actually have increased skill or knowledge in the areas that are identified. You may want to add other extra-credit items depending on your interest and on the opportunities at your college.

To keep things simple, each specific item within a group can add only one point to your overall KHS. You may have more than one item within a group (for example, you may know three foreign languages), but you can earn no more than five points for each of the seven groups discussed in this chapter.

GAIN SOFTWARE EXPERTISE BEYOND MICROSOFT WORD AND EXCEL

In chapter 4, I stressed the importance of knowing how to use Microsoft Word as one of the written communication skill sets. In chapter 9, I included the use of Microsoft Excel as one of the quantitative analysis skill sets. Being able to use these programs well is an essential element in most jobs today.

However, if you have basic competence in the primary operations of several other software packages, you could add one point of extra credit to your KHS, because that kind of knowledge could make you more qualified for some jobs. Some of the most important programs are listed below by function. Microsoft FrontPage was mentioned in chapter 4 as part of electronic communication enabling you to set up your own personal website. It is mentioned here because if you become a website maven in jobs that are not website oriented, you can have a significant advantage over others. (Please note: You can receive no more than five KHS points even if you master more than five of the software programs listed.)

Adobe Illustrator
Adobe PageMaker
Adobe Photoshop
Lotus Notes
Microsoft Access
Microsoft FrontPage (a more advanced level than the
   minimum discussed in chapter 5)
Microsoft Publisher
QuarkXPress
Quickbooks Pro
Statistical Analysis System (SAS)
Statistical Package for the Social Sciences (SPSS)

MASTER IN-DEPTH KNOWLEDGE OF ANY FIELD

In the beginning of this book, I wrote that skill beats the knowledge you can gain in college every time. That is true, but because life is a crapshoot, knowledge can sometimes make a big difference.

If two job applicants have an equal KHS score and one is a Civil War history buff just like the boss, who do you think will get the job? And who do you think will be paying visits to the boss's house to move around toy soldiers, not to mention cannons, on a detailed miniature replica of the battlefield at Gettysburg? Areas of in-depth knowledge are valuable because they may possibly connect with your boss or colleagues. In-depth knowledge will help you have bond-building conversations with people that you need to work with.

What knowledge area is most likely to help you in your work life is not relevant here. With so many specialized areas, it makes little sense to pick something because it has a higher probability of a successful "hit." Follow your interests, and it's likely that on many occasions you'll find it useful in conversations with others at work.

In-depth knowledge, like some of the other extra credit areas to be discussed, is particularly useful in careers populated by those who think they are, or want to be, in the elite of our society. Showing off in-depth knowledge is part of your membership card to join the cultured and well educated.

As you move up the career ladder, you will come in contact with people who are more highly educated and who have the cultural benefits roughly associated with wealth. Having the knowledge frequently associated with "high-class people" can't hurt you, and not having it can hurt you. Give it a shot and see if you can lose your self in scholarly study, but don't let it get in the way of improving your skills in the basic ten Know-How Groups.

The chances of any given area of knowledge paying off are a matter of chance and therefore can add only one point to your KHS score. Only your top five areas can be used, so the most you can add is five points. The five areas must be in distinctly different fields.

ACCENT FOREIGN LANGUAGE SKILLS

In this increasingly global society, developing foreign language skills is a good idea, especially if you are gifted in learning foreign languages. The major foreign languages to learn are Arabic, Chinese, French, German, Japanese, Russian, and Spanish. Some languages less frequently learned—such as Swahili, the languages of northern and eastern Europe—would be useful. For general job preparation, such foreign language skills are not likely to be valued, but employers, colleagues, and customers will view your mastery of one or more foreign languages as an extra piece of evidence that you are smart and adaptable. Spanish is an exception and can almost be a required skill in areas with a large Spanish-speaking population.

As is the case in the other areas, we will allow one point for each foreign language to be added to your KHS, up to a limit of five. However, you must be fluent in speaking, reading, and writing the language. Many college foreign language departments tend to focus on literature and the culture of the country (which counts as knowledge and not skill) and do not devote much energy to the conversations you are likely to have if you visit that country. Traveling to the country where the language is spoken and working hard to engage in conversations with the locals makes good sense if you are serious about foreign language skills. Extra credit points can only be earned if you have the capacity to carry on serious conversations or read a wide range of materials in the foreign language.

EMPHASIZE ARTISTIC AND MUSIC KNOWLEDGE AND/OR SKILL

Like the other extra credit items, interests that you may have started in childhood and continue as part of your college education can be counted toward your KHS score. You can earn one point for each specific skill or knowledge up to a maximum of five points. Count one point for each instrument you play, type of art you can produce, or your knowledge of particular periods of art or music. Just as with in-depth knowledge and foreign language skills, it's possible that someone above you in your organization will either have similar skills and knowledge or be impressed by someone who does. It will help you bond and converse with those you work with.

What type of art and music can be used to earn extra credit points? The answer is any type that has not been in the current pop culture mainstream for less than ten years, unless the artist or musician is dead, in which case five years is enough. Being a fan of the Dave Matthews Band might help with colleagues close to your age, but it will probably lose cache with older coworkers, who might think pop music is short-lived and best left to the younger generation. Fifteen years from now, your expertise and love for DMB may be quaint and interesting; until then it is plebian. Under this formulation, Elvis deserves one point.

STRESS SPORT SKILLS

Tennis and golf are the two sports with the highest potential payoff because they are the sports of the successful, especially in the business world. They are also important in the government and nonprofit world because those worlds want and need business support. So take some tennis or golf courses if available and/or make it your business to develop a high skill level in at least one. A word of warning: do not tell your boss you can play tennis when you have a serve that goes in a high arc, and he or she has one that knocks your racket out of your hand.

Participating on an intercollegiate sports team for at least one year, no matter what sport, earns one point. The experience will give you something in common with a few individuals you meet in the world of work. Even if you were third string, you can use the experience to bond and engage in conversation. Many employers who played on intercollegiate athletic teams see the discipline and teamwork they developed when they played to be a key to their success.

Colleges offer experiences in various sports, sometimes for credit, but always as an extra-curricular activity. Joining the ski club or intramural sports can have big payoffs.

No more than one point is given for each sport you are either very skilled in or have spent at least one year on an intercollegiate team. Once again, the upper limit is five.

We have not talked about knowledge of sports here. Being able to talk intelligently about college or professional football or basketball can help you with your peers and those you report to. However, this is so common that no extra credit points are given just for sports knowledge. Watching ESPN ten hours a day is not the way to earn extra credit points for your KHS.

PURSUE PLEASURE ACTIVITIES

Certain pleasure activities are treated as skills for credit in college. The most widely offered are wine tasting and cooking. These can be important in social situations, and one point is available if you really know what you are talking about. Horseback riding is another pleasure that you might want to pursue, although you may want to argue whether or not it is a sport. Gardening can also be useful as an area of common experience. There are so many areas that might be viewed as pleasures that we need to put a limit on how many you can count as extra credit for your KHS. The limit in this case is two.

The kinds of knowledge and skills discussed in this chapter obviously have benefits beyond your success in the world of work. Some would argue that as a whole, with knowledge playing the paramount role, they represent the real purpose of a college education. I take no position on this question because the "real purpose" of a college education, in the abstract, is meaningless. Your purpose is the real purpose, which is why it is up to you.

From the perspective of general preparation for your life or work, these extra credit items are clearly secondary. You may become a professional in one of these areas, and that should figure in your job-specific KHS, which will be discussed in the next chapter. For example, if your interest in literature stimulates you to seek a career in the book industry, then skills related to writing and editing as well as your content knowledge of trends in publishing will be important.

To make one or more of these areas pay off once you get into the workforce or even in your interview, you need to recognize two very important principles.

- Pursue an area because you enjoy it and have some aptitude for it. The term "dilettante" is used to identify people who dabble in many areas but lack depth in any. You do not want to be labeled a "jack of all trades, a master of none."
- The likelihood that any one of these "extra-credit" areas will definitely impact your career is low. If they do, it will be a matter of happenstance. Being prepared for luck, however, is a matter of genuine and serious hard work.

USEFUL RESOURCES

Given the large number of possibilities for extra credit, it is not useful to provide books on specific areas. However, because this chapter raises the issue of learning for the sake of learning, it might be useful for you to read about the goals and purposes of a college education beyond the specific goal of a higher KHS.

Bright College Years: Inside the American Campus Today by Anne Matthews (Simon & Schuster, 1997). This book takes a broad view of the impact of college on students. It may help you gain perspectives on the variety of learning experiences.

College: The Undergraduate Experience by Ernest L. Boyer (Harper & Row, 1987). This book is the starting point for understanding the way in which colleges attempt to educate their students. It is critical of many undergraduate programs for their emphasis on specialized rather than general knowledge.

Cool Colleges for the Hyper-Intelligent, Self-Directed, Late Blooming, and Just Plain Different by Donald Asher (Ten Speed Press, 2000). The book describes schools and programs that the author says will provide a better intellectual experience. In doing so, he also provides a good overview of the variety of non-KHS skills you can learn from colleges.

Higher Learning by Derek Curtis Bok (Harvard University Press, 1986). Written by a former dean of arts and science and president of Harvard University, this book will help you understand why the KHS is not on the top of the list of most faculty.

PART TWO

BOOSTING YOUR KNOW-HOW SCORE

YOU PAYS YOUR MONEY AND YOU TAKES YOUR CHOICES.

—PUNCH

CHAPTER 12

MAKING KHS-FRIENDLY COLLEGE, PROGRAM, AND COURSE CHOICES

Once you choose a college, your decisions about your education have only just begun. There are colleges within universities and programs within colleges. Each college has hundreds of programs and thousands of courses. You will be faced with making important choices throughout your college career from a large number of confusing options.

One of the major benefits most students see in going to college is getting away from parental authority or, in the tradition of America's number one value, general freedom. However, freedom is not just freedom *from* the control of others; it is also the freedom *to* make your own decisions. You will make more decisions in the first two weeks of college than you have previously made in a year about every facet of your life.

Choices, first of all, require you to be clear to yourself about your goals. They also require that you gather the information necessary to weigh the benefits and costs of various options as well as live with the uncertainty that comes from any action intended to have a future impact. To be really good at making these choices you should already have a high KHS, especially with respect to gathering information, asking and answering the right questions, and problem solving. But, ironically, gaining these skills is one of the purposes of a college education. The best way to deal with this irony is to be flexible and to realize, as hockey superstar Wayne Gretzky put it, "You miss 100 percent of the shots you don't take."

The way you learn to make good decisions is simply by making decisions or choices. And when it comes to the choices you make about colleges, programs, and courses, make those choices yourself. Your educational choices impact on *your* future, and that means you must take full responsibility for them. If you don't make the decisions based on your own perceptions and desires, you'll find yourself in unrewarding circumstances. As a faculty adviser, I have seen students take courses because their parents demanded it, or it would give them bragging rights back home, or their best friend is taking the same course and wants a buddy. Invariably these students have had a tough time completing their programs and acquiring the know-how skills necessary for a successful life.

You can canvass your friends for information and perhaps their views on the benefit and costs of a specific course or program. You can bounce your plans off your parents and relatives, especially those who know something about college education and respect your right to make your own choices. Ultimately, though, you must make decisions that feel right for you.

So, let's get back to you. The most important source for making your choices lies within your own goals. What do you want to learn from college? What kind of a career do you want? If you are like most people entering college, you don't have very clear goals about your career future—other, perhaps, than some idea about the amount of money you want to make, where you want to live, and what you do *not* want to do. On the other hand, if you're sure you're going into a specific career, don't be surprised if that goal changes over time.

Raising your KHS as a goal for your years at college provides a solid road map for the choices you face. It will allow you to keep your options open for specific careers while at the same time preparing to be successful in the career you finally pursue. I have already noted in the previous chapters that improving your KHS does not have to be the only goal of your college education. Other goals like minimizing debt, learning for the sake of learning, and having fun also influence your choices. However, this chapter speaks only to building your KHS. It provides you with a set of guidelines to use in making decisions about colleges, programs, and courses as you build your KHS. These guidelines are based on my experiences working in higher education for forty years as well as the existing research on higher education. For almost any guideline presented below, you will be able to think of exceptions. The guidelines are intended to help you make judgments about how KHS-friendly colleges, programs, courses, and teachers—whether faculty, staff, or other people in professional roles—are.

The chapter is organized according to the layers of choices you face from the broadest to the most specific. Like most things in life, the more specific levels will have the biggest impact. As you read the sections below, you will clearly see this. However, the choices you make at one level will shape the choices you will be able to make at more specific levels.

LAYER 1: COLLEGE CHOICE

You can develop your KHS at any college, but some are more helpful than others. Therefore, selecting a college should not be based primarily on the desire for a high KHS.

LAYER 2: PROGRAM CHOICE

Majors usually comprise less than 25 percent of your credits and in no case more than 50 percent, so even if the major does not help your KHS very much, you can supplement it by careful course choice. So if you are an art major, rejoice! Tell your parents to relax because you plan to get a high KHS along the way by taking skills courses.

LAYER 3: COURSE CHOICE

Courses will take time and if they don't do much for your KHS, they may be a significant roadblock. So choose carefully.

LAYER 4: CHOICE OF INDIVIDUALS TO CONNECT WITH

These choices are by far the most important force for your KHS development as well as your general learning. If you don't connect with faculty, staff, or others in professional roles outside of the college, you will have an anemic KHS.

Each of these four layers of choices will be discussed in this chapter as you seek to develop your KHS.

CHOOSE A COLLEGE

Your choice of college does not have to be driven solely by your KHS. There are many other factors to consider. However, if you are serious about your work future, see how KHS-friendly your possible choices are and include that in your decision. The guidelines presented below are directed at choosing a traditional four-year undergraduate college or university. Some of the suggestions are not directly relevant to part-time students or those taking advantage of nontraditional programs. However, when assessing these nontraditional college options, keep your KHS in mind.

LOOK AT MANY COLLEGES

The skills described in chapters 1 through 10 can be practiced and improved at any college, but some make it more difficult than others. The brief comments below will alert you to what to watch out for.

A major source of tension for most students is whether or not they should attend a "high-prestige" college. From a KHS perspective, this tension is unnecessary. Your KHS will not benefit substantially by the reputation of the institution, and there is an important trade-off to consider. At a high-prestige college, you will learn more from your peers perhaps, but you will also be faced with tougher competition in getting some of the experiences you will need for your KHS. If you need competition to drive your learning, such schools might be the place for you. If you can internalize your own standards and apply them to your own development, a high-prestige school is not a good choice for increasing your KHS.

In general, private colleges and universities are more likely to be KHS-friendly than most public institutions. Private institutions are likely to have better computer support and allow access to faculty and staff more readily. They are also likely to have fewer closed classes in those courses offering skills than public institutions. However, public institutions have one thing in their favor. Because public institutions tend to serve more people with lower incomes, their programs are more likely to prepare students for the workforce and therefore be more KHS-friendly.

As far as your KHS goes, the decision to go to a junior or community college for your first two years has mixed consequences. On the one hand, you will lose the first two years to build a base for activities and relationships with staff and faculty that you would have had if you had gone to a four-year school. On the other hand, you may have the opportunity to take more applied and hands-on courses at the two-year school. You may also be able to hold down a part- or full-time job more responsibly than would be possible at a four-year school. Usually the decision to go to a two-year college first has more to do with finances or personal reasons. If you do go to a two-year college, be sure to complete your associate's degree because doing so will allow you to avoid most lower-division required courses at the four-year school. For the most part, these requirements do little for your KHS.

LOOK AT METROPOLITAN LOCATIONS

The location of the institution may limit opportunities for internship, career services, and public-community service. College and universities located in or near metropolitan areas of at least 200,000 people have a distinct advantage for raising your KHS. Those in rural areas or very small towns are going to have fewer government, nonprofit, and business organizations that provide experiences and jobs while you are taking classes. If you choose a college more than fifty miles from a metropolitan area, you should plan to spend at least two semesters in off-campus programs. You may be better off in the mid-size metropolitan areas rather than the very large ones especially if you are seeking experience in the media, government, and, to some extent, business. At Syracuse University, there may be one hundred wanna-be TV sportscasters while in New York City, there are probably two thousand in college in any given year.

Schools located in faraway places are also less likely to have speakers and adjunct faculty who can bring real-world experience into the classroom. Even in a medium-sized city, the district attorney can speak to a class dealing with the criminal justice system and only lose two hours of her workday. A three-hour round-trip drive makes such a visit much less likely. Adjuncts who have both the academic background and real-world experience can meet a class in the evening two nights a week conveniently.

LOOK AT LARGE UNIVERSITIES

Large universities with a variety of liberal arts and professional programs will give you a larger variety of courses, in which you can practice the skills you need to develop, than smaller colleges. That does not necessarily mean more opportunities to develop those skills, but more variety.

Large universities will allow you to develop your own internal drive because there will be more students competing for the attention of faculty and more students in activities outside class. Large universities are more like the real world than small colleges if only because they are more complex. However, if you go to a small college, a semester or two off campus and good internship and job experiences can easily compensate.

Concern for your KHS score should not be the determining factor in the size of the college or university you choose. There are plenty of opportunities at both, but you may need to plan more educational off-campus activities if you choose a small college.

USE MULTIPLE SOURCES TO
GATHER INFORMATION

The choices you will make concerning colleges, programs, and courses all
require that you gather information. For that reason, I'll present the
guidelines for this section now so you can apply them when researching
your college choice.

Checking out the opportunities for you to develop your KHS and
explore your career options is no easy task. It requires time, the use of
multiple sources of information, and a strategy suggested by the skill set
described in chapter 8 called "Detect BS." Whenever possible, conduct your
research using the following four sources:

- Program descriptions
- Admissions representatives
- Faculty from the programs you are thinking about attending
- Students from those same programs

If you want to find out about the availability of internship for credit,
you can survey the material on program requirements to see if internship
credit is mentioned. However, that is only a beginning. You need to ask
admission representatives, faculty, and students some specific questions
about the kinds of internships available. Look for consistency from all your
sources.

SCOPE OUT CAREER SERVICES

Make sure the institution makes career services a high priority. Ask how
many full-time and part-time professional staff members provide career
services. Watch out for the use of graduate students as advisers. Some
can be competent, but they usually are around for less than two years and
may not know much, especially if they went to graduate school straight
out of college.

Ask what software programs they have purchased to help students.
They should subscribe to eChoices, Discover, or SIGI Plus. If they have
paid for access to all three, that indicates more commitment. The most
valuable of the three is eChoices, which provides information about professions, resources for learning, and frequent updates about job conditions. It

also contains self-evaluation procedures and planning devices to help you think about your career. This service is discussed more in chapter 18.

Ask for data on placement rates for new college graduates in the fields you are thinking about. Check with seniors and recent graduates to find out their experiences with career services and gaining employment. Find out how many employers visit the campus in job fairs and in other ways.

CHECK OUT COMPUTER FACILITIES

A few schools require that you bring a computer with you or give you a computer, but most leave it up to you. If you are serious about improving your KHS as well as getting a high GPA, come to school with a decent computer. You do not want to be pulling all-nighters in a computer cluster with lines of students waiting behind you and mass hysteria permeating the atmosphere. If you cannot afford to purchase a decent computer for college, I suggest you wait until you have enough money to do so. The cost of a computer and printer will be about 1 percent of the total money you spend on college. That 1 percent will contribute immensely to most of your skills. To go to college without a working computer and printer would be like someone with bad eyesight buying a ticket for a movie and not having eyeglasses. It makes no sense.

At times, however, you will need to use computer facilities on campus because you cannot purchase all the software you need yourself. Therefore, you want to do an audit of the computers and computer software. Check to see if they have all of the software listed below (and explained in chapter 11) available to students.

BASIC SOFTWARE

Adobe Illustrator
Adobe PageMaker
Lotus Notes
Microsoft Access
Microsoft FrontPage
Microsoft Publisher
Quark XPress
Statistical Analysis System (SAS)
Statistical Package for the Social Sciences (SPSS)

Other software that should be available will vary according to the program you are in. For example, if you are an architecture student, you will want to make sure the school has Photoshop, Autocad, and Form V. Also, ask students how crowded and reliable the computer facilities are around mid-term and the last week of the semester.

RESEARCH INTERNSHIP OPTIONS

Some colleges and universities have invested money in hiring professional staff to help you get on- and off-campus internships while others provide little help. You should look at the entire institution to see if there is a centralized office for internship administration, and look for the programs in which you are interested. Some schools like Northeastern and the Rochester Institute of Technology will have semester internships, usually called co-op programs. Many places do not have institution-wide co-op programs, but programs within the schools do. These programs give you more experience, but they also may take longer to complete and have less flexibility. Remember the more credit you earn and more integrated into the academic program structured work experiences are, the higher your KHS. See the next chapter for more on this. As in the case of career services, you do not want to rely only on printed material and information from admissions.

CHECK OUT COMMUNITY SERVICE PROGRAMS

In your freshman and sophomore years, you may not be ready or permitted to take a formal internship program. However, you can perform community service that will enhance your KHS. You want to go to a school that encourages and supports public- and community-service activities. "Public" and "community" refer to government organizations and private nonprofits, respectively. Check with students and determine whether or not the college or university is a member of Campus Compact, an organization that was established to promote community-based learning throughout the United States. Institutions that are members are more likely to take service learning seriously than those that are not members.

You may want to check into the existence and strength of a co-ed service fraternity such as Alpha Phi Omega. APO is a national co-ed service fraternity dedicated to developing leadership, promoting friendship, and providing service to humanity on campus, in the university community, and even at the regional and national levels. If one of these service fraternities does not exist on your campus, it may mean that other supports are so strong that such organizations are not needed. Conversely, it may be more likely to mean that community and public service is not strongly supported by students and the institution. Checking for the strength of the Habitat for Humanity chapter is also a good test. Habitat chapters are part of an international nonprofit that builds homes for the poor. They frequently have solid local and national support as well as strong interests from students. If a strong one does not exist on a campus you are considering, see if it's a sign that either the college does not support public and community service or the kinds of students who attend the college are not interested in performing service. In either case, you should consider this a serious negative.

CHECK INTO CREDIT FOR OFF-CAMPUS PROGRAMS

The big question here is what percentage of students get off-campus credit for semester-long programs in D.C., a state capital, or overseas. Any number under 20 percent raises serious questions about the support provided to those wanting to venture out into the real world for a semester. You also want to check for an office that supports off-campus semester-long experiences. Keep in mind that some colleges have cooperative arrangements with other institutions and thus no central office. The key is not that the college has its own overseas or off-campus programs. The key is that students actually take advantage of the opportunities.

A percentage below 20 percent may mean that the college or university places academic roadblocks to off-campus programs. It may also mean that students at that college are so weak in their KHS that they do not seek off-campus experiences. Also check for specific programs if you are planning to be in a highly structured program like architecture or social work. Some of these programs incorporate well-structured off-campus experiences while others do not.

CONSIDER ROTC PROGRAMS

Although the military is not for everyone, the benefits to your KHS make the Reserve Officer Training Corps (ROTC) program, offered by the Army, Air Force, and Navy (includes Marines) at over one thousand colleges, something you should explore. The programs carry full or partial scholarships to your college for many of the recruits (under current funding in 2003) and summer pay in exchange for an obligation to serve four years once you graduate.

The choice of academic programs is open, but scholarship opportunities are usually limited by your choice of major. The nonacademic component of ROTC and the courses specifically taught by military personnel can build your KHS. This is particularly true with respect to work ethic, physical skills, and the full range of people, communications, and problem-solving skills.

After graduating from college, you will be commissioned as a second lieutenant (or ensign) as a junior military officer (JMO). You would enter your respective service and attend specialty training in whatever career field assigned (e.g., pilot training, intelligence, maintenance, logistics, security forces, services, public affairs, and communications). You would then be assigned to a base, post, or ship.

Once the active-duty service commitment is met, many officers leave the military and transition to rewarding civilian careers in government and business. College graduates who have had some military experience are in high demand in the world of work according to an article by Dave Moniz in the *Christian Science Monitor.*[1] The article points out that when a business manager from Merck, a major pharmaceutical manufacturer, "screens resumes submitted in response to a newspaper's advertisement no more than 1 in 10 candidates is hirable. When he works with military head-hunters, the number of employable candidates rises to about 7 in 10." Those odds may make it worthwhile to you to consider schools with ROTC programs.

CONSIDER NONTRADITIONAL OPTIONS

The term "nontraditional" applies to a large number of programs in which the course or degree credit is not generated by traditional classes in which you have forty-five hours of seat time for a three-credit course. Nontraditional learning takes many forms, including assigning credit for work experience that is supplemented by reflection, distance learning through the Internet, and programs that meld traditional classroom activities with independent study. Three underlying forces have created the growth of nontraditional programs: dissatisfaction with classroom-based teaching; the importance of learning through experience in an increasingly skilled workforce; and the needs of people who are not able to take off four years to go to college full time.

Some nontraditional degree programs do a great job in enhancing your KHS. However, these programs require a maturity and self-direction that is rare among most people and particularly those under twenty-five years of age. Still, you might want to learn about some of these programs just to be aware of them and to give yourself ideas about different approaches to developing your KHS.

For-profit organizations like Dale Carnegie Training (discussed in the Useful Resources section of chapter 3) or Microsoft Office User Specialization certificate program (discussed in chapter 9) provide opportunities to learn many of the KHS skills. A publication described at the end of this chapter lists hundreds of such opportunities. Some colleges will accept the training provided by these organizations for elective credit. See if the colleges you are investigating do.

USE GUIDES WITH CAUTION

Several of the books and websites that provide information and ratings on college are mentioned in Useful Resources at the end of this chapter. These types of sources may have an explicit bias such as what schools have programs that will help you make a difference in the world; others, such as the Fiske books and *U.S. News & World Report* annual publication, are supposed to be objective and reflect no biases. They provide rankings that feed into a competitive frenzy that should have no place in your thinking if you are primarily concerned with enhancing your know-how. Remember that your goal is developing the skills from the ten Know-How Groups at any college you go to.

I want to comment on *U.S. News & World Report*'s *America's Best Colleges* because it is so widely used and quoted. Every fall this publication provides rankings for hundreds of colleges and universities. The major ranking formula is complicated and integrates a large variety of factors that do not touch directly on acquiring skills. I recommend that you not use the rankings heavily in your decision making for that reason. Instead, use the annual report's section on what seniors have to say with respect to the items like "participated in a community-based project as a part of a regular course" or "completed a Practicum, internship, field or co-op experience or clinical assignment." The responses are "never," "sometimes," "often," and "very often." The higher the percentages of the last two categories are, the better in terms of developing most of the KHS categories of skills. The findings for this survey come from the National Survey of Student Engagement, which is sent to 620 four-year schools. Unfortunately, many schools do not allow the results to be made public for their schools and others refuse to even allow the survey to be taken. If schools you are looking at are not on the list or will not provide you with the information when you ask, you should seriously question their commitment to undergraduate education.

In addition, *America's Best Colleges* provides specialized rankings of schools, which are useful from a KHS perspective. I have listed six of them in the order of importance for providing the opportunity for you to develop your KHS.

- Internships/Co-ops (for reasons discussed in chapters 13 and 14)
- Service learning (because you gain credit for well-developed placements; see chapters 14 and 15)
- Undergraduate research/creative projects (to help you connect with faculty; see chapter 14)
- Study abroad (for reasons discussed in this chapter and chapter 14)
- Learning communities (because you share learning experiences with people you live with, which has a positive impact on your people skills)

In using this publication and other ranking publications, remember that books and rating schemes can only provide a rough screening device for making your own decisions.

The program you take in college needs to be viewed in layers. If you are at a university, the first layer is the college or school in which you are registered. Second, within any college, there may be different degree requirements. They are usually broken down into general, sometimes called distribution or core, requirements and major requirements. The choice of program may impact your KHS, particularly if you are forced to take a lot of requirements that are taught in a conventional manner. However, almost all programs allow for electives in which you can take the courses you need most for your KHS. This brings up the third layer: the courses you choose to fulfill your requirements, which will be discussed in the next section of this chapter. Highly structured programs with a lot of requirements and an outside authority dictating much of the curriculum have few electives. Most majors, particularly in liberal arts programs, allow for a great deal of variety.

One significant choice you face is between liberal arts and professional schools or programs. Some colleges specialize in liberal arts, but they also offer some professional school–type programs. In liberal arts or arts and sciences programs, you major in one of the traditional disciplines or in an interdisciplinary program. A typical list follows.

TYPICAL MAJORS IN LIBERAL ARTS

SOCIAL SCIENCES	NATURAL SCIENCES	HUMANITIES
Anthropology	Astronomy	African-American Studies
Economics	Biology	English
International Relations	Chemistry	Fine Arts
Political Science	Earth Sciences	Foreign Languages
Psychology	Geography	Literature
Public Policy	Mathematics	History
Sociology	Physics	Philosophy
Women's Studies		Religion

All programs can be used to improve your KHS if you plan carefully. The biggest problem from a career perspective that students have when majoring within a liberal arts program is they think of their major as a gateway to a specific career. A liberal arts education prepares you for all types of careers and not just those that require graduate education.

Undergraduate professional school programs are also a good choice for raising your KHS. The next table lists the programs that are usually housed within a school or college at the university or can be floating programs in smaller colleges. The majority of students who go into professional school programs may not end up in their intended profession because professional school programs offer a great deal of general education and a relatively small amount of technical training. As in all the generalizations presented in this chapter, there are major exceptions to this rule. For example, a program in drama can be run as one long audition and require that most of the course work be directed at developing actors. Another example is accounting in business or management schools in which graduates are ready to pass the CPA exam and work as accountants.

PROFESSIONAL PROGRAMS BY SCHOOL

ARCHITECTURE
Architecture

EDUCATION
Communication Sciences and Disorders
Education by subject (Art, English, Mathematics,
    Music, Reading, Science, Social Studies)
Elementary Education
Higher/Postsecondary Education
Inclusive Elementary and Special Education
Physical Education

**ENGINEERING AND
COMPUTER SCIENCE**
Engineering (Aerospace, Bio-, Chemical,
    Civil, Computer, Electrical, Environmental,
    Mechanical)
Computer Science
Systems and Information Science

**HUMAN SERVICES AND
HEALTH PROFESSIONS**
Child and Family Studies
Dietetics
Hospitality and Food Service Management
Nursing
Nutrition
Social Work

INFORMATION STUDIES
Information Management and Technology

MANAGEMENT
Accounting
Business Administration
Entrepreneurship and Emerging Enterprises
Finance
General Studies in Management
Marketing Management
Organization and Management
Retailing and Marketing

PUBLIC COMMUNICATIONS
Advertising
Broadcast Journalism
Graphic Arts
Magazine
Newspaper
Photography
Public Relations
Television-Radio-Film

**VISUAL AND
PERFORMING ARTS**
Art
Design
Drama
Fashion
Museum Studies
Music

The point is that liberal arts programs are not as irrelevant to your KHS as some think, and professional school programs are not on target to getting you a job in a specific industry as others believe. That is why your selection of programs must be guided by the question, "What skills am I good at and like performing?" rather than, "What job will this major get me?" Chapter 17 will help you begin to explore these questions. If you learn nothing else from reading this book, remember that the general skills you develop in college are the foundation for your success in any profession.

To support this view, you should know that spokespersons for almost all professional degrees like the JD, MBA, MPA, and MSW say that the degree you took as an undergraduate is not critical for admittance to their program. In fact, they emphasize diversity in the backgrounds of their students. These professional school programs actually look for the same skills as employers, along with high scores on the standardized graduate school examinations like the GRE, GMAT, and LSAT. In most cases, your GPA is not as important as your skills and test scores.

Based on my experience with students over the past thirty years, I advocate a program in which you have a professional school major or minor *and* a liberal arts major or minor. Unless you are one of those few students who have a complete commitment to either becoming a scholar in a liberal arts field or following a highly specialized professional field like chemical engineering, you should have at least a minor in a field outside of your primary school program. If possible, try to take two majors from different schools if you are at a university. These combinations are important for your KHS because different programs emphasize different skills, and the ability to navigate between two programs will develop the skills described in chapter 9 (asking and answering the right questions) and chapter 10 (problem solving).

SELECT COURSES

The course recommendations for the ten Know-How Groups in chapters 1 through 10 make it clear that you have to plan carefully to find course work that will enhance your KHS. Concerning these recommendations, there is both bad new and good news. Here's the bad news:

- The majority of courses you take will not have KHS skills as a primary goal.
- Some courses will be focused primarily on skills like writing, statistics, and speech communications, but even these courses may not deliver what they promise. They tend to be heavy on theory and light on practice.
- Many college professors rely on lectures and recall tests, which are not KHS friendly.

But there is good news. These roadblocks can be overcome if you follow the three "remedies" discussed next. You can practice and develop your basic skills through much of your college course work while also getting good grades and your degree. The remedies will show you how to make course and instructor choices and follow a proactive learning approach that will help you enhance your basic KHS skills. If you do this, college is probably the best place you can be to develop the basic skills you need for success in the world of work. Follow these suggestions, and you will be able to use much of your course work to raise your KHS.

SEE YOUR COURSES AS OPPORTUNITIES TO DEVELOP YOUR KHS

You will take many courses that are not directly related to your KHS for graduation requirements of one kind or another. Even these requirements can give you an opportunity to develop many of the skills if you use them for that purpose. Business students taking a chemistry course as a general educational freshman requirement can develop skills like paying attention to detail, using numbers to reach conclusions, and learning to ask the right questions. If the course has a community-service requirement in which they tutor high school students in chemistry, then almost every one of the ten basic Know-How Groups can be practiced. Most courses will provide you with an opportunity to develop some KHS skills only if you take advantage of the opportunity to do so.

Even the most academic and theoretical courses provide an opportunity to improve your KHS. They will also provide you with an opportunity to develop listening and writing skills or, if they use numbers, quantitative skills. Being required to take so many of these courses is far from ideal, but you can turn a negative into a positive with the right approach. Above all, don't get frustrated with these requirements because, if nothing else, they will provide an opportunity for you to improve your work ethic and your ability to solve problems.

Furthermore, even though many courses may not help you with the basic KHS skills, they could help you in gaining the knowledge or skills for extra credit. As noted in chapter 12, having a passionate interest in a subject that has no direct application may help you in your career in unforeseen ways. In addition, courses aimed at higher-level skills beyond the basic KHS skills that are related to your professional interests may also be available.

DO NOT RELY ON INTRODUCTORY SKILL COURSES TO DEVELOP YOUR SKILLS

Most colleges offer "skill" or "tool" courses in writing, speaking, foreign language, and a vast array of quantitative and computer skills. Taking them, particularly at the introductory level, may help you get started on developing a skill. However, that is far from guaranteed and in any case cannot replace the real-world application you will need.

There are many reasons why introductory tool courses may not help you develop the KHS skills in oral and written communications, computer usage, and quantitative analysis, but they need not concern us here. Even if you take a course that helps you, skills are not something you get from one course. They need to be practiced over a long period of time and applied in different situations. So practicing in every course you take will ensure that you can apply them when you start on your career.

FIND KHS-FRIENDLY INSTRUCTORS

The instructor is always more important than the course, so do some serious investigation of the courses you choose. The best place to start is *not* with the official course catalogue. The write-ups are brief and frequently not informative or accurate. Instead, obtain a copy of the course syllabus *before* you sign up for the course. The syllabus can be viewed as a contract between you and the instructor.

This advice sounds obvious, but may not be so easy to follow. First, many instructors do not prepare the course syllabus early enough to allow you to get the information ahead of time. If that is the case for a course you are interested in, sign up for one or two backup courses, go to the class the first day, and get the syllabus. If the instructor has taught the course before, get an old copy of the syllabus. Second, the instructor might not stick to the syllabus, or it might be so vague that it tells you very little. The remedy for this is to check with students to find the "real syllabus." Finally, email the instructor or make an appointment to conduct a brief interview.

The basic questions to ask when choosing courses and instructors that you hope will enhance one or more of the ten basic Know-How Groups significantly are the following:

1. WHAT KINDS OF TESTS AND ASSIGNMENTS ARE REQUIRED?

Avoid courses based on multiple-choice exams, which rarely, if ever, measure the application of skills. Take courses that have off-campus field experience. (The vital importance of courses and programs that have incorporated some type of fieldwork will also be explored in the next chapter.) Look for words in the syllabus like "logs," "labs," "fieldwork," and "community service."

2. HOW IS YOUR FINAL GRADE DETERMINED?

An instructor who weighs class participation and projects is likely to be looking more at your skill levels than your content mastery. Instructors who give a mid-term and final are not going to be concerned with your skill development. Be wary of instructors who grade on a bell-shaped curve. This practice occurs primarily in the sciences and mathematics but can happen in any course. It usually signifies that the instructor is not clear about standards, and that competition for the sake of competition seems to be the primary educational strategy. Curves may also reflect the tendency of faculty to teach too much at too high a level for the class so that grades are determined by how far the best can go. This is not usually a good way to help students develop their skills because the standards are muddled to the professor, and they will be even more confusing to you.

3. HOW ARE COURSES CONDUCTED?

Avoid professors who think teaching is telling or reading and who give recall tests. They may help you with your attention to detail skills and your ability to figure out what is wanted, but so will any course. Professors who use methods to engage students in debate and use active learning techniques like classroom exercises are always preferred. I'm not suggesting that you avoid a class from a professor who is a great lecturer, but instead check to see if the examinations ask for more than recall or simply figuring out what the professor wants. Conversely, some professors who allow open class discussions that are unstructured and team projects that are not tightly evaluated are not helping you develop your skills any more than a teacher reading from notes that are thirty years old. Discussion sections, in which big lectures are broken into small groups and are run by a graduate student, may not allow for hands-on learning. Also, the quality of the discussion section depends on the quality of the graduate student. So ask students who've had the class what they think.

4. IS THE INSTRUCTOR BOTH STUDENT ORIENTED AND STANDARDS DRIVEN?

This is a very important question. Professors must finely balance two loves—the love for their subject matter and the love for their students. The balance is important for your own KHS development. If the teacher throws the subject to you and then says, "Show me that you are almost as knowledgeable and as smart as I am," the skills value will be diminished. There may be value in this approach especially with respect to the skills of asking and answering the right questions and problem solving, but there will be little opportunity for anything else. If the teacher is trying to entertain you, the value to your skill development is minimized, except as a powerful example of how not to be honest. An email to the instructor before the class starts may help you here. The answers may help you figure out the kinds of standards set for the course. If you get no response, the instructor is either not student oriented, not well organized, or not into email.

5. IS THE INSTRUCTOR ACCEPTING OF THE NOTION OF KHS?

Even those professors that have the right combination of support for students and standards may not do a lot for your KHS. They may have a very narrow and specialized view of higher education, which is that you are to become a scholar just like them. They can work with you on a one-on-one basis so that you understand the major research and theoretical questions they grapple with, but not much more. Unless you think you might want to be a scholar like your professor, this type of professor may do little to help you improve your KHS. You will find many professors who have this orientation, so you should explore this question.

Search for professors who send you out to test your knowledge and ideas in community service or related fieldwork. For example, if you are learning to master survey research, take the class in which the professor makes you design, conduct, and analyze a survey for a real-world client rather than one who has you read several books on survey research design and gives you a multiple-choice test. Almost every field can supply real-world experiences as part of the course, even if it is presenting your knowledge to a local high school class. If that is not possible, professors can run simulations and exercises, give real-world case studies, or bring in outside speakers who are active in the field to give you a sense of the real-world dynamics. These are the professors who will boost your KHS the most.

FIND CONNECTIONS

The most powerful source of raising your KHS while you are in college is developing learning relationships with faculty, staff, and community people who will help you develop your skills. The more you are able to find these individuals, the more you will be able to raise your KHS score. I will begin this section talking about how to connect with faculty, who may be your most important starting point. However, know that some of the most important "KHS teachers" in college will not be faculty members.

THE FACULTY

The kinds of connections you make with faculty do not necessarily have to be ones where you sit on one end of a log and your professor on the other discussing her or his subject and then moving on to the meaning of life. This idyllic image is frequently the one that students, faculty, and administrators hold of what college is all about. Except for the few students who want to connect at the most sophisticated level of the professor's field so they can pursue their Ph.D. and a life of scholarship, intense faculty-student relationships are not usually functional for raising your KHS. In fact, these relationships may take valuable time away from practicing the essential skills.

Student-oriented faculty members usually have too many students, and they need to take strategic actions to help you move to the next level. Therefore, judge by the quality of interactions you have with them rather than the quantity of time they spend with you. A faculty member who writes on your first paper that you need to learn how to use commas better and then praises you on your next paper for doing so can make a big contribution to your KHS. Faculty members who alert you to scholarship and internship opportunities through email can make a huge difference in your education. If you strategically consult with key faculty on limited occasions throughout your college years, you can benefit enormously. Initially, the faculty member should take time to meet you and learn your interests. Once this is done, don't look for bonding experiences but for guidance as you develop your skills. When you schedule an appointment with a faculty member, prepare a list of questions you want to ask and show the professor that you are reading off the list.

One of my most outstanding recent graduates who obtained a fabulous job when she graduated provides the following advice:

I've seen it many times—students who inevitably take a course because they heard the professor was lenient or buys drinks for the students after a night class. But what do they end up with? An easy A, and nothing more. The most valuable resource I found during my college years was my connections with the faculty, beyond that of a recommendation letter or an occasional pat on the back.

She also had some advice about irritating professors, like me.

*Don't judge a book by its cover and do NOT drop out of a class because it's difficult or because the professor is an ass. Coplin pushed me, infuriated me, and at times made me feel two inches big. But something kept me coming back, kept me enrolled in his courses, and eventually I majored in his field of expertise. It took me four years to realize it was the personal challenge this professor lay before me that other professors had yet to do. Instead of being spoon-fed an assignment, he informed us of the ultimate goal and then left us high and dry to figure it out on our own—for an **entire** semester. It was extremely difficult, but it taught students to avoid procrastination, to explore a new path, to fend for themselves, and most important—to think on their own. I started with one major; he challenged me to take on two. I was prepared to study abroad in London with all of my friends; suddenly I was studying in Hong Kong knowing no one. I started my college career as the naïve girl from Iowa, yet ended it as the senior class marshal of the university. How? I developed healthy relationships with the university faculty and worked my tail off to impress them. It worked.*

You should be looking for faculty who:

- Suggest goals for your education
- Provide you with advice and learning opportunities to achieve those goals
- Evaluate your performance with respect to those goals
- Kick you in the butt

To connect with faculty, you need to find the connecting point. Usually that point is a genuine interest in what the professor is studying. Offer to become a research assistant or read a manuscript the faculty member is writing. Even going up right after class and suggesting how the lecture or class exercise might have been better would work. However, do these things because you are honestly sincere, not because you just want to raise your KHS or, even more disgusting, want to get a good grade.

STUDENT CONNECTIONS

Don't overlook connections that you make with your peers. As a freshman or sophomore, upperclassman can also prove to be very useful. First, you will find "colleagues" to develop your skills and expertise as you work on shared projects. Second, students with whom you've worked and who graduate before you can be helpful making job connections when you graduate. They may alert you to a job opening at their organization as well as provide you advice on where the jobs are. Connecting with fellow students on academic work and projects outside the classroom is extremely important.

OTHER KHS CONNECTIONS

As you move through your college career, professionals other than faculty may play an important role in helping you develop your KHS. One place to make these connections is through student organizations or residence hall activities. The professionals who manage these activities have a lot to teach when it comes to KHS skills. Work closely with them, and encourage them to accept a coaching role toward you.

You should also work with career counselors and, if appropriate, campus chaplains. A good source of connections would be helping the admissions department with campus tours or working for the alumni giving program.

Not all connections to professionals can be found on campus. Off-campus adults whom you meet through public or community services or internships or jobs can become your de facto teachers if you show them you share their goals and value their opinions. Support a program director at a nursing home or community center to help the clients. Not only will these relationships lead to better skill development, they may open doors to career paths you never thought about. You may not find a mentor for life, but I can guarantee you that you will find connections that will boost your KHS and enhance your exploration of professions.

USEFUL RESOURCES

America's Best Colleges by the editors of *U.S. News & World Report* (U.S. News & World Report, most recent edition). Published every fall, this publication provides rankings for hundreds of colleges and universities on a variety of dimensions. As noted previously, the general ranking is not the one most useful for your KHS.

Bears' Guide to Earning Degrees by Distance Learning by John B. Bear and Mariah P. Bear (Ten Speed Press, most recent edition). First published in 1974, this book is updated frequently because the distance-learning options are expanding. As supporters of distance learning, the Bears are not afraid to be critical of many of the existing programs.

Cool Colleges for the Hyper-Intelligent, Self-Directed, Late Blooming, and Just Plain Different by Donald Asher (Ten Speed Press, 2000). This book describes schools and programs that the author says will provide a better intellectual experience. The author admits a strong bias toward small liberal arts schools, but he also favors colleges that provide hands-on activities. Even if you are not interested in any of the schools discussed in the book, it will help you to get a better perspective as you look at schools you are interested in.

The Fiske Guide to Colleges by Edward B. Fiske (Sourcebooks, most recent edition). A widely used general screening guide, this book has a checklist to help you decide between a small and a large college and between a liberal arts school and a university with several professional schools.

How to Transfer to the College of Your Choice by Eric Freedman (Ten Speed Press, 2002). This book provides a solid discussion of reasons for transferring and how to go about it. It does not focus on your KHS but will help you improve your KHS if you do transfer.

Major in Success: Make College Easier, Fire Up Your Dreams, and Get a Very Cool Job by Patrick Combs (Ten Speed Press, 2003). This book shows you how to relate your dreams about careers to what you learn in college. The book oversells the possibilities of dream careers, but as you develop your KHS, you will learn to adjust your dreams to your skill levels.

Making a Difference: College and Graduate Guide by Miriam Weinstein (SageWorks Press, most recent edition). The book lists a wide variety of undergraduate colleges (also graduate schools) that integrate community service and activities with course work. These colleges are more likely than others to provide learning opportunities that will help you build your KHS.

Reserve Officer Training Corps (ROTC) (Army: www.armyrotc.com, for about 575 colleges; Air Force: www.afrotc.com, for about 300 colleges; Navy/Marines: www.nrotc.navy.mil, for about 130 colleges). Make sure the college you choose has an ROTC program if you have any inkling whatsoever that you might be interested.

FOR THE THINGS WE HAVE TO **LEARN** BEFORE WE CAN **DO THEM,** WE LEARN BY **DOING THEM.**

—ARISTOTLE

CHAPTER 13

CREATING YOUR OWN APPRENTICESHIPS

TOPICS

EXPLORE APPRENTICE-BASED EDUCATION • BUILD YOUR
BASE • LAND GOOD SUMMER JOBS AND INTERNSHIPS •
MAKE THE MOST OF YOUR EXPERIENCES

Aristotle presents an ironic challenge to new college graduates looking for their first job after college. Most job descriptions call for experience, but you can't get the experience without the job and you can't get the job without the experience.

Before the early twentieth century, the apprentice system, in which a beginner worked with a professional in the field, was the way to get the experience and grow into the job. That is how Benjamin Franklin became a printer with virtually no formal education. Being an apprentice means having a teacher and mentor who will encourage, demonstrate, provide ample learning opportunities, and correct.

Apprentice education is the best form of education in every field, but in the modern world there are too many wanna-be apprentices and not enough faculty to serve the wanna-bes. Consequently, colleges cannot provide an apprentice system for the majority of undergraduates. Given the underlying economics and the trend toward distance and web-based learning, there is little hope for improvement. Email can help close the gap between the professor and the student but, in most cases, not enough to develop the kinds of apprentice relationships you need.

Even if there were enough college faculty members to provide apprenticeship experiences to all college students, they could not provide good apprenticeship experiences in most cases. Most college faculty, especially in arts and sciences programs, have studied their subject but not been a "player" themselves. They can analyze the modern American novel but have not written a novel. They have written books on political leaders but have not been a political leader. Consequently they are not equipped to give you an apprentice experience themselves. These faculty members are important to your general education but may be limited in how much they can help your KHS.

There are two important exceptions to this rule, however. First, those students who want to take up the academic trade of scholarship and teaching can benefit greatly if a faculty member treats them as a junior colleague. This happens in many situations. Frequently, college students become research assistants to the point of being co-investigators and even co-authors with faculty. Second, faculty members who have extensive nonacademic experiences can create apprenticeship relationships through their contacts or in their own work outside academia.

Fortunately, you can have apprentice relationships during your college years with experienced mentors and teachers both on and off campus. The solution to Aristotle's irony is a string of educational work experiences or mini-apprenticeships. The apprenticeships will not be as long and intense as those Benjamin Franklin received from his brother and others to become a master printer, but they can become powerful learning experiences. Having a set of work experiences under the guidance of a professional can provide the support you need for an outstanding KHS. Recognizing the need for such experiences, most colleges are doing a good job in helping you get them.

Apprenticeship-type experiences are essential to your preparation for a rewarding work life for several reasons. First, every one of the ten Basic Know-How Groups can be developed during these experiences depending on what jobs you are assigned.

Second, practicing the skills in real-world situations is a powerful learning engine. It means that when you do well, you will be praised in a genuine way, and that when you mess up, you will suffer real consequences. Receiving praise from a professional in the field you aspire to can motivate you to high levels of performance just as being chewed out by the same professional can move you even higher.

Finally, these experiences are important for your future work life because they give you a chance to see what kinds of jobs exist and whether or not you like them. The enormous haystack of professional fields that you face can be explored by these real-world experiences. You may find your work inherently interesting and the skills you exercise fulfilling, or alternatively, you may realize that what you thought you would like to do is no longer rewarding. These experiences are more powerful and educational than reading books about careers and searching the Net.

For these reasons, what you do between semesters is as important for developing your basic skills as what you do during semesters. The time during both winter and summer semester breaks should be used to develop skills and acquire new experiences. Your public service, part-time jobs, or internships (paid or unpaid) are more important for your KHS than your major and the classes you take.

I base this assertion on what I hear from alumni, who routinely tell me that their internship and job experiences were the most important part of their education and urge me to provide even more opportunities. Often the difference between college graduates of the program who obtain satisfying careers and those who don't is related to their summer jobs or internships between their junior and senior years.

Employers are also unanimous about the value of summer work experiences. As one human resource director said, "Sure, it's great to have a fun summer job, but I'd rather see something with a lot of responsibility that needs skill."

EXPLORE APPRENTICE-BASED EXPERIENCES

There are four opportunities for apprentice-type experiences:

- Public or community service: These are usually in the local community but sometimes away from campus such as the Habitat for Humanity "spring break trips." Such work is not paid and may or may not earn credit, depending on your college and program.
- Internships for a business, nonprofit, or government agency: "Internships" are usually credit bearing and sometimes paid. They can be taken during the semester or in the summer and can be on or off campus, but are usually the latter. Some organizations will call paid positions "internships" in order to make it clear that it is not a permanent job and also to reduce fringe benefit costs. Internships can earn any number of credits depending on school and program policies and the availability of faculty oversight. The standard is forty-five hours of work for each semester credit hour.
- Part-time jobs during the academic year: These jobs can be on or off campus and, by the use of the term "job," are always paid. They usually do not generate academic credit, but give it a try.
- Full-time jobs during any period you're not a full-time student, usually in the summer: These jobs are paid but they can also earn internship credit. The key feature here is that you work thirty to forty (or more) hours a week, and you receive wages.

I have lumped these four "types" together because they all have the potential to provide apprenticeship opportunities. The best opportunities for developing your KHS skills come when the organization provides you with a staff member or experienced volunteer to train and mentor you.

In addition, the four types frequently overlap. For example, the difference between an internship and a job is one of convenience for some employers. The term *internship* usually implies that academic credit will be earned. Internships frequently, though not always, are unpaid. For obvious reasons, paid internships are better than unpaid ones, but in certain fields paid internships are impossible to obtain. So the line between internship and job is not clear. Moreover, sometimes you can get credit for a job and sometimes public service morphs into a paid position. This is no different from the real world where companies often give what are in effect internships before permanent employment. Think of these as types of opportunities in which you can have short-term apprenticeships.

What are the tradeoffs among the four types of educational work experiences? All four types of experience can be powerful in raising your KHS, just as all can be an enormous waste of time. Public and community service is the easiest of the four types to obtain. The downside to public or community service from a learning perspective is that some of the agencies are not well enough organized to use you effectively, and frequently they provide little training or mentoring by the staff or volunteers. Things are frequently chaotic, especially if the agency deals with youth. Chapter 15 describes the benefits of service activities during your college years.

Internships have the most educational potential because inherent in the idea of an internship is that learning will occur. First, the organization offering the internship is likely to take some responsibility for making sure that you learn something and not just do gofer work. Second, as we have noted throughout the book, courses that integrate field experience are better suited for skill development. If the internship experience is part of a class and there are structured assignments and time for reflection on skills, you can make giant strides in many of the ten Know-How Groups. Third, you earn college credit, which means that you have more time and less traditional academic pressure to limit your investment in the internship. Some college programs have a co-op requirement. A co-op is usually a semester-long (or even longer) full-time internship that is a requirement of the program and carries credit with it. Usually occurring in the junior or senior year, you are expected to act as an apprentice for a company or agency. Frequently, a salary is paid by the host organization.

However, this is an ideal view of internships—their quality depends on both the college and the placement site. The site and your college may not have adequate resources invested to make it the kind of learning experience it can be. Many times, internships are open-ended poorly defined activity. This can be work if the placement site has it together. However, if the organization is out of control and support from your college is weak, you may be in for an unpleasant experience. This does not mean you will fail to learn from the experience and should avoid it. It does mean that you have to put in extra effort to make it a learning experience yourself.

Jobs, whether part-time or full-time in the summer, can make a major contribution to both your skill development and your career exploration. This is true even though the primary purpose of a job is for you to do what the employer needs to have done rather than your learning particular skills or knowledge about a business or organization, as it is in an internship. However, you need to select a job that promises some education and is not continuously repetitive. Waiting tables, being a lifeguard or camp counselor, or driving a forklift are OK for your first summer, but they are not likely to be a learning experience worthy of the summer between your junior and senior year.

Some students opt to go for a higher paying job even though it will provide poor career and skill development. They will choose a job that pays $12 an hour that they did last summer over one that pays $8 an hour but is directly related to a career goal. When you are paying $15,000 to $30,000 a year for your college education, going for a job that pays $4 an hour more or $1,280 over an eight-week period does not make a lot of sense. A summer job that gives you access to a full-time job when you graduate or, alternatively, helps you come to the conclusion that the field you have chosen is not so hot after all is worth much more than $1,280.

There are no clear-cut rules about paying versus non-paying jobs. Even a job as a camp counselor, which some might view as just a summer of fun, can contribute greatly to your KHS. And a summer job scooping ice cream—if it also includes hiring, training, and firing workers—can mean more to a future employer than your having taken a management course or volunteered in a senator's office. Determine what skills you will be gaining from your experiences. Good choices about work and internship experiences are essential to a high KHS and, therefore, a top-of-the-line career.

BUILD YOUR BASE

Would you like to land a summer internship between your junior and senior year at a major corporation where you receive $20 an hour? How about adding to that salary a subsidized apartment, plane tickets home for the weekend, a broad and nurturing educational experience, and the promise of a job if you perform well in your internships? If you think this is too good to be true, think again. Every year hundreds of students end up in this summer job heaven. Thousands find summer jobs that are not quite so profitable in the short run but just as valuable in the long run.

Most large corporations offer summer internship programs. However, only some of them are what you might label "dream internships." The four described below are included to illustrate the point.

- AT&T offers a Finance Summer Internship Program for finance, accounting, economics, or business administration juniors or seniors with a cumulative GPA of 3.5 or higher. You receive an AT&T corporate finance assignment (in such areas as auditing, business case development, financial analysis, investor relations, treasury, tax, competitive and industry analysis, and many more). AT&T provides interns with a competitive compensation package, including paid holidays and vacation days. As an intern, you receive support from a management team, which includes orientation, career-counseling sessions, facility tours, team-building activities, and community service events.

- The General Motors Intern Program is offered to students with goals in engineering, business, or manufacturing. You must be enrolled as a full-time student at an accredited university, with evidence of academic excellence and leadership potential. Interns participate in real-world work situations related to their academic programs. This full-time program is unpaid, but interns are provided with company-paid housing and a travel lump sum.

- The CIA Internship Program is geared toward majors in computer science, finance, electrical engineering, physical science, economics, geography, non-Romance languages, international relations, national security studies, military or foreign affairs, or political science. Students must be U.S. citizens, have a minimum GPA of 3.0, and must successfully complete a background check, as well as medical and polygraph examinations. The program is paid with benefits, and provides practical work experience that complements a student's academic studies through either (1) a combination semester and summer internship or (2) two ninety-day summer internships.

- Microsoft has an intern program in Seattle, Washington, perfect for business or information technology majors. Not only is it paid, but you are also provided with other benefits. There are free flights to and from the internship, subsidized housing with free cable, electricity, water, and housecleaning, help with shipping your belongings from home, subsidized car rental, free bus pass, free health-club membership, free Microsoft training seminars, intern events and parties, free drinks, free clothing, and software discounts.

This list of dream internships is not at all comprehensive. There are many more, but they are highly competitive and frequently require a scientific or computer background. They can also disappear if the company hits hard times. While not all corporations offer internships like these, most do offer some kind of internship or co-op program for college students. All it takes is a little persistence and research. Information on how to find internships appears in the next section.

How do you get one of the dream internships or a great summer job? You follow a master plan that guides your activity from the first day you arrive on campus. That plan enables you to get such a summer internship between your junior and senior year. I am a firm believer in hitting the ground running. Students who begin their college career by building a base of experiences outside the classroom are almost always more successful than those who do not. If you are already beyond the freshman year, all is not lost. Get started now.

During the first semester of your freshman year, visit some faculty members or graduate students whom you think you can connect with and offer to do some extra research. Take positions, either volunteer or elected, in your residence hall or with student groups. Do some off-campus public service. Do these things both to help you develop your skills and to make connections for bigger and better things. I am not a big fan of student government at the college level because it attracts too many people whose KHSs are low and exposes you to their adolescent ways. However, try your hand at it, especially the areas that deal with allocating money.

During the second semester of your freshman year, get involved in one serious commitment on campus and one off campus. I say "one" because you do not want to spread yourself too thin. Too many students overcommit when they get on campus. Even if you don't suffer academically, you will not learn as much as you would if you focused on a small number of activities. Spreading yourself too thin does not look good to future employers. As a human resource person from a major financial corporation said:

Our company wants to see someone with persistence and drive. We'd rather have you have one job and work your way up, than many different jobs. That's an immediate red flag when I see applicants with a job list the size of their resume.

This applies to community service as well as internships and jobs. You should explore a variety of opportunities throughout your college career, but ultimately employers are wary of people who do too much and appear to have a shotgun approach.

Although student groups are a viable place to start either on or off-campus activities, look for opportunities provided by the university faculty and administration. For on-campus activities, most colleges and universities want their best students to serve as student "hosts" to school visitors or as peer advisers. The competition for these positions is not as great as you would assume, and the payoffs can be enormous. A peer academic adviser works directly with a higher administration official and could end up as a student representative to the board of trustees. Some faculty members also use undergraduates as research assistants, teaching assistants, and tutors. If you find a faculty member who's looking for an assistant and are interested in the subject, take this path.

Your coursework may help you get off-campus experiences even in your freshman year. A growing number of lower-division courses in colleges throughout the country have a field-service component. A political science course may give credit for your work on a political campaign. A freshman writing course may require community service to provide experiences about which you can write. Even if courses are not offered, most colleges have offices that place students in volunteer positions in all kinds of nonprofit and government agencies.

In addition to volunteering, or what is usually called public or community service work, you can also seek paid positions, even in your freshman year. If you have college work-study, these positions cost the hiring department about thirty cents on the dollar, which places you in high demand. Even without work-study, college students are frequently hired on campus. A particularly valuable college job is to work for the alumni fund-raising office, for which you solicit alumni for contributions. People who can stand the rejection of cold calling and can be successful at getting contributions are in short supply. It will give you a look at the field of sales and at the same time give you credentials as someone who can do a difficult job.

During your second year, build on those experiences you found most enjoyable and educational the first year. Perhaps you want to become a resident adviser, which provides both leadership experience and significant financial support. If you were active as a volunteer in residence hall associations the first year, your chances to win the RA position the second year are much greater. Or, you liked the peer-advising program—perhaps you can be elected or appointed to the advisory board. Or, you work with a professor, and this leads to more advanced work in which you learn how to use statistical software. Or, you become a staff assistant to the campaign manager for the politician you worked for in your freshman year. Your paid positions can also lead to higher levels of work that develop many of your skills. You might manage other workers at sports events or supervise a small snack bar operated by food service. Or, you get hired at the local Boys and Girls club to run a pregnancy prevention and self-esteem program for teenage females because you were valuable as a volunteer to the person who ran the program the year before.

The trick is to make your initial position a learning experience for one or more of the ten Know-How Groups. This does not necessarily mean finding an exciting and interesting experience like working in the chancellor's office to help set up receptions for the rich and the famous or becoming a statistician for the football team. It may mean dishing out food in the resident hall cafeteria or stocking books in the library. How can working for food service be a great learning opportunity? The answer is that first it will build and demonstrate your work ethic. If you do a good job and show leadership by suggesting to your supervisor a better way to do things, you will quickly move into a management position. Serving in a management position during your sophomore year will develop your people skills. It could lead to a high-paying summer job or a management position the next year. Employers salivate when they think they can hire someone who will relieve them of the people problems they face every day.

A former student obtained one of those dream summer internships with a consulting company during the summer between her junior and senior year. By October she had a firm offer with a sizable signing bonus because of her outstanding performance that summer. Her college career started off in social work but ended up in communications and arts and sciences. However, it was her extracurricular activities that made the difference. Below is a list of activities from her first three years that helped her earn the internship:

FRESHMAN YEAR

- Joined the rowing team for a semester and then decided it was too time-consuming given the learning payoffs.
- *Unsuccessfully* ran for president of her hall council.
- Devoted a small number of hours to community service.
- Joined a sorority.
- Impressed two professors: one gave her an office job and the other some community service activities.
- Decided that her initial enrollment in the School of Social Work did not meet her long-term goals.

SUMMER BETWEEN FRESHMAN AND SOPHOMORE YEAR

- Obtained an internship as a marketing assistant for a cardiology firm in her hometown that provided priceless experience for a college sophomore. She realized that marketing was not her aspiration, but that she enjoyed working with people.

SOPHOMORE YEAR

- Changed majors, choosing to dual in policy studies in the School of Arts and Sciences and public relations in the Newhouse School of Public Communications. Both programs supported applied learning.
- Elected to the position of recruitment chair for the Panhellenic Association, the governing body of the sorority system.
- Worked with a professor on class projects.

SUMMER BETWEEN SOPHOMORE AND JUNIOR YEAR

- Obtained an internship in Washington, D.C., with Independent Sector, a research and lobbying group that represents close to one thousand nonprofits.

JUNIOR YEAR

- Became an undergraduate teaching assistant.
- Became a literacy tutor for the Center for Public and Community Service at an after-school program for Spanish-speaking children.
- Elected president of the Panhellenic Organization.
- Took a senior-level course in benchmarking that required a team project for a community agency. In February of that year, an alumna who works for one of the top consulting firms made presentations to a senior-level class and recruited for its Summer Scholars Program.
- Interviewed and was selected for the position at the consulting company.

That summer, she worked for the consulting firm on a state government project. She was able to combine the knowledge from all her college experiences to serve the company well. At the end of summer, she received an offer for full-time employment when she graduated. She accepted the offer (with signing bonus) and was able to spend her senior year dedicated to things other than finding a job.

The steps that this undergraduate took to land the dream summer internship and also a very high-paying position for someone with just a bachelor's degree—equal to the starting salaries of many MBAs and MPAs—are interesting from a number of perspectives. First, in her freshman year she undertook some activities that were false starts, if not downright failures. The lesson that was demonstrated by her eventual success was her ability to be decisive in changing programs and activities while having a firm idea that she wanted to develop her skills. Second, she undertook a variety of activities and stuck with them. Community service, research and teaching assistance to professors, and leadership in a sorority remained a constant throughout her career. Finally, luck played a role because it just so happened that a member of the consulting firm, who was also a former alumna of the program in which she was enrolled, made a classroom presentation and was looking for people to apply for the summer program. Good fortune is important, but those who work hard are more likely to get it.

Paying your dues and doing well academically when you start college can open the doors for better volunteer and higher paying positions while in college. Most important, it will lead to a high KHS and many exciting job offers. With a solid base of experience early in your college career, you are ready to search for outstanding job and internship opportunities during your last two years of college. If you are reading this book as a sophomore, junior, or senior, you have not entirely missed the boat. You can do something right now to get on board.

Landing a good internship or summer job is a result of two processes: (1) locating them and (2) convincing the organization that you are the one for the position.

THE SEARCH

The way you search for a community service project, an internship, or a part-time or summer job is no different from the way you will search for your first job after college, which means this is great practice. The first step is to figure out what kind of position you are looking for. You will need to be clear to yourself about your goals for the experience and then do a systematic search for a fit. Decide what kind of selection criteria you want to have—wage, stipend, credit, additional benefits, or company size. Don't be afraid to be selective in your search for the best position—even if you think you won't get your top choices. Eventually you may have to ease up on your selection criteria, but aim high when you start out.

Your search for the "perfect" internship or job opportunity should employ both an inside and an outside strategy. The inside strategy depends on your contacts. If you have pursued my suggested course of action for your freshman and sophomore year, you'll have a solid network of people who might be able to lead you in the right direction. Use family and neighborhood ties to locate job and internship opportunities. Ask peers who are a year ahead of you for leads. They are in the same boat as you and should be willing to share information. Former interns will be able to call up their internship coordinator and give them a heads-up that your application is in the mail. Some professors, usually those who also have a "skills-oriented" approach to their courses, have a handful of direct alumni contacts who want to give back to their college and can offer good advice and possibly even work experiences.

The outside strategy is hard work. It involves consulting books, websites, and offices on campus to get advice and assistance. This strategy is time-consuming and, to an extent, hit-and-miss, but if you dedicate yourself to it, you are likely to gain a valuable internship. Matt and Susan are two of my students who found excellent summer internships early in their college careers using the outside strategy. The advice and recommendations below reflect their own experiences finding internships. They suggest you use books, the Web, and campus resources.

BOOKS AND OTHER PUBLICATIONS

There are tons of internship reference guides available in annual editions that are described at the end of this chapter. These books list internships by field and location, and information such as selectivity, organization size, and application requirements. The books can be great springboards from which to launch the rest of your internship search.

These books are usually found in the reference section (along with college guides and SAT prep materials) in bookstores and libraries. Because libraries are apt to only carry outdated versions, Matt and Susan discovered that spending an afternoon or two at a large bookstore was the best way to go. Take along a notepad and pen and be prepared to find a lot of information. Of course you can always purchase a book, but they found this to be more cost-effective. (Just don't get caught by the friendly sales associates.)

One word of caution though: don't take reference guide information as an ultimate, or true, source. Matt and Susan found that the write-ups weren't always accurate and sometimes provided an overly flattering view of organizations. If you find an opportunity particularly appealing, investigate these agencies or companies by contacting their website or internship coordinator.

There are also good books that give you more complete advice on the internship and job search as a whole—from finding one, to getting one, to making the most out of your experience. In addition, you may find newspapers, magazines, and trade or other journals provide valuable leads.

WEBSITES

Several clearinghouse-type websites enable you to search for internship opportunities that match certain variables (e.g., location, field, and time period) of your choice. Matt and Susan were primarily searching for non-profit, government, or public service internships, but these websites also serve those interested in business, media, environment, science, and other fields. A few of the most helpful sites they found are listed at the end of this chapter.

Another excellent way to use the Web is to research agencies and companies you have identified as being possibilities. Once you find an organization you might want to work for, bring up their web page and find out more information. Usually, internship information is located in the "About Us," "Contact Us," or "Jobs and Opportunities" section of websites. If you find nothing on the website about internships or summer jobs, don't assume that the organization doesn't offer any: websites are often not kept up-to-date, especially at small organizations. In this case, email or the telephone is the best way to go. Ask the receptionist for an internship coordinator or the human resources department. Agencies may have never hired interns before and therefore will not publicize such opportunities. But, if you are highly motivated and very much interested in the work of a particular organization, contact that organization and inquire about the possibility of interning. If you demonstrate a specific knowledge or skill base, agencies may very well create a position just for you. Until you talk to an actual human being, don't assume anything.

One thing Matt and Susan found useful about using websites is that they create a domino effect of leads upon leads upon leads. Look in the "Sponsors," "Partners," and "Links" sections of an agency's website to find links to other organizations that are similar in mission or field.

Finally, remember to work from the ground up. If you are interested in a particular subject or societal problem, do a general web search (www.yahoo.com or www.google.com) on organizations that attempt to address these issues.

CAMPUS RESOURCES

The most centralized source of information on your campus will be the career center or, if your college has it, the office for promoting and administering internships. These offices purchase a wide variety of publications. They have specialized sources for such fields as the media, music industry, animation, resorts, sports, and environmental positions.

Matt and Susan also jump-started their search with a visit to their campus internship office. Although they did not end up using the services of the office to get credit (discussed later in this chapter), they did take advantage of the resources that the office provided to them. The office had decades' worth of internship search guides, file folders of newspaper clippings, recruitment flyers, and application materials. Don't underestimate the knowledge of the staff at these offices—they have helped students find excellent (and not-so-excellent) opportunities, and it's at least worth a conversation. In the best-case scenario, the staff may be a transition to the inside strategy: maybe they can hook you up with a former intern or an alumnus or alumna who can help you seal a position.

Using these strategies to find your internships is one thing; getting one is another thing entirely. Once you have decided what you are looking for, create a resume and a cover letter. Your cover letter and resume should highlight those experiences that best demonstrate your KHS. Talk about real-world experience in addition to your academic performance. Be sure to emphasize computer skills if you have them (and if you don't have them, develop your knowledge through computer classes or self-help books).

Those doing the hiring for your internship or part-time job are just like employers. They want to know your KHS. They will not demand as high a KHS as employers will, but they are interested in specific skills like writing, teamwork, and computer savvy. They will also want references, not just from faculty, but also from previous supervisors of community service, internships, or jobs.

One of the simplest ways you can impress a prospective internship agency is by sending your application, cover letter, and resume early. If you are applying for a summer internship, this means getting your application out by early January. Internship coordinators will not expect this timely behavior and will be impressed with the way you plan ahead. Susan, who interned with the Children's Defense Fund in the summer of 2002 between her freshman and sophomore year, a feat in itself, can attest to the importance of being prompt:

When I was doing my internship search, I had more than one agency place me high on their list of potential interns because they received my application in the first week of January. This is really rare for college students, who tend to put off the internship search and application process until a few days before the deadline, which for the summer is usually sometime in March. My internship coordinator at the Children's Defense Fund actually told me later that one of the biggest reasons she accepted me was because she was so impressed with my timeliness.

Another easy way to show self-reliance and dependability, even in the application process, is to pick and choose what kind of assistance you get from your college or university. Getting academic credit for your internship experience is great if it will help you graduate on time or early. It also helps you get a better learning experience in most instances. However, if you don't need the credit, you're just paying the university extra tuition. Your internship coordinator may also be relieved at the absence of paperwork and evaluations to fill out as well as impressed that you are so willing to spend time doing something with no direct compensation (in the case of an unpaid internship).

The advice on credit needs to be tempered with caution. Some organizations demand that credit be associated with the internship so they do not have to treat you as a regular employee, and there is pressure on you to do well. This is particularly true in the media business. In addition, if you have a faculty member who will provide advice and help you reflect on your experience, the credit charge might be worth the cost even if you do not need credit. Ask other students about their experiences and then decide.

If this is your first time searching for an internship or part-time job, keep in mind that you may not get that "dream" position the first time around. If you are rejected from an organization that you really wanted to work for, call up their internship director and ask how your application could be improved the next time around. Your failure could be the ultimate learning experience and help you get the job in the future. In fact, sometimes the best opportunities may lie in the most unexpected (and sometimes unglamorous) positions.

For example, be willing to take "pay your dues"–type positions. Cold call sales positions with reputable firms that give you ample training may be unspectacular and difficult but could be a great learning experience. They definitely will appeal to future employers in many fields. Working in a business like Kinko's, where customer service along with the ability to learn how to operate different machines, can provide you with a base and ultimately lead to a management position.

Taking a position in something like data entry will help you improve and streamline your skills in highly useful computer programs. Though the job itself will likely be boring and monotonous, the skills you will learn are in such short supply that you will eventually make good money and be a target of recruitment for excellent internships and permanent employment. This tip is especially relevant if you are staying at your college for the summer or live in a college town. Many professors do research and will be looking for short-term employees to do data entry and preliminary analysis. Susan was able to use her computer software application skills as a selling point in her cover letter and resume:

I remember clearly two of the coordinators I interviewed with being absolutely floored that I, as a freshman, knew both Microsoft Excel and SPSS. When I actually started interning, I was amazed at how many times I was helping department heads with computer problems they were having with these software programs. I even was able to show one staff member how to streamline a project using Excel. These skills can really get you far.

One final tip: go to temp firms. If you can demonstrate skills in demand, a temp firm will find you work, either part or full time. The firm takes a cut, but the money you receive will be competitive with what you would get if you found the job yourself. Moreover, the firm will prepare you for the job and find you another one when the first is over. Temp positions get you inside the company so that you can build your own network and make it part of your inside strategy the next time you look for an internship or part-time or summer job. National temp firms provide a good starting point, but every city has local firms that can be equally useful. Use the Yellow Pages or the Web to find them. According to several of my students, one of the best national firms for college students seeking a professional career is OfficeTeam, a division of Robert Half International.

MAKE THE MOST OF YOUR EXPERIENCES

Several books are discussed at the end of this chapter to help you get the most from your internship, but I want to emphasize that the key is your attitude. See your internship as an opportunity to raise your KHS and, at the same time, as an opportunity to be both proactive and professional. This attitude is crucial—not only with regard to internships but also to anything you do for your career future, whether it is an internship, a summer job, or your first job out of college. Look at all experiences as an investment in developing your basic skills.

There may be times after you have begun an internship that you do not see much potential for growth in your skills. If you have made a sincere effort to explore skills for all ten Know-How Groups, you should move on unless there are financial, legal, or moral commitments that you made when you took the position. "Sincere effort" is the key phrase here. My first thought when students tell me that their internship supervisor was incompetent or did not keep them busy is that the student either did not try hard enough or was not capable of performing in that position. Whether in volunteer, internship, or paid position, you must prove your worth to your supervisor. Demonstrate a commitment to learning and a commitment to perform at the highest possible level. Search for additional work and for information that might help you identify additional work. If you are eager, even to the point of being a pest, your supervisor will want to hire you when you graduate and will be willing to provide you with a recommendation.

Or to put it in different terms, an internship or work experience is like a test you don't want to fail. It may be a lousy test or an unfair test, but treat it as a challenge that you will meet. A passive attitude of "they didn't have anything for me to do" is not acceptable, even if they really didn't have anything for you to do. Taking the initiative to find something to do is important if you have a weak supervisor. If you have a strong but busy supervisor, you need to make sure she or he recognizes your competence and talent the first day on the job. As soon as supervisors learn to trust your ability to do what needs to be done with as little supervision as possible, you will find yourself extremely busy. They don't want high maintenance employees whose messes they have to clean up. Matt had firsthand experience dealing with these challenges as an intern for a political lobbying group in the summer of 2002:

> The first couple of days at my internship, no one was giving me anything to do. The majority of the other interns accepted this and sat around complaining of being bored. Every time I would start to get bored, however, I would remember a conversation I had with Professor Coplin during which he said that I was "self-motivated." This always inspired me to seek out more work, no matter how menial; I literally made thousands of copies during the first few weeks. Because of this work ethic, however, I was put in charge of a major campaign initiative and had a very rewarding experience.

If you have a successful internship job experience, you should cultivate the relationships you developed with both your peers and your supervisors. Peers who interned with you may help you network in the future just as you might help them. Supervisors can be instrumental in hiring you in the future, either directly or indirectly. They can provide a letter of recommendation, which you should try to obtain before you leave the job. Even more important, they could help you as a reference to be contacted by future employers through email or a phone call. When identifying a supervisor to serve as a reference, don't go after the big cheese like the CEO or the senator unless you had daily contact with him or her. Instead, go after your immediate supervisors because what they say will be more credible and specific.

If you have a poor experience in any of these apprenticeship-type activities, reflect on the reasons. Finding out that you are not cut out to be a journalist after a summer working on a local newspaper is not a bad thing. As Louis Blair, the head of the Harry S. Truman Foundation, says, "The main difference between a successful person and an unsuccessful person is that the successful person has had a lot more failures!" Or to put it in the Zen perspective, "There are no wrong turns, only wrong thinking on the turns your life has taken."

Let me give you an example of wrong thinking in which a student placed his desire to get a great learning experience above the need to be professional. One of my students was an intern at a law firm and was supervised by a paralegal. When the paralegal asked him to make some copies to be provided to the court, the intern quit and was quite rude in the process. This student overlooked the fundamental reality that as an undergraduate intern in a law office, you are not going to write a legal brief. You pay your dues and make copies so you can attend professional meetings, do some very basic research, and get debriefed. In fact, many newly graduated lawyers do the same thing. In a field like law in which there is an oversupply of professionals, this little temper tantrum was not only unprofessional—it also helped to reduce the supply by one.

Neither unprofessional nor wimpy behavior in your jobs and internship experience will do. These experiences are like minor league training for the big leagues of your career. Grab the experience with the energy and seriousness that you plan to use in your first job out of college. If you don't, you will have missed a powerful opportunity to have an enviable KHS.

Finally, whether you get your apprentice experience from community service, a job, or an internship, enhance your skill development by recording daily (or at least weekly) what you did, what you learned from it, and how you could have done it better. These notes will help you refresh your memory a couple of years later when you are in a job interview. At the same time, they will help you learn more while you are going through the experience.

Action Without Borders (www.idealist.org). For those interested in a public service internship, fellowship, summer job, or volunteer opportunity, this is the website to search for thousands of opportunities by country, state, area of focus, and time period. The site also includes a "career center" with lots of resources and helpful hints for those interested in the nonprofit world.

The Back Door Guide to Short-Term Job Adventures by Michael Landes (Ten Speed Press, 2002). Use this as a source for a summer job in which you can develop skills and explore your interests. Many of the positions described are primarily for fun and adventure, but there are volunteer opportunities and internships, too.

Everett Public Service Internship Program (www.everettinternships.org). The Everett organization provides dozens of agencies with grants specifically for paying wages to student interns. These internships are selective and in high demand, but if you are accepted as an Everett intern you will get paid and participate in exclusive lectures and activities with other Everett interns.

The Insider's Guide to Political Internships: What to Do Once You Are in the Door, edited by Grant Reeher and Mack Mariani (Westview Press, 2002). For students who have internships with politicians and government, this book is a valuable guide on how to get the most from the experience. Read this book to get a clear idea of what to expect from a political internship.

Internships for Dummies by Craig P. Donovan and Jim Garnett (John Wiley, 2001). This book is the most comprehensive general source of advice for any type of internship. It tells you how to search for and land internships and, most important, how to gain an experience that will enhance your KHS.

Internship Programs (www.internshipprograms.com). You must register to use this site (it is free), but then you have access to searching thousands of opportunities in cities across the country. You can also post your resume on this site and allow prospective employers to recruit you. The site certainly isn't comprehensive, but it will give you ideas and leads.

National Student Internships and Jobs (www.internjobs.com). Browse a database of internships available globally and nationally by searching keywords or location. Employers can also post their internships and entry-level jobs openings online.

Peterson's Internships (Peterson's Guides, most recent edition). This is one of the best internship directories available. It offers over 50,000 U.S. and overseas listings for summer, semester, and year-long internship opportunities at over 2,000 organizations.

The Princeton Review Internship Bible by Mark Oldman and Samer Hamadeh (Random House, most recent edition). Thousands of internship entries listed by location and field of interest are found in this guide. Includes information on selectivity, compensation, academic requirements, and application procedures.

The Riley Guide (www.rileyguide.com). There's lots of information on this site to help guide your job and internship search. Resumes, cover letters, networking, and interviewing are all covered. Best of all, you can search thousands of internships, apprenticeships, volunteer opportunities, part-time and temporary employment, and occupations by discipline and industry.

Rising Star Internships (www.rsinternships.com). This site is about posting and searching. Students can post their resumes and search for internship openings by fields from accounting to zoology. Employers post intern and job openings and search for interns who match their qualifications.

"I LIVED A LIFE THAT'S FULL. I TRAVELED EACH AND EVERY HIGHWAY."

—PAUL ANKA, SINGER-SONGWRITER

CHAPTER 14

EXPLORING OFF-CAMPUS SEMESTERS

TOPICS

BUILD YOUR KHS WITH OFF-CAMPUS PROGRAMS •
WEIGH OVERSEAS EXPERIENCES VERSUS EXPERIENCES IN
THE UNITED STATES AND CANADA • EARN CREDIT FOR COURSE
WORK • CONSIDER THE NEGATIVES • FIND PROGRAMS

Undergraduates are increasingly earning a semester's worth of credit in another location. Some students spend two or three semesters off-campus and still graduate on time. An enormous variety of opportunities for semester-long and summer off-campus study exist both in the United States and around the world. From a KHS and career exploration perspective, spending one or two semesters away from campus has potential benefits that usually outweigh the risks.

Like everything you do in college, you can make the off-campus experience pay off for your KHS and career options. You can also choose to use the experience to have a good time or explore a subject that might count as extra credit rather than specifically develop the skill sets from the ten Know-How Groups. Even if building your KHS or exploring a career is not your primary goal, it is pretty hard to be off campus for a semester and not raise your KHS.

The following Know-How Groups will be enhanced regardless of your primary goal for off-campus semesters:

- Establishing a Work Ethic. An off-campus semester means that you will face a host of new logistical tasks, starting with the application process at your home institution, which will enhance your time-management skills as well as your ability to kick yourself in the butt. Money management will be a major challenge. You not only have to bring enough money, but you need to use credit and possibly banking facilities in a new place.
- Developing Physical Skills. Staying well in a new environment will be even a bigger challenge than on your own campus.
- Communicating Verbally. You will need to communicate with a whole new set of people, including peers, administrators, and faculty.
- Working Directly with People. You will have to work with a whole new set of people, including peers, administrators, and faculty.
- Using Quantitative Tools. You'll practice these skills particularly if your semester is overseas, where dealing with currency conversions requires more intense number crunching than most people are used to.
- Asking and Answering the Right Questions. Given the increased uncertainty surrounding your new environment, you will be more vulnerable to those who BS, and you will also have to pay attention to detail, especially when traveling.
- Solving Problems. You'll face new situations on a daily basis that require solutions.

These seven Know-How Groups will improve even if you are just taking college classes at a different location with a group of friends from your home institution. However, you will gain much more if you choose an off-campus semester in which the major learning component is field experience, either through an internship or assigned activities by the instructor. Students are increasingly choosing programs in which there is not just a wholesale transplant. They choose programs in which they learn art at local museums, or they complete an internship in a local nonprofit or government organization. They also choose programs that have specific offerings like marine biology or archeological digs. They may also choose programs to develop their foreign language skills by living with a local family in a foreign country. In these types of programs, more than the basic skills listed previously are developed. Skills from the other Know-How Groups are developed along with extra credit skills listed in chapter 11. Some of these programs will also introduce you to professional skills not contained in the ten basic groups.

Off-campus semester programs as a place to learn and enhance your KHS are uniformly recognized by graduate schools and employers. They know that students who like to deal with new situations and are able to take risks to improve themselves usually pursue off-campus programs. Graduate schools value foreign experiences because they help prepare students to work in professions that have a global reach. All employers like to hire people who can accept the risk of new challenges. Employers also highly value internship experiences, which are associated with many off-campus programs, whether within or outside the United States. A semester spent working for a legislator in a state capital will not only help your law school application but also appeal to lobbying firms.

I strongly recommend that you plan an off-campus semester once you have completed your sophomore year. With two years of course work under your belt, you will be able to apply the skills you have been learning in the classroom in a different setting, which is key to being ready for a rewarding and exciting career.

WEIGH OVERSEAS EXPERIENCES VERSUS EXPERIENCES IN THE UNITED STATES AND CANADA

If you are only going to take one semester off-campus, you are faced with a decision to go overseas or to a program within the United States or Canada. (I have included Canada with the United States because of the similarities between the two countries.) What is the right decision?

The answer is like everything else in life, "It depends." The general rule is that going out of the United States and Canada is better than staying in the country because you will be stretched and tested more. However, there are many exceptions and considerations. First, there is the money question. Overseas, if nothing else, requires significant travel expense. Second, if you have a specific interest such as politics or medicine, an internship-based semester working as a White House intern or for the National Institutes of Health would make more sense than an overseas placement that did not provide similar internships. Third, if you see the experience more as having fun than enhancing your basic skills, an overseas placement might make more sense.

More than 150,000 U.S. students participated in a study abroad program in 2000–2001 according to the Institute for International Education.[1] That figure has tripled since fifteen years ago. While the majority of students go to Europe (63 percent), programs in Latin America and Asia have increased in popularity over the last decade. The most popular options are one-semester programs, although some experts advocate a full year abroad.

An overseas experience means that twenty-four hours a day, seven days a week you will be trying to make sense out of the unfamiliar. The lack of familiarity with the physical environment, including toilets and transportation facilities, will be less important than your lack of familiarity with the language. Unless you go to an English-speaking country, your relationships will depend on makeshift attempts to communicate. If you are seeking to master that language and have taken some courses, the experience will sharply improve your language skills. The fact that you will have to learn conversational language to adjust to daily life will be a huge learning experience in itself.

The depth of the challenge will be directly related to the amount of time you spend away from peers from the United States. If you live with buddies from your college in a housing situation controlled by your university, you'll be much less challenged than if you live with a host family. Even so, you'll have plenty of opportunities to be confused by your inability to communicate when you leave the confines of the familiar.

It should also be noted that there are some clear benefits to studying in an English-speaking country. Because there won't be a language barrier, you will be able to immerse yourself in a different community and culture much more quickly. The depth of your experience may grow as you find it possible to communicate easily with the locals. If you try hard enough, you may find yourself experiencing small—but nonetheless important—parts of the social and community structure that you may have otherwise missed. This benefit also stands for domestic off-campus programs that send you to other areas of the country.

Almost any student who has had an overseas experience will rave about it as this student did when she wrote me six months after graduation about her experience in Hong Kong.

For eighteen years I lived in a homogeneous bubble where Caucasian, middle-class Christians were the overwhelming majority. Diversity was a concept, not a reality. New York was enough of a culture shock! But I took a risk, hopped on a plane, and came back a different person—more educated and open-minded. Hong Kong was a learning experience—educationally, culturally, and professionally. I gained international experience that employers value in today's economy. I interned for the Fortune Global Forum where every year, Fortune magazine hosts this forum for over 250 of the world's top CEOs with prominent guest speakers. During my internship, the forum was held in Hong Kong where I met and worked with such well-known leaders as Gerald Levin (CEO of AOL Time Warner), Bob Seltzer (CEO of Ogilvy), Bill Clinton, Thaksin Shinawatra (Thai prime minister), Jiang Zemin (president of the People's Republic of China), Jack Welch (CEO of GE), etc. The forum was surrounded by political controversy and it became my responsibility to inform the Hong Kong and New York contacts of the international events around the world. Just last week I sat prepping a senior financial analyst for GE, who was traveling to Shanghai for a possible sales expansion opportunity, about the people, culture, and what to expect in Asia's economy today. You don't get that kind of exposure sitting around your sorority house discussing last week's episode of Friends.

A particularly intense experience at coping with different situations is provided by the Semester at Sea Program run by the University of Pittsburgh. Here is what one of my students wrote about her experience in the program:

The diversity of the trip forced me to modify certain parts of my personality. Because I visited ten countries in three months, I benefited from brief introductions to a huge variety of languages, people, and culture. In order to travel within, I had no choice but to be flexible and adaptable. My appreciation and acceptance of differences grew

*with each country visited. I had to cooperate with fellow
travelers, communicate with locals, and put in very long,
tiring, difficult days at times. I learned that being flexible,
patient, cooperative, alert, and determined yielded wonderful results. These rewards were in the form of firsthand
knowledge of conditions around the world and a drive to
"think out of the box." The most difficult adjustment I
made on the trip was to be continually resourceful. When
I spent five days in a country, if I wanted to see or do
something, I had to find a way to do that in a short time
frame, no matter what obstacles stood in my way.
Sometimes, this meant changing travel plans, taking risks,
or being a little bit scared, but the persistence always
paid off.*

These two students had unusually good overseas experiences, but
you can see how being placed in a foreign environment can create powerful
learning experiences.

An off-campus experience within the United States and Canada will
present you with fewer day-to-day challenges if only because differences in
language will not permeate everything. However, you will be faced with
new geography and the daily chores that were much easier at college.

If you choose off-campus semesters within the United States and
Canada, you need to be more selective about the nature of the program,
the quality of the course requirements, and the value of the internship or
work environment in which you find yourself. In general, the stronger the
local control by the university over the courses and hands-on experience,
the better. Even if you get in an overseas program with poor courses and
loose structure, you are still overseas.

Most domestic off-campus programs will require an internship experience of at least two, and as many as five, full days a week. The days will
usually run the regular work hours of 9 to 5 and may involve overtime,
plus you will have assignments and classes. Together, this experience will
make you work much harder than you work on campus. The biggest challenge for many students with whom I have talked is learning to deal with
"a real professional job."

One former student of mine thought he was a hard worker because
he carried eighteen credits and was in all kinds of activities on campus,
yet he almost had a meltdown during an internship at a high school in
New York City. He had to get up 5:30 in the morning and take the subway
to arrive at the school by 7:30. He frequently did not get home until 9 P.M.

because of classes held in another location and other activities. Not being able to run to the residence hall for a little nap or relaxation just about ruined him. It took eight weeks before he got adjusted to working in the real world because he did not control his free time. He reflects back on that experience as preparing him for working in his first job, and he is doing quite nicely.

A domestic program off-campus that requires a job-like internship can be more difficult than an overseas program in which there is no major internship. You may find a program with a four- or five-day-a-week internship overseas, but it's not as likely. This may be a crucial advantage to a domestic program.

EARN CREDIT FOR COURSE WORK

In any off-campus semester, your first goal should be to earn the academic credits you need to graduate on time. If you cannot earn a full-semester worth of credit, do not go into that program. Although most colleges accept most credits from many programs, check this out very carefully. You don't want to spend an extra semester at school because your college refused to accept nine of the fifteen credits you took in Botswana. You want to see a written commitment either in a policy statement by your college or a memo confirming what you have been told. Never accept the spoken word in a matter as important as this.

The best way to be sure you will get the credit is to enroll in a program run by your own college. This will keep your hassles to a minimum in getting credits accepted. If your school does not offer such programs, it probably has formal relationships with other colleges and organizations that do. If so, your next choice would be to enroll in one of those programs. Only after you have exhausted both of these alternatives should you enroll in a program run by a college, university, or institute that does not have a formal relationship with your home institution. If you do, make sure your home college and program will accept the credit. You will probably be required to take a leave of absence from your home school and enroll in the college providing the experience. There may be some extra hidden fees if you do that. To ensure you don't fall behind in credits from your off-campus experience, you must begin the exploration two semesters before you go off-campus and have it buttoned down by the first month of the next semester.

You can usually take twelve to eighteen credits during your off-campus experience. If you are ahead in the pursuit of your degree, drop to twelve credits since the more free time you have to explore your environment or just to have fun, the better. Most programs are designed to generate fifteen credits.

The benefits of course work off campus to your KHS and your preparation for your future career can best be explained by looking at their comparative advantage over courses you might take at your home college. The following statements are generalizations and therefore may not apply to your particular situation, but they provide a starting point.

CLASSES THAT ARE REQUIRED FOR YOUR DEGREE BUT THAT YOU DON'T RELISH TAKING MAY BE EASIER OFF CAMPUS

This assertion is true if only because the classes will be smaller. Many programs will not offer these kinds of required courses, but some will. You are more likely to find them if you take an off-campus program run by your own school or a program affiliated with your school. Taking such courses may not be optimal for your experience since the course may not make use of the new location, but occasionally it makes sense. Most programs will provide you with a syllabus in advance if you request one, and you can determine if the required course will be tailored to the host culture in some way, such as with local speakers or field trips.

CLASSES ARE MORE LIKELY TO HAVE FIELDWORK OF SOME KIND

Those programs that are well developed will try to offer courses that take advantage of the location. They will incorporate field trips, lectures by subject-matter experts and practitioners in the area, and actual fieldwork ranging from an internship at a nonprofit to studying vegetation in a nearby desert. Choose programs that have internship experiences for the same reasons we have emphasized through the book and particularly in the previous chapter. Fortunately, most overseas programs are increasing the field or internship elements of their course work.

FACULTY MEMBERS WILL BE DIFFERENT FROM THOSE IN YOUR HOME SCHOOL

Even if the college ships someone over, the faculty member may be more relaxed and have a different perspective. However, the use of local people is more common and likely to provide a very different educational experience. This applies to both domestic and foreign programs. In domestic programs, the faculty members are likely to be part-timers who have real-world applications to present to you. Foreign faculty will have a different take on most subjects than faculty at your college. In general, different is better.

STUDENTS WILL BE DIFFERENT

Most programs have groups of students who are not necessarily from the home university. This will make for better class discussions and more peer learning than occurs in your home school.

CONSIDER THE NEGATIVES

The biggest single downside to off-campus programs is no matter what they tell you, it will cost you more (unless you get a paid position), and that is even more true for overseas programs. The tuition will be the same, but that does not include travel, moving an extra semester, and ending up in places where daily expenditures are higher. You may not be able to get a job in another city or country. Occasionally, off-campus programs that require a substantial internship carry a stipend or the intern-hosting organization could provide a salary. You may also be able to find grants that support study in particular countries or through specific organizations—ask at your on-campus financial aid and study abroad offices, and check online financial aid and scholarship resources at the end of the chapter. There are currently substantial grants and scholarships sponsored by the U.S. government for study in Asia and other non-Western regions. This may offset the additional costs or at least help you break even. In programs overseas where the standard of living is low, housing and food costs may be lower. In any case, carefully compare costs on campus and off.

The next biggest risk that you face in taking a semester off is breaking the continuity that might be needed by your academic program. You may take a course in the fall, leave in the spring, and get back in the fall but not be able to take the sequence to the course until the next spring.

This will depend on your academic program and the frequency with which courses are offered. You will also break the continuity of the extracurricular and academic commitments that you have developed during your first two years in college. This can be a major drawback, especially if going off-campus means losing a good job or the progress you have made developing your own program or initiative. The only surefire way to mitigate this drawback is to adequately plan ahead. If you know in your freshman year that you are going to be studying off campus during the spring of your junior year, you can plan around that semester. This will give you time to schedule your classes so you don't miss a sequence, to negotiate with your employer, and to find a replacement to take over in leadership positions you may hold.

The chaos caused by going away one semester can use time and energy that would be better put to your course work or your career exploration. It could increase stress and cut down options for summer jobs and upcoming opportunities. If you want a summer internship in New York City but are in Austria for the spring semester, you could have trouble. If you want to apply for a scholarship or special award for your senior year, it may be difficult to get the information about when applications are due or participate in selection processes. Email is wonderful but doesn't always work. Some places would like to conduct interviews. Moreover, you will not have as much support from the college's intern placement office and faculty members if you are away.

The break can even be more serious if you are not sure what you want to do after you graduate. In my experience, most students put thoughts about the future on hold while they are away, especially overseas. The intensity of the experience seems to prevent long-range planning for many. If you are away during the fall semester of your senior year, you will miss most of the campus visits by the large corporations, and you will get back in the spring in a funk. Graduate school applications, and taking the tests for those schools, usually must be completed no later than February 1, which gives you little time if you arrive back in the United States in late December.

Finally, the question of safety and health needs to be considered. How serious those issues are depends on where you are spending the semester off campus as well as your specific living arrangements. It also depends on the status of your health and how careful you are about keeping yourself safe. The risks may be slightly, but not significantly, higher than remaining on campus. Other than staying away from countries where there is a civil war, or the potential of one, and taking the health precautions and safety recommended for tourists, most overseas locations are at least as safe from criminal acts and disease as your home college. Global terrorism has made some areas more risky.

Much of the advice provided in the previous chapter on finding internships also applies to the search for off-campus semester programs. Decide on your goals and then do a search using books and websites. Your college career or internship office will also be a big help. The sites listed for finding internships can also be used for finding semester programs in the United States.

For overseas programs, most colleges and universities have a study abroad/international office, or a study-abroad adviser who can review options and policies for off-campus study. Start with this office or person to save yourself a lot of wasted time and trouble. You'll receive a list of study-abroad programs they approve for credit, in addition to their own, and you may be able to retain your scholarships and other institutional aid if you attend one of these programs. Study-abroad offices may also have a list of programs for which your home college will definitely not award credit. For instance, if you are a language major, you may be required to go to a foreign institution to study abroad rather than a U.S.-sponsored program that offers advanced language courses for Americans. The study-abroad adviser will be familiar with many of the programs you have heard or read about and can fill you in on a program's strengths and weaknesses.

Overseas semester programs vary. Most emphasize the geographical aspects of the experience and present a general program, but an increasing number of programs closely tie the geographical location to a topical focus of the experience. Broadly based university-supported programs like those offered by Boston University, the Institute for the International Education of Students (IES), the Semester at Sea, and Syracuse University are in the first category. Specialized topical programs like the Theatre Conservancy in England through Rutgers University and the Woods Hole SEA Semester, which focuses on marine biology and tropical conservation, are in the second category.

Given the large and growing options, you should spend some time gathering information. The section at the end of this chapter will suggest some general resources. The best source of information on the potential for all these programs for your KHS is from students who have experienced these programs, preferably from your own campus.

There are excellent study-abroad websites (see list at end of chapter) that allow you to sort through the growing variety of options sponsored by universities, nonprofit organizations, and corporations. You can search by region/country, discipline, or language of study. Or you can search by duration of program: academic year, semester study, summer programs, or intersession. Once you have narrowed your search to programs that seem to fit your needs and interests, consult the individual program websites for details about courses, living arrangements, and costs. Whether your search for programs begins with the Internet or with your school's study-abroad adviser, in the end it is your home school's study-abroad adviser or college dean who must finally approve a program so you receive credit.

The programs you find online will include everything from small "island" programs (with no connection to universities abroad) to "immersion" programs in which you take all your classes at foreign universities alongside host-country students. Full-immersion programs will take you beyond the ten Know-How Groups into specialized skills that could be useful if you plan to seek overseas employment.

If none of the hundreds of formal program offerings that now exist suits you, you can create your own fifteen-credit-hour-away-from-campus experience. If you are a very strong student and can find the right on-campus program or at least a faculty member, you can find yourself a placement at a nonprofit and ask for some portion of the credit. Usually nine credits is an upper limit for experience credit (graded pass/fail), but you can sometimes get up to fifteen through independent study courses. To get to fifteen credits, you could propose two independent study courses for a grade that you can complete while you are away. Alternatively you could take any number of distance-learning courses offered by your school or some other school that will be accepted by your home school. To make your own semester-away program requires a strong and trusting relationship with at least one faculty member. If you think you might want to try a self-designed program, get started on building that relationship right away.

Council on International Educational Exchange (www.ciee.org). This valuable and friendly site provides comprehensive coverage of educational exchange programs. CIEE offers some good services, but the study-abroad programs listed on this site are strictly their own. It administers work- and travel-abroad programs for students and recent graduates, such as international volunteer opportunities, and teaching English in Asia.

Institute of International Education (www.iie.org). This site lists some substantial financial aid and scholarship programs for undergrads and grad students studying abroad, particularly in Asia and other non-Western sites.

International Education of Students (www.iesabroad.org). This website guides you to the programs offered by the Institute for the International Education of Students, which has strong relationships with universities in more than a dozen countries and will help you transfer credit to your home college.

Peterson's Study Abroad (www.petersons.com/stdyabrd/sasector.html). This site is one of the best comprehensive online resources, especially from the point of view of being user-friendly. You can also purchase the book, *Peterson's Study Abroad* (Peterson's Guides, most recent edition), one of the most widely used directories.

Study Abroad Information Source (www.studyabroad.com). This user-friendly site provides comprehensive coverage and claims it is the number one online search site. Unlike others, the site takes browsers directly to sponsors' web pages.

Washington Internship Program (www.washingtoninternship.com). This site provides information on opportunities for a variety of semester-long internships and course programs in government agencies and nonprofit organizations in Washington, D.C. For other websites for programs outside of Washington, use the sites listed in chapter 13.

WE DON'T LIVE TO EAT. WE EAT TO LIVE. IN THE SAME WAY, OUR LIVELIHOOD EXISTS TO SUPPORT OUR LIFE, NOT THE OTHER WAY AROUND.

—BERNARD GLASSMAN AND RICK FIELDS, IN
INSTRUCTIONS TO THE COOK: A ZEN MASTER'S
LESSONS ON LIVING A LIFE THAT MATTERS

CHAPTER 15

DOING WELL BY DOING GOOD DURING YOUR COLLEGE YEARS

TOPICS

BUILD YOUR KHS BY VOLUNTEERING • VALUE VOLUNTEER OPPORTUNITIES—EMPLOYERS DO • EXPLORE CAREERS • CULTIVATE INTEGRITY

You were probably introduced to the idea of community service in your high school or through your family or religious institution. You may think that working in a food pantry, tutoring economically disadvantaged youth, or reading to someone in a nursing home is only for the unselfish and pure. I have called this thought one of the "curses" of Mother Teresa. The other curse is that total dedication of one's waking hours to doing good is necessary. They are curses because people use this unreachable model as an excuse for not doing anything.

If Mother Teresa were to be viewed as a role model, it would be best to examine how she got things done and follow her lead. Except for computer skills, which became important in the last years of her life, Mother Teresa had a very high KHS. She was a master of communications, a person who knew how to find answers to the tough questions, a stellar problem solver, a first rate BS detector, and she was great with people. The standards she set for leadership are hard to match, but if you are going to do anything to honor her life, be as effective as she was in promoting a better world.

Just as Mother Teresa honed her KHS skills on serving others, you can do the same in preparing for a successful work life. Working for the public good during your college years and after can provide you with valuable experiences in the job force.

But that is not really the point of the quote by the Zen master at the beginning of this chapter, is it? His point is that money is not everything. It is a tool for your happiness, not the definition of your happiness. That point is very hard to deliver to beginning college students who are spending and/or borrowing huge amounts of money in order to have a rewarding career. That is why I'm not going to tell you to do good because it will make you happy and spiritually satisfied, even though it is true. This chapter tells you why doing good in college will lead to a great life of work.

"Doing good" for the purposes of this chapter means any kind of work you do as a volunteer or for credit either on or off the campus. It applies to volunteering at the rescue mission or a local community tutoring program as well as what you might do for student organizations and for faculty and staff committees. These volunteer activities, especially if they involve leadership positions, can be a critical source of KHS development.

BUILD YOUR KHS BY VOLUNTEERING

It might seem harsh to say, but the truth is that nonprofit organizations usually have no choice but to give you experiences before you are really ready for them. For example, a local community center might like to have a monthly newsletter to distribute but does not have the funds to hire a professional. If you have some basic skills in Microsoft Publisher or have taken an introductory public relations course but have no real experience in producing a newsletter, the center might be willing to give you a shot. From someone with no experience, you now have an opportunity to be a newsletter designer, editor, writer, and publisher. If you do a reasonably good job, you could have a product to put in a portfolio when you seek a paying job with a private organization.

One of my students did a study for a local nonprofit on how members of the organization liked the organization's newsletter. He conducted a phone survey and wrote the results up for this organization. The study was helpful to the organization but even more helpful to the student. He brought a copy of his study to a job interview with a national association in the construction business. One of the major jobs they wanted him to do was to conduct yearly surveys on their publications. My student said, "Well, I just happen to have a study I did for an organization in Syracuse on its newsletter, and here it is." He was hired on the spot and never looked back.

Summer and semester internships are easier to get at nonprofits than businesses for the same reasons that they provide viable sites during the semester—namely, lack of skilled staff. Businesses are likely to have paid internships except in areas of high student interest like TV stations and law firms. Many nonprofits may not be able to offer a salary or a lump sum stipend, but many do.

Volunteering and working in nonprofit internships can give you critical experience that will enable you to build your KHS. For that reason alone, it is valuable to prospective employers. You can grow from someone who has little experience with Excel or Access to one with substantial experience. It is one thing to say to an employer, "I took a course in which I learned Excel" and quite another to say "I worked for the Salvation Army creating Excel spreadsheets to generate graphs for a grant proposal."

Doing good without a credit or monetary payoff is viewed by many employers as valuable for another reason. Such work can mean that you are the type of person who can work for something bigger than yourself. The step from good citizen in the volunteer sector to a team player within the business world is small.

Most companies want to hire someone who is both competitive and a team player. If you can do both, you are more likely to get the job and more likely to excel on the job. They want to see students who helped their college host applicants, served on the residence hall council, participated in student government, or tutored kids in a community center. They know that fitting such activities into your busy schedules shows good time management skills and a good heart.

A word of warning is in order, however! Employers become concerned if they see a lot of scattered activities, especially if it comes with a weak GPA. You need to focus on a few do-good activities and still maintain a respectable GPA. Don't become a community service junkie!

EXPLORE CAREERS

Working as a volunteer for a nonprofit or government agency will expand your contacts for future job exploration. Nonprofits have boards of directors from all over the community. You can meet them at social functions or meetings and talk to them about your future. Adults love to play Daddy or Mommy to college students, and they frequently have very good advice. If you are sitting next to the right person at a dinner, you can conduct an informational interview before dessert.

If you undertake volunteer activities and internships with government and nonprofit organizations during your college years, you may find a career that you want to pursue. You may discover you want to teach, do police work, work as a district attorney, or run a community center. You may learn that you do not want to sit in front of a computer all day or that you do not like the chaos of a small, underfunded organization. Even if you don't go into nonprofit work, you may find the skills you exercise as a volunteer are the type of thing you like to do. If you enjoy performing statistical analysis for a nonprofit in the summer, you may want to think about a position in market research when you graduate. If you enjoy meeting people and explaining the mission of your nonprofit, you might want to explore a sales position after you graduate.

On the other hand, from your experience with a nonprofit, you may decide that you want to work for one when you graduate. More than 7 percent of the American workforce is employed by nonprofit organizations; federal, state, and local governments employ another 15 percent.[1] Every job you can do in the business world, you can do in the nonprofit and government world. By volunteering during your college years and then taking internships, you can explore the advantages and disadvantages of employment outside of business.

The yearly salary of people working in these positions ranges from the low teens to high six figures. People who help others or work in public service are not necessarily going to be poor. It depends on their talents and on what they want to do with their lives.

But the truth of the matter is that a person performing the same duties as someone in a for-profit business will receive less money working either for the government or for the nonprofit sector. Accountants working for the government make less than those who work for private firms. But there are other advantages. Government positions sometimes carry lucrative pensions. For example, some teachers in New York State who retire after twenty-five years of service receive close to 100 percent of what they were paid when working. Even where the pensions are not as generous, you can retire at fifty, get a pension, and take on a new career. Nonprofits do not usually have strong pension programs, but they are much more generous about vacations and family-friendly policies.

The bottom line is that the money is not as good as it is in the business sector, but the perks may offset it. Moreover, if you work in a field in which you help others, you can be happy that you are making a difference. A feeling of doing something good for others can be an added bonus to a rewarding job.

The final reason for doing good during your years at college is that it will help build and reinforce a sense of integrity in everything you do. Integrity is the practice of being open and truthful toward others. Employers want to see evidence of integrity in their employees because that is the basis of trust.

One way to develop and show integrity during your college years is to present a record of consistent volunteer work with one or two nonprofit organizations. If you devote four years to Habitat for Humanity on campus and take part in a least one of their spring-break trips, you are demonstrating integrity. If you work your way up through the Greek system from being an officer in your fraternity or sorority to a position on a university-wide body, you are showing that you have persistence and commitment to serve others.

Moreover, taking on volunteer positions will enhance your capacity for integrity, if only because you will be associating with a group of people who can see beyond their own narrow self-interest. As Miguel de Cervantes has Don Quixote say, "Tell me what company you keep, and I'll tell you what you are." If you move up through a student organization, you will face additional responsibilities, including dealing with people who have competing interests and who lack integrity. Working with people who ask you to break the rules will give you a taste of what you will face in whatever profession you pursue. It will prepare you for a world where integrity is in short supply.

USEFUL RESOURCES

Campus Opportunity Outreach League (www.cool2serve.org). This group, formed by students in 1984, will help you explore a variety of options, including their own leadership training program.

How You Can Help: An Easy Guide to Doing Good Deeds in Your Everyday Life by William D. Coplin (Routledge, 2000). A no-guilt approach to doing good, this book will provide you with the range of activities that can be undertaken as a meaningful but limited part of your life.

Making a Difference College and Graduate Guide: Outstanding Colleges to Help You Make a Better World by Miriam Weinstein (Sageworks Press, 1999). Already listed as a source to help you choose the right college, this book will give you ideas of what you can do in college, any college, to make the world better.

IT'S DÉJÀ VU ALL OVER AGAIN.

—YOGI BERRA

CHAPTER 16

THINKING BEYOND COLLEGE

TOPICS

CONSIDER THE GRADUATE EDUCATION ALTERNATIVE •
EXPLORE THE PROFITABLE ALTERNATIVE • VALUE THE
DO-GOOD ALTERNATIVE • BUILD YOUR POSTGRADUATE KHS

Fortunately, your skill development does not stop once you leave college. In fact, it will grow much more in the first few years following college than during the entire four years of college. This is true whether you go to graduate school, get a temporary job or internship, or start on a full-time job in your career area. In this chapter, we'll talk a bit about graduate school as well as how to acquire skills without going to graduate school. The purpose of this chapter is not to guide your career development after college but to alert you to what lies ahead so that the decisions you make in college are better informed.

Regardless of which of the first three paths you take right out of college—graduate school, the profit sector, or the nonprofit sector—the idea of continuously improving your skills will always serve you as you move through your work life. We'll take a look at the idea of lifelong learning in the last section of this chapter, but now let's look at your options that follow graduation.

Graduate school is becoming increasingly popular—maybe too popular according to Randall Collins. In an editorial entitled "The Dirty Little Secrets of Credential Inflation!" in the *Chronicle of Higher Education,* he writes, "[M]any people believe that our high-tech era requires massive educational expansion" and if it keeps up, "janitors will need Ph.D.'s and baby sitters advanced degrees in child care."[1] In an article, two Stanford Business School researchers, Jeffrey Pfeffer and Christina Fong, maintain that with the exception of some of the elite schools, an MBA is not correlated with higher salaries over the long run.[2]

Keeping these comments in mind, ask yourself, "Is graduate school a good investment for me?" If you are going to be a doctor, lawyer, or professor, you have no choice. You have to get what is called the "union card." For most other fields, neither a Ph.D. nor even a master's is required, and in some cases an advanced degree may make you look overeducated for the job you want. In fact, if you are able to get into GE's Financial Management Program (FMP), described later in this chapter, the GE website says, "If someone successfully completes the FMP, other advanced educational degrees or certifications are not required to succeed at GE." This statement may be self-serving for GE because it is designed to entice talented people to join up, but from my experience with several alumni, it is true. Because most graduate education is costly and financial aid is less available than it is for undergraduate education, look very carefully at the potential benefits of corporate training versus the costs of graduate education.

The most important question to ask yourself is what a graduate degree can do for your skills. If you already developed your basic KHS in college, the answer is that graduate school will introduce you to new skills, especially in quantitative analysis and research. It should also reinforce existing people, analytical, and problem-solving skills. Graduate programs will also help to improve your grasp of professional concepts and terminology. Those programs that have a deep commitment to fieldwork-based learning will be the most powerful in improving your skills.

If for some reason you left college without developing the basic skills in the ten Know-How Groups, graduate school can accomplish what your college education did not. First of all, most of your peers, if you go to a halfway decent program, will have those skills. Just associating and competing with them will raise your level. In addition, they will have other more advanced skills than you might have, which they will help you learn. Second, graduate programs tend to be more skill oriented. They will have some courses that provide the opportunity to develop basic and advanced skills. Third, most good graduate programs will have significant internship or fieldwork requirements.

If you go to a graduate program, you will want to follow the advice throughout this book on how courses and non-course activities can be used to develop the skills you need. Choose the programs and courses that give a primary emphasis to skill development. For example, if you are in law school, take as many clinic credits as possible. Choose a graduate program that requires a semester or even a yearlong internship.

It makes more sense to go to graduate school for a master's program if your undergraduate program left you poorly prepared. But if you already have a high KHS, the advantages to graduate school do not lie primarily in acquiring critical skills. Instead, they are related to career exploration and development. First, graduate programs will help you explore careers by getting you closer to practitioners than you were in your undergraduate program. Faculty members in graduate programs are usually accomplished in their profession or have had at least some experience. Moreover, some of the students in your classes will have already been in the field, and you can learn a great deal from them. Second, any good graduate program will have a lot of resources devoted to getting you a job or at least an internship leading to a job. Third, the friends you make in graduate school will be in fields related to the one you choose. Consequently, you will have a built-in network that will help you find and keep jobs.

Another value to graduate school is what might be called "the growing-up factor." Most people in the work world are not ready to take anyone under twenty-five seriously. The four years of college fills the time until you are twenty-one, if you started college right out of high school. If you look young or feel you are not quite ready to deal with professionals over the age of thirty, taking a couple of years to mature may not be a bad idea. Graduate school, however, is a costly way to tread to water. If warehousing yourself to grow up were the only reason you are going to graduate school, I would suggest working for at least two years in an entry-level job. Many companies hire people right out of college with the assumption that they are really "interns" and will leave after two years. Consulting companies, which are really high-class temp firms, will send you off here and there for six-month gigs. A job with a consulting company may be viewed as a short-term commitment to figure out what you want to do when you grow up.

A special word about law school is needed because too many people are going to law school with no commitment to becoming a lawyer or much of a clue about how the law degree will help them. Many of my students went to law school in the 1990s, and they are not happy campers because of these negatives:

- Law school costs $100,000, and financial aid is minimal compared with undergraduate programs.
- Law school, according to most students I have ever talked to, is HELL. Many law professors are brutal to their students.
- Law schools tend to attract highly competitive and insecure people who help to make it even more HELL than intended by the professors.
- People with law degrees have serious trouble getting jobs.
- Many jobs, especially at the entry level, in the legal profession tend to be boring.

The trend for students to obtain a combination degree consisting of a law degree and a Master's of Public Administration (MPA) or Master's of Business Administration (MBA) does not seem to make much sense. An MPA or MBA is good enough for most jobs. As mentioned above, appearing to be overeducated can be a negative. If you have any of the following characteristics, however, the negatives listed above may not be as important:

- You have relatives in the law business who will hire you.
- You have wanted to be a lawyer for as long as you can remember.
- You like to argue and your parents said, "You should be a lawyer"— unless they are secretly thinking, "You should suffer the hell of going to law school."
- You want to move high up in government circles, which requires having the law credential and being able to read legislation. Like it or not, a large number of elected officials started out in law.
- You have this burning desire to lock up bad guys, to protect others from the arbitrary and capricious application of the law, or to fight some injustice (like child abuse or consumer fraud).

The message about graduate school is mixed. Except for professions requiring the credential, it should not be viewed as an automatic decision. Even for such professions, two or three years of work will bring clarity of purpose to your decision to go to graduate school. As far as your KHS is concerned, graduate school can raise your general levels and introduce you to the more specialized skills and the perspectives of the profession you choose. The primary value, however, of most graduate school programs is to help you explore careers and get you into a career network.

If you do decide that graduate school is right for you and you have strong motivation, great undergraduate preparation, and a stellar KHS, you may want to aim for the top and have your way paid at the same time. A number of prestigious scholarship programs (including the Truman, Rhodes, and Marshall Scholarships) pay for two years of graduate school and may also provide a stipend. These programs look for a very high KHS, extensive service to others, and an extremely high GPA. They also provide supplementary educational activities like high-level internships and access to the alumni networks for previous winners.

EXPLORE THE PROFITABLE ALTERNATIVE

Going after a job in business, especially with established corporations, is the most frequently chosen alternative by new college graduates. Although the job market is competitive, persistence pays off. This alternative makes sense not only because you get paid but also because it provides a learning experience. Most companies have a training period, which itself is valuable. Once you are on the job, you will develop your KHS even more.

Many of the largest corporations offer two-year positions that do much better in technical training and raising your KHS than most graduate schools, and they pay you a reasonable salary while they are doing it. One of the oldest, best-known, and largest programs is the Financial Management Program (FMP) of GE. If you are good enough to get in such a program, take it over graduate school. GE runs five entry-level leadership programs in addition to the one on financial management: Commercial Leadership, Communications Leadership Development, Edison Engineering Development Program, Information Management Leadership, and Operations Management Leadership. These two- to two-and-a-half-year programs combine four to five rotational assignments across different GE businesses with formal classroom studies. Other companies like Johnson and Johnson, Lockheed Martin, and the Lincoln Financial Group have similar programs.

Most Fortune 500 Companies have training programs for new-hires. In part, these programs are designed to socialize you into the culture of the corporation and the procedures that need to be followed. Many corporations, however, go far beyond that by providing programs that range from three months to two years. When interviewed by any company, ask about the training programs that are offered and use the answer in deciding which job to take.

If you cannot land any satisfactory entry-level position, all is not lost. In fact, an excellent option, which could have as good, if not better, long-term payoff than a traditional entry-level corporate job, is to go to a temp agency. I know many people whose first job was through a temp agency, and they are now on a path to success. To give you a clear idea of how the temp scene works, one of my former students provides a description of her experience. She writes:

> *I moved home after graduation. My dad suggested I sign up with a temp agency immediately and . . . look for a "real job." A temp agency interviews you and tests your competency in some basic skill areas like word processing, alphabetizing, and arithmetic. Then you call every morning (this is really important) until they give you an assignment.*
>
> *I had no corporate experience, but basic office skills got me a position in an operational department of a stock brokerage firm. The temp salary was about $25K. My first two days were entirely spent filing account paperwork—the test of whether I was a complainer or willing to work hard. I spent the next weeks and months preparing daily management reports for the staff to work from, supervising other temps, analyzing client accounts for compliance with industry regulation, and executing cashiering transactions in client and house accounts. After two months, I was offered a permanent position, at about $28K.*
>
> *I was promoted quickly through the operational levels, found a good mentor, and with his help landed a career opportunity in project management about a year after I was hired. So after 5 years, I'm making $58K using my knowledge and skills gained on the job and from some of my college experience to solve problems in technical and operational processes that have regulatory or financial impact on the company.*

With a reasonable salary and a future in the company, this alumna has many options. She could have a profitable career in the company. She could go on the job market and search for a better job. Or, she could go to graduate school to change career areas or to move up faster in the field she is in. Her five years of experience and outstanding performance would enable her to get into a much stronger graduate program than if she had applied right out of college. All this from a temporary position!

VALUE THE DO-GOOD ALTERNATIVE

Another solid alternative, especially if you cannot get or do not want one of the for-profit training options and you are not ready for graduate school, is to join Teach for America, the Peace Corps, or AmeriCorps. These organizations provide two years of experience that will help you figure out what you want to be, money to pay off loans or additional schooling together with a salary, and a network for career building. Alumni of Teach for America and the Peace Corps have gone to the best graduate programs and landed jobs in the most well-established corporations. You will have little difficulty following their paths if you participate in either organization. To learn more about these options as well as others, check out the websites of these organizations listed at the end of this chapter.

Another do-good option is to join the military. If you are in good physical shape and not risk-adverse, the military offers college graduates enormous opportunities. We talked in chapter 14 about the valuable KHS education provided by ROTC programs at many colleges and universities. If you did not take one of these programs in college or did not go to a service academy, it is not too late to join the military once you graduate. You can apply to an officer candidacy training program, which requires a four-year commitment. This is a competitive option, but I have had students take it and benefit greatly. If you decide to stay in the military for twenty years, you can retire with a solid pension and start a new career.

BUILD YOUR POSTGRADUATE KHS

If you decide not to go to graduate school or to put it off for a while, your skills education will not stop. In fact, every decision you make throughout your work life should be viewed as enhancing your KHS. Lifelong learning is no empty phrase. It is the key to a successful career.

If you approach your job as this book suggests you approach your college education, you acquire more skills. You will be an apprentice to a more senior member in the organization in your first few jobs. Eventually you will become that senior member acting as teacher and mentor.

I encourage my students and you to think of your work life as an educational experience. In your twenties, you are learning skills and exploring career options. That is why some of the strongest companies set up training programs, sometimes two years in length, and create a long-term plan for "professional development." The term *professional development* means providing employees with new skills. An employee who stops learning is an employee who is not likely to move up—and who is quite likely to be moved out.

If your job requires that you continually learn, the strategies suggested in this book for college will also serve you well at work. Your decisions about career paths and projects as well as your volunteer activities within and outside your organization will determine how much you learn. In a sense, choosing options on the job is similar to the planning outlined in chapter 18 for how to approach college. You will take on new tasks to help develop skills you think are important or to learn about different kinds of career options.

The long-term benefits of a commitment to learning in your career are substantial. You will be excited to go to work every day because you are learning something new. Your employer will see that excitement and be ready to assign you new tasks. You will have opportunities that will open many paths to you. As you grow, your skills grow too—and vice versa. That's why I say to always keep the skills in mind.

USEFUL RESOURCES

AmeriCorps (www.americorps.org). A network of national service programs, AmeriCorps engages more than fifty thousand Americans each year in intensive service to meet critical needs in education, public safety, health, and the environment.

Lucas Group Military (www.military.lucascareers.com). This is one of the many websites of an organization that helps place military officers. The range of jobs that ex-military people get and the salaries are listed on the site.

Making a Life: Reclaiming Your Purpose and Passion in Business and in Life by Mark Albion (Warner Books, 2000). Written by a former Harvard Business School professor who decided that life was too short to stay in a job that had no purpose beyond making money, this book will help you think about how to have a fulfilling career.

Peace Corps (www.peacecorps.gov). The Peace Corps was formally authorized by Congress in 1961, and its mission is to "promote world peace and friendship." There are seven thousand Peace Corps Volunteers currently serving in seventy countries around the world. All assignments are for two years plus three months of training in your country of service. Peace Corp alumni have a strong network and use their experience to pursue graduate study and rewarding careers.

So, You Want to Join the Peace Corps by Dillon Banerjee (Ten Speed Press, 2000). Written by a Peace Corps member from 1994–1996, this book is organized around seventy-three questions, which are the titles of short chapters. Several appendices contain basic documentary information from the Peace Corps, but you will have to check the Web for the latest information.

What Color Is Your Parachute? A Practical Manual for Job-Hunters & Career-Changers by Richard N. Bolles (Ten Speed Press, most recent edition). By far the most widely used career-hunting book on the market, it was initially written for job changers. It also helps those looking for a job right out of college.

Teach for America (www.teachforamerica.org). Teach for America is the national corps of outstanding college graduates of all academic majors and backgrounds who commit two years to teach in urban and rural public schools. Since its inception in 1990, more than ten thousand exceptional individuals have joined Teach for America.

PART THREE

PLANNING YOUR SUCCESS

"I ALWAYS WANTED TO BE SOMEBODY, BUT I SHOULD HAVE BEEN MORE SPECIFIC."

—LILY TOMLIN, COMEDIENNE

CHAPTER 17

USING YOUR KHS TO EXPLORE PROFESSIONAL FIELDS

TOPICS

IDENTIFY YOUR PROFESSIONAL INTERESTS • BEGIN THE
SELF-REFLECTION PROCESS • SCAN THE PROFESSIONS •
LOOK AT SPECIFIC FIELDS IN-DEPTH TO FIND SKILLS •
APPLY WHAT YOU HAVE FOUND TO YOUR KHS

The Know-How Groups presented in the first ten chapters provides a picture of those skills needed for professional careers commonly pursued by college graduates. I use the term "profession" or "professional field" to refer to any work that might be found in business, government, or non-profit organizations that usually, but not always, require at least a two-year or four-year college degree. It may also require passing a test or having experiences that must be certified in order to receive a license to work in the field. Professionals are people who share similar jobs and belong to associations that seek to raise the standards of their performance through conferences, publications, training, and award programs. This is as true for physicians as it is for people in retail sales.

The higher your KHS, the more likely you will be hired and succeed in a professional career. This basic KHS is the one you need to improve while in college regardless of what type of job or career you pursue.

The spirit behind the KHS can also be used to help you assess your inherent potential strengths for the specific professional fields you might enter once you leave college or, in some cases, graduate school. By seeing yourself as a "professional" in whatever field you pursue, you are accepting the single most important underlying principle of this book and one of the attitudes most valued by employers: a commitment to continuous self-improvement. Good professionals are in a perpetual state of learning and improvement. You may change your professional field a few times or you may stick with one throughout your work life, but whatever the case, always strive to improve yourself.

A good way to explore a professional field is to construct a specific KHS for a profession that may be of interest to you. This chapter introduces you to the range of professions and discusses how you can go about creating your own KHS for a profession of your choice. But first, you need to learn how to identify your interests and talents. Only then can you begin your search for a professional field of interest.

Believe it or not, you have been exploring professions your whole life. Remember when you wanted to be a police officer or teacher, or when you thought you'd be the next football superstar, TV news anchor, hot-shot lawyer, or U.S. senator. Those were ways of "trying out" different careers. Now it's time to look at potential careers in a new way and to deal with reality. "Dealing with reality" doesn't mean you can't shoot for the stars. You should always aspire to achieve your dreams. But the good news of reality is this: there are millions of stars out there. The bad news—well, not bad but certainly challenging—is there are even more paths to those stars.

Exploring professions is like looking for a needle in a haystack, but much worse. When you look for a needle in a haystack, you at least know you are looking for a needle. When you approach the gigantic haystack of professional fields and the jobs associated with them, you are not exactly sure what you are looking for because you don't know what your "needle" is. The haystack is not your biggest problem. Your biggest problem is *you*.

If you're the kind of person who needs to reduce uncertainty prematurely, you'll be onto something that is obvious, like doctor, lawyer, engineer, or some role model played up in the media. If you're the kind of person who buckles under pressure, you'll give up in despair and avoid this question until sometime in the distant future. Both of these responses are counterproductive. A better response is to realize that you are in a long process of self-exploration that may never end in certainty about what you want to do when you "grow up."

To come up with an answer as a high school senior or lower-division undergraduate is in most cases premature. We all know someone who said they were going to be a physician when they were eight years old and actually became one. However, if you are like me, you know many more who said they were going to be a physician or lawyer but are now in completely different professions.

Faced with the uncertainty generated by this overwhelming number of choices, it is natural to turn to your parents and family. Although what you do for a living must be your choice, your relatives may have some useful advice. Some students think they are committed to following in their parents' footsteps. Others are absolutely sure they will never do what their parents do. In my experience, such firm decisions (either way) are a mistake. The advantage of following in parental footsteps is that more doors will be open for internships and jobs, and you will have built-in mentors. These are not trivial advantages. Don't reject them solely because you "want to make it on your own," or your parents themselves tell you, "Don't do what I did." Conversely, be sure you really want to pursue that career rather than take the easy way out.

Exploring career options is a long and complicated process that can be explained in three steps: (1) self-reflection, (2) scanning professional options, and (3) in-depth assessment. Unlike the steps in front of a building, these three steps are not sequenced. Self-reflection will lead to scanning and perhaps more self-reflection after your in-depth assessment. An in-depth study via an internship may lead to self-reflection or scanning. The three steps are really in a circle.

STEP ONE: BEGIN THE SELF-REFLECTION PROCESS

Using tools provided by your career-service office can help self-reflection, but you can actually start on your own by using some of the same tools. The earlier you start, the sooner you will be able to narrow down your choices and develop the skills, knowledge, and experience you will need to succeed in those fields.

I have provided two very simple diagrams that my students have found useful. They represent only an initial set of screens to start thinking about your career futures. Like all such tools, their purpose is to help you to think, not to make a decision.

The first diagram is the Career Triangle, which assumes all careers are some combination of working with physical things, people, and information. The diagram has some examples of careers to illustrate how it can be applied. However, there is a lot of variation in these fields, so different specializations would be placed differently in the diagram. For example, a teacher of industrial arts would be higher in the "physical things" dimension than the English literature teacher.

This diagram can be used to record where you think you are at this stage in your life with respect to both your talents and your preferences. The Career Triangle is a very simple first cut. There are several well-known and extensively used frameworks identified at the end of this chapter that ask you more specific questions about your likes and dislikes.

The two points on the bottom of the Career Triangle—people and information—have a direct relationship to the ten Know-How Groups. The first six groups are related in many ways to people; the last four are related to information. As you develop your KHS, you may decide where you want to be between the dimensions of "people" and "information" on the basis of what you like to do and what you are good at. A high school teacher, for example, balances mastery of information and working with students.

Thinking about what you like to do and what you are good at raises an interesting point about thinking about a professional field. Do you select one in which you do what you like to do or one in which you are good at the required skills? Most of the students I deal with like to work with people rather than information, but they may be very good at some of the information skills. When they realize they like doing one set of skills but are happier performing others, they become quite confused and even depressed.

You will never find a career in which *all* the tasks are pleasant or fulfilling, which is one of the reasons why you get paid. Moreover, as you move through a profession, you will have opportunities to perform a variety of skills, some of which you will like better than others.

Look at any profession in which you eventually will be spending most of your time doing things you like *and* you are good at. I say "eventually," because your entry-level position may not be very pleasant at all. To put it in concrete terms, you may get your first job because you can work in Excel and spend a lot of time working with information in a cubicle in front of a computer. If you are good with people and want to work with people, you will move into management in a few years and get out of the cubicle.

You can easily create your own version of this diagram. I recommend that you place two marks on the diagram and revisit it annually. Place an *L* for what you like to do and an *S* for where you have the most skills and talent. Use the examples in the diagram to think about it.

Once you have thought about the Career Triangle, you are ready to ask a few more specific questions. The Career Field Explorer is designed to help you explore your desired career by looking at eight dimensions represented as lines between two extremes. Where do you want to be on those lines five years after you graduate? Place an X on each of them to help you think about the field in which you would like to exercise your favorite skills. In the right-hand column, indicate how important the dimension is to you by writing 1 for low, 2 for medium, or 3 for high.

THE CAREER TRIANGLE

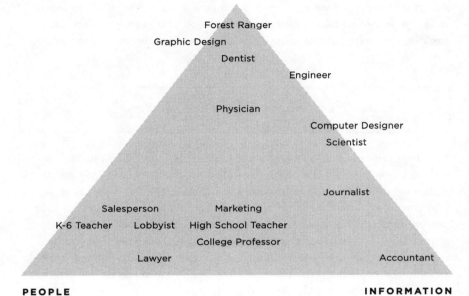

PHYSICAL THINGS

Forest Ranger

Graphic Design

Dentist

Engineer

Physician

Computer Designer

Scientist

Journalist

Salesperson Marketing

K-6 Teacher Lobbyist High School Teacher

College Professor

Lawyer Accountant

PEOPLE **INFORMATION**

THE CAREER FIELD EXPLORER

CAREER DIMENSION	PRIORITY
(Spectrum of extremes)	(Rate from 1 low to 3 high)

Average Salary ||||||||||||||||||||||||||||||||||||||||||||||||||||||||| Top 5%   _____

Work No More than 40 Hours per Week ||||||||||||||||||||||||| 80 Hours   _____

Do-Good Field |||||||||||||||||||||||||||||||||||||||||||||||||| Money-Making   _____

Near to Where You Now Live|||||||||||||||||||||||||||||||||||||||| Far Away   _____

Little Traveling ||||||||||||||||||||||||||||||||||||||||||| Lots of Traveling   _____

Economically Risky ||||||||||||||||||||||||||||||||||||||||||||| Not Risky   _____

Orderly ||||||||||||||||||||||||||||||||||||||||||||||||||||||||||| Chaotic   _____

Professional Graduate Education |||||||||||||||||||||||| No More Degrees   _____

Your responses to these two diagrams—the Career Triangle and the Career Field Explorer—represent the start of your exploration of professional fields you may want to pursue. You will also need to explore other resources that look into your skill and interest areas. Three of the most widely used resources are described at the end of this chapter. You can work on this self-evaluation with the career services office at your college.

STEP TWO: SCAN THE PROFESSIONS

The term *profession,* as already noted, can apply to a field as highly controlled as medicine to one like retail sales, in which entry is easy but a high level of professional competence is difficult. The fields can be grouped into two categories: those that require either a specific undergraduate or postgraduate degree and/or a specific certification (like an accountant, nurse, physician, or lawyer) and those that have no degree or credential requirement. The tables that follow list some of the more common professions in the two categories according to eChoices, a computer service that is described in the next section of this chapter.

Now that you have applied the Career Triangle and the Career Field Explorer, you are ready to make some tentative selection from the lists provided in the following tables of professions. If none of the two lists provide you with an appealing option, use other resources including counselors, family, books, and websites. The purpose of this scanning process is to help you start to think about your future. Spend a limited amount of time in making your initial selection, because the purpose of the scan is to help you figure out what skills you want to develop in college rather than to require you to settle on a specific career.

SELECTED ENTRY-LEVEL PROFESSIONAL POSITIONS REQUIRING ADVANCED STUDY AND/OR CERTIFICATE[1]

Profession	Degree and/or Credential Requirement	Website
Accountant	Degree in accounting or a closely related field; some work experience may be required	American Institute of Certified Public Accountants www.aicpa.org
Architect	Professional degree in architecture (usually acquired from a 5-yr program at a 4-yr school), a period of practical training or internship, and a license, which includes the two former requirements as well as passage of all sections of the Architect Registration Examination	American Institute of Architects www.aia.org
Archivist	Master's degree in history and/or library science and substantial practical or work experience	Society of American Archivists www.archivists.org
Audiologist/ Speech Pathologist	Most states and the District of Columbia require the following for licensing: a master's degree, 300–375 hours of supervised clinical experience, a passing score on a national examination, and 9 months of postgraduate professional clinical experience	American Speech Language Hearing Association www.asha.org
Clergy	Many denominations require that clergy complete a bachelor's degree and a graduate-level program of theological study	The Academy of Parish Clergy www.apclergy.org
Clinical Psychologist	Master's degree and frequently a doctoral degree is required for employment as a psychologist in most fields. Psychologists in independent practice must meet licensing or certification requirements in all states and the District of Columbia	American Psychological Association www.apa.org
College and University Administrator	Most positions require a doctoral degree	National Association of Student Personnel Administrators www.naspa.org
Food Scientist	Master's degree or doctoral degree is required for basic research	Institute of Food Technologists www.ift.org
Instructional Coordinator	Master's degree is required to work in this profession	National Education Association www.nea.org
Lawyer	Four years of undergraduate study followed by 3 years in law school. Advanced law degrees may be desirable for those planning to specialize, do research, or teach.	American Bar Association www.abanet.org
Librarian	Master's degree in library science is required for positions in most public, academic, and special libraries, and in many school systems.	American Library Association www.ala.org
Medical and Psychiatric Social Worker	Master's degree in social work is generally required for positions in the mental health field, public agencies, and is usually necessary for supervisory, administrative, or research positions. A doctorate usually is required for teaching and some research and administrative jobs	National Association of Social Workers www.naswdc.org

SELECTED ENTRY-LEVEL PROFESSIONAL POSITIONS REQUIRING ADVANCED STUDY AND/OR CERTIFICATE[1]

Profession	Degree and/or Credential Requirement	Website
Medicine and Health Service Manager	Master's degree in such areas as health services administration, long-term care administration, and health sciences is the standard credential for most generalist positions in this field	American College of Healthcare Executives www.ache.org/career.htm
Operations Researcher/ Analyst	Master's degree and high level of computer skills are required	Institute for Operations Research and the Management Sciences www.informs.org
Optometrist	Four-year professional degree program at an accredited optometric school preceded by at least 2 or 3 years of preoptometric study at an accredited college or university. All states require optometrists to be licensed	American Optometric Association www.aoanet.org
Pharmacist	Pharmacists must be licensed—to obtain a license, one must graduate from an accredited college of pharmacy, pass a state examination, and serve an internship under a licensed pharmacist. Most colleges of pharmacy require 1 or 2 years of college-level prepharmacy education	American Association of Colleges of Pharmacy www.aacp.org
Physical Therapist	All states require physical therapists to pass a licensure exam after graduating from an accredited physical therapy program	American Physical Therapy Association www.apta.org
Physician	Four years of undergraduate school, 4 years of medical school, 3 to 8 years of internship and residency, and a license depending on medical specialty. Some fields have additional requirements	American Medical Association www.ama-assn.org
Researcher and/or Professor	Master's degree for more professional opportunities; Ph.D. for most positions in postsecondary institutions, which takes 4–10 years of graduate school	Search under the specific profession you are pursuing—example: "Economist"
School/ Vocational/ Career Counselor	All states require school counselors to have state school counseling certification. Depending on the state, a master's degree in counseling and 2–5 years of teaching experience may be required for a counseling certificate	American Counseling Association www.counseling.org
Teacher	All 50 states and the District of Columbia require public school teachers to be licensed, and require at least a bachelor's degree (in education or another field) and completion of an approved teacher training program with a prescribed number of subject and education credits and supervised practice teaching	American Federation of Teachers www.aft.org
Veterinarian	Prospective veterinarians must graduate from a 4-year program at an accredited college of veterinary medicine with a Doctor of Veterinary Medicine (D.V.M. or V.M.D.) degree and obtain a license to practice. All states and the District of Columbia require that veterinarians be licensed	American Veterinary Medical Association www.avma.org
Vocational Rehabilitation Counselor	Most vocational and related rehabilitation agencies usually require a master's degree in rehabilitation counseling, counseling and guidance, or counseling psychology	National Rehabilitation Association www.nationalrehab.org

SELECTED ENTRY-LEVEL PROFESSIONAL POSITIONS NOT REQUIRING ADVANCED STUDY AND/OR CERTIFICATE[2]

Administrative Services Manager

Artist

Athletic Trainer

Audio-Visual Specialist

Budget Analyst

Computer and Information Systems Manager

Computer Programmer

Computer Security Specialist

Computer Support Specialist

Computer Systems Analyst

Construction Manager

Consultant

Cost Estimator

Credit Analyst

Data Communications Analyst

Database Administrator

Dietician/Nutritionist

Editor

Employee Training Specialist

Employment and Placement Specialist

Employment Interviewer

Farm Products Purchasing Agent

Financial Counselor

Forester

Government Service Executive

Graphic Designer

Health and Safety Engineer

Human Resources Manager

Industrial Production Manager

Insurance Claim Examiner

Interior Designer

Interpreter/Translator

Job and Occupational Analyst

Loan Officer/Counselor

Market Research Analyst

Medical/Clinical Laboratory Technologist

Meetings and Convention Planner

Newscaster

Occupational Therapist

Parole and Probation Officer

Postal Worker

Property Manager

Public Health Educator

Public Relations Specialist

Purchasing Agent

Real Estate Appraiser

Recreation Facilities Manager

Recreation Worker

Reporter

Residential Counselor

Sales

Set Designer

Social Services Manager

Social Worker

Tax Examiner/Revenue Agent

Technical Writer

Transportation Manager

Utilities Manager

Wholesale and Retail Buyer

Writer

STEP THREE: LOOK AT SPECIFIC FIELDS IN-DEPTH TO FIND SKILLS

Once you have identified some professions that interest you, you are ready to acquire information on those fields. Gathering specific information on a field should be done one field at a time. I suggest that you first use a program like eChoices and then examine relevant books and websites. (Access to eChoice services can be obtained from your high school or college guidance counselor as well as public libraries, if they are subscribers. More than fifteen thousand subscribers are located in North America.) Finally, you should undertake one or more informational interviews.

If your college or high school has eChoices, you have a powerful tool for gathering detailed information about various professions. eChoices, which was briefly discussed in chapter 12, provides the following kinds of information on any of the 655 professional fields it lists. There are other programs including SIGIPlus offered by ETS and Discover that offer similar information, but eChoices appears to be the most comprehensive.

Note that eChoices lists relevant websites, which can be used to search for additional information. Also do book searches on the Web, and visit libraries and bookstores to come up with some books on the field. Also, write to professional associations for additional information.

THE TYPES OF INFORMATION eCHOICES PROVIDES ON PROFESSIONAL FIELDS[3]

GENERAL INFORMATION
- Description
- Typical Tasks
- Field of Work
- National Career Pathways
- Career Clusters
- Specialties and Similar Occupations
- More Information (lists professional associations and websites)

SKILLS AND ATTITUDES
- Education, Training, and Work Experience
- Transferable Work-Content Skills
- Basic Skills
- General Workplace Skills
- Suggested School Courses
- Aptitudes
- Career Areas
- Work Values
- Interests
- Myers-Briggs Types

NATURE OF THE WORK
- Physical Demands
- Physical Abilities
- Work Conditions
- Work Hours and Travel

ECONOMICS OF THE PROFESSION
- National Earnings
- State Earnings (of the state in which your school is located)
- National Employment and Outlook
- State Employment and Outlook (of the state in which your school is located)

As part of your study of a field, conduct at least one informational interview. Informational interviewing is a technique in which you find someone who has the job or career you think you might want, and you ask them all about it. These interviews will help you decide if you really want to pursue that career. You might ask questions like "How did you get to your current position?" or "What do you like best and least about your current position?" Internships, part-time jobs, and job shadowing (following an employee around for a day or two) can help you to get a more complete picture by giving you an experience in the field and access to people whom you can interview. By the time you enter your senior year, you should have in-depth information using the range of sources for at least three professional fields.

APPLY WHAT YOU HAVE FOUND TO YOUR KHS

Although this research will provide you with a broad but still incomplete picture of the professional field you study, start the research early in your college career. Continue throughout your college years as you gain experience in identifying the skills that are considered essential to success. Build a list from this research so that you adapt your KHS for your own purposes. If you think you want to be an accountant, for example, you could add the ability to interpret a balance sheet to your KHS. The research will help you plan course and non-course activities in college that will improve your KHS. The research will also help you see the relevance of the ten KHS groups as well as suggest which groups you may want to develop beyond the MSL. It may also suggest additional skills that you will need that are not part of the KHS groups.

You may not be ready at this point in time to create a specialized KHS because you are not sure of what professional fields you want to pursue. However, as part of your preparation for your working life after college, before the start of your sophomore year, explore at least one profession you are now considering. This will help you see how to develop more specialized skills and to think about other potential professions. By completing a list for one professional field, you will have a base for comparing other fields and jobs as you move closer to your senior year.

Every professional field requires skills beyond the basic ten Know-How Groups—skills that employers would expect their employees to have or develop. For many fields, the specialized skills are higher levels of the skills listed under our basic ten. This is true for the field of journalism, for example, in which higher levels of writing and asking questions are required. In other fields, such as graphic design, there may be skills not listed in our basic ten. Some corporations prefer to provide specialized skill training. However, they also want to see if you have the ability and desire to develop into a professional. For that reason, it makes sense for you to be aware of skills needed beyond the basic ten (which, of course, you'll need) and to begin developing them.

For many professions, the basic skill sets contained in the ten Know-How Groups constitute most of what you need to prepare for that field. You may want to give extra weight to some skills, like the information-gathering skills in chapter 7, if you plan to go into law. However, some fields require skills that are not in the basic ten. For example, art and architecture require good manual dexterity for drawing and building models. Professional jobs associated with computer development require extensive experience with software and programming. In some cases, the discussion of extra credit items in chapter 11 might be helpful. If you are looking at a profession that requires skills beyond the basic ten, you can create a specialized skills list and construct your own KHS.

Using the approaches described and calculating a new KHS that will help you plan your activities in college is not, however, as important as doing the three-step exploration discussed previously. Try to do this by the first semester of your sophomore year, but if you are past that, don't fret. You can start today and still have a successful future if you complete the three steps just discussed. This is a case, though, in which doing it sooner rather than later is important because what you learn in that exploration process could change your plans for the remainder of your college years. As I point out in the next chapter, planning is the key to success.

eChoices (www.bridges.com). Although eChoices is available only through schools, public libraries, or other organizations providing job support, you can visit the Bridges website to learn more about it. The same company offers a free online resource at www.careercurrents.com. Every day the site provides engaging features about various occupations and articles about building skills and exploring education programs. You can also sign up for a free weekly email newsletter full of career exploration and skill-building articles.

Making Vocational Choices: A Theory of Vocational Personalities and Work Environments by John L. Holland (Psychological Assessment Resources, 1997). As a supplement to Richard Bolles's *What Color Is Your Parachute?* (see below) and the discussion at the beginning of this chapter, you may want to explore the list of six basic job activities identified by Holland. These are found on the Learning for Life Resource Center's website (www.learning4 liferesources.com/holland_codes.html), which provides an excellent overview of the Holland system as well as sample assessments to begin finding out what your work personalities may be.

What Color Is Your Parachute? A Practical Manual for Job-Hunters & Career-Changers by Richard N. Bolles (Ten Speed Press, most recent edition) has sold more than eight million copies since it was first published in 1970. The book is revised annually. Written primarily for people changing jobs and careers, *Parachute* provides a more elaborate discussion than the questions raised by the Career Triangle and the Career Field Explorer presented earlier in this chapter. If you want to explore beyond the discussion presented in this chapter, complete the activities presented in Bolles's Flower Exercise: A Picture of the Job of Your Dreams. You may also find his website (www.Job HuntersBible.com) helpful.

THE BEST WAY TO PREDICT YOUR FUTURE IS TO CREATE IT.

—PETER DRUCKER, MOST INFLUENTIAL MANAGEMENT CONSULTANT IN THE TWENTIETH CENTURY

CHAPTER 18

BUILDING YOUR SKILLS AGENDA

TOPICS

SPEND TIME ON TASK • PLAN FOR A HIGH KHS •
DEVELOP A MODEL KHS LEARNING PLAN

Thinking about what you want your basic KHS level to be and, if appropriate, constructing your KHS to incorporate extra credit and profession-specific skills allow you to plan your college strategy for gaining the skills needed for a successful work life. Now, if you could only figure out how to raise your KHS, along with everything else, while still enjoying yourself at college!

This chapter will help you create your own plan for your years as an undergraduate. The purpose of any plan is to achieve your goals, whether it is a football game plan, a business plan, or, in this case, a plan to develop the skills you need to succeed in the workplace. A plan is never set in stone. It needs to change as you progress through the game of life, but it serves as a starting point. An original game plan may work, but you need to make adjustments to it if your opposition throws up an unexpected defense. In the career game, reality is your opposition whether that means job applicants you compete against, the changing labor environment, or new technologies.

This chapter provides three tools to help you plan your college years so you can achieve the MSL for each of the ten Know-How Groups.

The first step in making your plan is to decide how hard you will be working on your KHS compared with the other college activities. How much time and energy will you put into raising your KHS versus having fun, getting good grades, or learning for the sake of learning? The fact that you've read this far indicates a considerable commitment to developing skills in college that will enhance your work future. Your commitment is important. Saying you are committed, however, is only a very small first step. Getting off your butt, our first skill set discussed in chapter 1, is the key.

An example from an outstanding student, artist, and musician (with a band that actually gets paid for performing) illustrates the point. The topic is far from academics but is directly applicable to the importance of commitment. He writes:

> *I have known many a band that has practiced once a week thinking that it would be enough, and maybe someone would hear them and sign them to a contract. But band members who want to play will get off their butts and do it themselves. This means putting together a professional press kit with a glossy photo, a band bio, and music sample, and sending it to every club in the area. It means keeping track of the club owners' names and phone numbers to follow up and get shows.*

Students who say that they will study hard if it is interesting are like members of a band who proclaim, "Just let us play our music, man, and we'll make it." It's no fun to do the mundane work of putting out information or practicing for hours every day just as it's no fun to practice typing, Excel, or public speaking skills. But being committed and working hard will help get you where you ultimately want to be.

A very clear measure of your commitment is called "time on task." How much time are you spending developing your skills measured by the KHS? Remember it is not what you say but what you do! Here are some telltale clues about your level of commitment to your KHS at this point in time. Would you prefer to:

- Lifeguard or have a relevant summer internship or job?
- Take easy courses to build your GPA and have plenty of time for your social life or take time-consuming courses that you know will enhance your KHS?
- Avoid Friday classes or take them because they would help with your KHS?

Building skills and exploring careers requires a long-term and continuing commitment. To be successful, you need to see your college experience as an investment in your career future. Your track record up to this point in time is revealing but does not define the future. It is never too late to work on your KHS.

How much time should you spend developing your KHS? There is no clear answer because it depends on how KHS-powerful your course and non-course activities are and what your current level is. (We'll discuss that in the next section.) If you want a KHS close to 100, you should spend between 500 and 1,000 hours a year. Divided by 365 days, that is between one-and-a-half to three hours a day or on average ten to twenty hours a week. Even if you work on your KHS 1,000 hours a year, you still have approximately 7,700 hours to sleep, have fun, make money, and do what you want to do.

Note that this recommendation does not refer to time you spend on academics. As we have suggested throughout the book, some of the course work you take will not contribute to developing a high KHS just as some of the activities you undertake to develop your KHS will not contribute to a high GPA. According to one study, "63 percent of students said they spend 15 or fewer hours on class preparation."[1] While the author cites experts who voice concern that this is not enough, the real question from a KHS perspective is this: how much time are you devoting to building your skills?

Let's take a look at how you might spend your time. The next two tables give you an idea of what your tables might look like. These are based on the time spent by Gina DeRosa, my research assistant for this book. She filled the two tables out for the year 2002, when she was a second-semester sophomore and a first-semester junior. She describes the process in her own words. Blank tables—one for courses and one for non-course activities—are available at www.tenspeed.com (search for *10 things*) so you can follow Gina's lead in completing one for your last twelve months for both course and non-course activities.

GINA'S TIME SPENT ON SKILL DEVELOPMENT IN COURSES (ONE CALENDAR YEAR)

Semester	Course	Total hours spent	% going toward KHS	= Hrs spent on KHS	Comment on relevance to KHS
Spring	Race & Literary Texts	90	20%	18	The primary value of this class was in taking legible notes and in improving my writing skills.
	Critical Issues for the U.S.	90	15%	13.5	The time I spent was on writing papers and taking legible notes.
	Methods in Public Policy Analysis	130	80%	104	The KHS-relevant work I did for this class consisted of making agendas, keeping track of contact dates, writing near-professional reports for a local agency, designing, conducting, and analyzing surveys, etc.— 2 words: TIME MANAGEMENT. The other 20% was class time and elementary tasks that really didn't relate to KHS skills.
	Nutrition in Health	35	20%	7	The only skill this class required was taking legible notes.
	Public Service Practicum (U-Reach-U)	45	80%	36	For this class, I had to teach typing to a group of kids at a local public housing complex, so I was able to work on my inter-personal, problem-solving, and teaching skills.
	Ethics and Value Theory	55	40%	22	The time I spent was on writing papers and taking legible notes.
	General Biology I	60	30%	18	My time in this course was spent mostly on taking legible notes and applying knowledge in our labs.
Summer	Introductory Microeconomics	60	30%	18	I spent most of my KHS time on taking notes.
	American National Government and Politics	70	30%	21	My KHS time was spent writing, mostly, between papers, essay exams, and tons of notes.
	Psychology of the Adolescent	65	20%	13	I spent most of my KHS time on taking notes.

GINA'S TIME SPENT ON SKILL DEVELOPMENT IN COURSES (ONE CALENDAR YEAR)

Semester	Course	Total hours spent	% going toward KHS	= Hrs spent on KHS	Comment on relevance to KHS
Fall	Microsoft Access	16	100%	16	This was only a 1-credit course, so I only had to spend a little time per week learning Microsoft Access, but each week I learned something relevant to improving my skills with Access.
	Intermediate Analysis of Public Policy	117	67%	78	I was a teaching assistant for Professor Coplin's freshman Policy course. As my position was "TA Manager," I learned and used such skills as time management, conversing one-on-one, building good relationships, working in teams, leading, keeping and using records, etc.
	Community Problem Solving	100	45%	45	I taught a community service course to five students. I learned and used such skills as teaching, leading, keeping and using records, using visual displays, applying knowledge, identifying problems, and creating solutions, etc.
	Social Work Practice Skills Lab I	50	15%	7.5	In this class, I learned a lot of one-on-one conversational skills but in the context of a counselor-client relationship, so nothing we did really targeted any specific KHS skills.
	Social Welfare Policy & Services	54	10%	5	I spent most of my KHS time in this class taking legible notes.
	Persons in Social Contexts	68	20%	14	The primary value of this class was in taking legible notes and in improving my writing skills.
	Foundations of Social Work Research	50	10%	5	I spent my KHS time taking legible notes, since the material we covered didn't leave room for developing KHS skills.

TOTAL HOURS: 1,115   AVERAGE: 37%   TOTAL KHS: 441

Gina writes:

*I took the thirty-eight skill sets identified in chapters 1
through 10 and thought about how each of the seventeen
courses I took in 2002 helped me to develop those skill
sets. Since I took courses in the summer, I had four more
courses than I would have normally taken in a typical year.
For each class, I calculated how many hours per week I
spent in the class and doing homework for it. In many
courses, the reading, lectures, and some of the activities
required memorizing content or relating specific facts and
concepts to each other, which I did not see as contributing
directly to my KHS. I found that the process of completing
this table was very subjective, [and] someone else who
may have taken the same course as I could feel as if he or
she gained more or fewer skills than I did from it.
However, I found this to be a useful exercise to evaluate
how much time I was spending on raising my KHS.*

The striking aspect of this table is that in Gina's opinion, less than
half of the time spent on course work helped her develop her KHS. That is
why your non-course activities are so important.

Gina's next table describes how non-course activities contributed to
building her KHS.

GINA'S TIME SPENT ON SKILL DEVELOPMENT IN NON-COURSE ACTIVITIES (ONE CALENDAR YEAR)					
Date	Non-course activity	Total hours spent	% going toward KHS	= Hrs spent on KHS	Comment on relevance to KHS
Fall–present	*Public Services Asst./Reference Asst. at school's Science & Tech. Library*	*350*	*20%*	*70*	*With these jobs I learned how to use library holdings and commercial databases, search the Web, pay attention to detail, converse one-on-one, and so forth.*
Spring	*Secretary of Habitat for Humanity (HFH) (school chapter)*	*70*	*30%*	*21*	*My job was to take notes at all of the officer and general interest meetings, and then send the information electronically through email to our officers and members.*
	ESF Liaison of Alpha Phi Omega (school chapter)	*60*	*30%*	*18*	*This position allowed me to present to groups, talk one-on-one, sell, lead, and manage my time.*

GINA'S TIME SPENT ON SKILL DEVELOPMENT IN NON-COURSE ACTIVITIES (ONE CALENDAR YEAR)

Date	Non-course activity	Total hours spent	% going toward KHS	= Hrs spent on KHS	Comment on relevance to KHS
Summer	Administrative Assistant for college's Public Affairs Dept.	100	20%	20	I learned how to use basic office equipment (which IS a valuable skill), and I also used random skills such as using word processing and identifying problems/creating solutions.
Summer–present	Manuscript Manager	200	70%	140	This job allowed me to refine the skills of: typing 35 WPM error free (by use of word processing tools), manage my time, converse one-on-one, send info. electronically, pay attention to detail, apply knowledge, identify problems, etc.
Fall	Vice President of Service of Alpha Phi Omega (school chapter)	80	50%	40	This position allowed me to sell, lead, manage my time, present to groups, keep and use records, manage, etc.
	Vice President of HFH (school chapter)	100	20%	20	In this position I basically oversaw committees within our own chapter, so I was able to use my leading and managing skills.
	Student Peer Advisor for the College of Arts & Sciences	10	70%	7	This job required me to meet with a group of freshman students for 7 hours one day and teach them all about our college and university, and help them get acclimated to college life. The other hour was spent emailing the students frequently to see how they were doing.
Fall–present	Co-Chair for school's first American Cancer Society Relay For Life event	15	80%	12	This position started in the middle of the semester, so I haven't had the opportunity to invest much time in it yet. However, the time I have spent has been on taking legible notes, presenting to groups, conversing one-on-one, etc.
TOTAL HOURS: 985			**AVERAGE: 43%**		**TOTAL KHS: 348**

Gina's description of her non-course activities might have included more hours if she had not been in school during the summer, but then her number of hours in courses would have been smaller. She completed 348 hours working on KHS skills through non-course activities for the year 2002 compared with 441 hours through course work. The total of 789 hours falls in the middle of the suggested range of between 500 and 1,000 hours that you should spend during each of your four years as an undergraduate.

Gina probably has a bigger commitment to her KHS than most students, but that is because she believes in the philosophy of this book. You do not have to make as big a time commitment at this point in time. However, you do need to look over the past twelve months and make an assessment.

PLAN FOR A HIGH KHS

In high school, you may have developed many of the skill sets we have discussed. You may already have a respectable KHS as high as 7. Alternately, you may come to college with few skills and a KHS of 2. If you have been in the workforce for a while or have extensive part-time job experience, your KHS is likely to be higher than if you have not.

The lower your KHS, the more time you need to spend to bring up your score. In any case, you should spend a minimum of 500 hours a year in course and non-course activities to improve your KHS. Now that you have determined how much time you did in fact spend last year on developing your KHS, you are ready to assess your current KHS. Using the table on the next page, you can figure out how you will close the gap. A blank version is available on the web.

The first three columns are taken directly from chapters 1 through 10. The next column, "Rate from 1–10 and Comment on Current Status," asks you to rate yourself on your current level for each skill. Generally you would assign yourself a "1" if you have not begun to practice a skill or if you just started, a "5" if you are making good progress on the development on a skill, and a 10 if you are an expert at a skill. After you rate your skill level, justify why you assigned that number. By doing this, you will have a basis for the last column "Plans" and a better idea of what you need to do to pull off that 10 for each skill set and a perfect score of 100.

Don't get discouraged if this chart seems overwhelming—it is actually a very simple chart to complete. By the time you begin your junior year in college (and if you stay on track), you should be over halfway to achieving the MSL for each of the skill sets.

Gina also completed this section, which appears in the example below. She writes:

Under "Rate 1–10 and Comment on Current Status," I rated myself according to how I measured my level of progress for each skill, and sometimes I wrote down courses and non-course activities that helped me to develop those skills. If I didn't give myself a 10 on a skill, then under the "Plans" section I wrote what I would do in order to begin developing that skill or to continue developing it.

This is obviously a very subjective and open-ended process, but you are the best judge of what you perceive the numbers to mean and how much progress you make with each of the skills. As long as you complete this chart in the same frame of mind all the way through, then you will have an accurate picture of where you stand.

GINA'S ASSESSMENT OF CURRENT STATUS AND PLANS TO RAISE KHS

Know-How Group Score*	Skill Set	Minimum Skill Level (MSL)	Rate Yourself 1–10 and Comment on Current Status	Plans
1. Establishing a Work Ethic Score: 26/4 = 6.5	Kick Yourself in the Butt	Like George Washington, you're able to tell yourself that you have worked hard enough to deserve everything you have pursued even if you fail to reach your goal.	7—I've had a lot of experiences where I've set some goals and made them, but I also failed to make them on occasion. I have vowed to keep motivated in the future.	Only time will help me become better at telling myself I've worked hard enough, and I'll make sure to try harder at achieving my goals.
	Be Honest	You have not lied or cheated from the moment you read this page.	9—I only lie when I'm sworn to secrecy, so that's why I gave a 9. Other than that, I'm honest with friends, family, coworkers, etc.	I'll continue to be honest with everyone I come into contact with—unless I'm sworn to secrecy!
	Manage Your Time	By your senior year, your assignments are done and ready for final proofing 24 hours before they are due.	7—I'm making good progress here. I get most of my assignments done about 24 hours before they're due, but not all.	I will try my hardest to get my assignments done and ready for final proofing 24 hours before they're due!
	Manage Your Money	You have no credit card debt, your checkbook has been balanced for 12 consecutive months, you owe no income taxes, and you have a clear idea of how much you owe and how long it will take to pay off your college debt.	3—I don't have credit card debt, but I definitely don't balance my checkbook and I have NO idea how long it will take me to pay off my college loans.	I'll try to start balancing my checkbook and figuring out what I owe in taxes, as well as how much and how long it will take me to pay off my college debt.

*total skill set ratings divided by number of skill sets in group

229

GINA'S ASSESSMENT OF CURRENT STATUS AND PLANS TO RAISE KHS

Know-How Group Score*	Skill Set	Minimum Skill Level (MSL)	Rate Yourself 1–10 and Comment on Current Status	Plans
2. Developing Physical Skills Score: 32/4 = 8	Stay Well	You do not miss or are not late for any classes during your senior year because you are sick or overslept.	8—I've only missed about 4 classes total due to illness. Other than that, I'm always there and on time!	I'll try to take good care of myself so that illness doesn't prevent me from attending class.
	Look Good	You present yourself well to whomever is your target.	7—I guess my wardrobe could use a little work, but I think I make pretty good first impressions on people.	I'll buy fancier clothes and hang out with more people who are similar to my potential employers.
	Type 35 WPM Error Free	You type 35 errorless words per minute.	7—I am close to this standard but need more practice.	Be conscious of the need to focus on speed and accuracy when typing.
	Take Legible Notes	You never go to a meeting without a pen and paper to take notes.	10—I take concise, and legible notes at every meeting I attend!	
3. Communicating Verbally Score: 24/3 = 8	Converse One-on-One	This skill requires an ongoing development, but by the time you graduate, you should be skilled at spotting miscommunications involving yourself or in conversations you observe.	7—There is always room for improvement. My boss sometimes claims I don't communicate clearly and on occasion there are misunderstandings with friends and family. I've been exposed to many different kinds of people in different situations and feel I can spot miscommunications at the drop of a hat!	Continuously be on guard that poor communications may be at the heart of a problem.
	Present to Groups	You do not let one classroom experience go by where you wanted to say something but did not.	7—Most of the time I have something to say in class, I let my voice be heard, but sometimes I hold back.	I will make myself talk more in classes when I have something to say.
	Use Visual Displays	You have created a PowerPoint presentation in at least one class and have used handouts in several small group meetings.	10—I had to do a PowerPoint presentation for a class I took in my sophomore year, and I have handouts for people at the majority of meetings I hold or attend.	
4. Communicating in Writing	Write Well	You can quickly and clearly write a proposal presenting an idea that others have to buy into.	6—I haven't had to do this too often, but I've done it enough so I feel confident in my ability.	Whenever I have the chance to write such a proposal, I will do so as quickly and effectively as possible. I plan to take more classes in which writing is a major component.
	Edit and Proof	When given a rough draft, you are able to spot lack of subject and verb agreement and a paragraph without a topic sentence as soon as you see them.	10—Working with Professor Coplin this summer, and having proofed many friends' papers, editing and proofing have become second nature to me.	

*total skill set ratings divided by number of skill sets in group

GINA'S ASSESSMENT OF CURRENT STATUS AND PLANS TO RAISE KHS

Know-How Group Score*	Skill Set	Minimum Skill Level (MSL)	Rate Yourself 1–10 and Comment on Current Status	Plans
4. Communicating in Writing Score: 28/4 = 7	Use Word-Processing Tools	You can create a professional-looking resume in a Word document that you can send over email. You can use the following functions: Spelling and Grammar; Cut, Copy, and Paste; Tracking; Bullets and Numbering; Find and Replace; Header and Footer; Styles and Formatting; Insert Table; Borders and Shading; and Word Count.	*7—I don't claim to be an expert at all of these functions because I haven't used them all enough, but I feel I'm fairly proficient with the Microsoft Word program overall.*	*I will practice writing in Word more and experiment with the different functions.*
	Send Information Electronically	You know how to use the Web as a storage facility for everything from papers to resumes, and you can use emails to send information (including file attachments). By the time you graduate, you have your resume set to send electronically.	*5—I don't store anything on the Internet, but I definitely have sent many emails, which contained important information for professors and organizations, and some include attachments.*	*I will start saving files on the Internet and use it to send out my resume to potential employers.*
5. Working Directly with People Score: 28/3 = 9.3	Build Good Relationships	You consciously seek to develop good relationships with your professors, landlord, teammates, or associates in student organizations as well as with the full range of people you meet in jobs and internships.	*8—I always try to maintain good relationships with everyone I come into contact with—whether it be friends, co-officers, classmates, professors, whoever. But there is always room for improvement.*	*I will continue to monitor my interactions with others.*
	Work in Teams	You are able to work cooperatively in a variety of team settings.	*10—I'm a very compromising, receptive person and I've worked in a variety of team settings where I've had to be cooperative with others.*	
	Teach Others	You have had at least three teaching opportunities in which you were successful in teaching others the skills they needed.	*10—I've definitely had more than 3 teaching opportunities and by virtue of being a leader in the student organizations I'm involved in. I need to strengthen my tendency to avoid conflict.*	

total skill set ratings divided by number of skill sets in group

GINA'S ASSESSMENT OF CURRENT STATUS AND PLANS TO RAISE KHS

Know-How Group Score*	Skill Set	Minimum Skill Level (MSL)	Rate Yourself 1–10 and Comment on Current Status	Plans
6. Influencing People Score: 20/4 = 5	Manage Efficiently	You have managed at least three other workers in a job or community service experience.	7—In my service fraternity, APO, I have to manage about 40 volunteers, and in Habitat for Humanity, I have to manage about 7 committee heads. I have not had experience in managing employees.	I will take a position in which I have to manage people in a business setting.
	Sell Successfully	You have had at least two different positions in which you have tried to convince others to buy a product, donate money, or sign a petition.	0—I don't like selling, and therefore I managed to avoid such positions.	I will try my best to take up positions in which I can practice selling an idea or product. I will take a course in grant writing.
	Politick Wisely	You have participated in one student organization activity and one college level activity in which you were involved in decision making.	7—I've been involved in student organizations since freshman year when I was involved in decision making. However, I have not had experi-ence in trying to shape the policies of large organizations	I will take a political science course in congressional lobbying
	Lead Effectively	You have held a minor or major leadership position in an existing organization or team project.	6—I've been an officer in 2 strong student organizations since the beginning of my sophomore year. This is such a difficult skill area, I feel I have much more learn.	I will take on more leadership opportunities as they open up. I will take a course in leadership.
7. Gathering Information	Use Library Holdings	You have used library catalogues and databases in a variety of fields.	10—In addition to having worked in a library since my freshman year and helping patrons to use such things, I've used them myself for classes.	
	Use Commercial Databases	You have used at least these commercial databases before you graduate: Lexis-Nexis, ProQuest Direct, FirstSearch, and Dialog@Carl.	10—I consider myself an expert at databases only because I've worked in a library at school for 2 years and my job is to use them to find information for others. I've also used all of the above mentioned ones for classes.	
	Search the Web	You can find the telephone number and address of someone you know, and you can use at least three different search engines. You can locate desirable internships and jobs through web searches.	8—I search the Web every day for personal and academic information. I may not use some of the formal search strategies available.	I will take the tutorial suggested in this book to learn formal search strategy techniques.

*total skill set ratings divided by number of skill sets in group

GINA'S ASSESSMENT OF CURRENT STATUS AND PLANS TO RAISE KHS

Know-How Group Score*	Skill Set	Minimum Skill Level (MSL)	Rate Yourself 1-10 and Comment on Current Status	Plans
7. Gathering Information Score: 48/6 = 8	Conduct Interviews	You have conducted at least two interviews about careers you may want to pursue before you are a senior in college.	*7—I haven't conducted formal interviews with people, but I've had many conversations with professors and people in general who have careers similar to what I'd like to pursue.*	*I will conduct a few formal interviews about careers I may want to pursue before I'm a senior.*
	Use Surveys	You have a reflex reaction whenever you get survey results to ask critical questions about the sample and the nature of the questions.	*8—I've seen enough surveys and taken enough research methods-based courses to be fairly proficient at this, but there's always room for improvement.*	*I will be more critical when I encounter or design surveys.*
	Keep and Use Records	You can keep a log of your daily activities that can document to someone else what you have done.	*5—I have maintained logs for internship experiences but have not developed and maintained a systematic record-keeping system.*	*I will begin to keep a log of daily activities.*
8. Using Quantitative Tools Score: 26/3 = 8.67	Use Numbers	You can determine the percentage change between your GPA in the fall and spring semester. If you can do this, you will be able to do just about any general calculating function you will face in the job world, including creating and adjusting projected budgets.	*10—I've had to create all kinds of budgets, and I'm able to use general calculating functions.*	
	Use Graphs and Tables	Whenever you see a group of numbers, you can display them by use of a graph or a table to make the point you want to make.	*8—I had to do this many times for a class I took, and I definitely think I'm an expert at it by now.*	*I realize that graphs and statistics can be used in many ways. I will take courses requiring their application to enhance my skills.*
	Use Spreadsheet Programs	You can visualize how to use a spreadsheet when you see a large amount of data that needs to be analyzed and can set up the spreadsheet and generate tables and graphs.	*8—I have used a spreadsheet program to produce a survey study for a community client. I have also used spreadsheets in several courses and in my work with organizations. I still need to learn additional features of these programs.*	*I will take several more courses in which spreadsheets will be necessary to give me additional practice.*
9. Asking and Answering the Right Questions	Detect BS	Whenever you read or hear something, you immediately ask yourself what motivated the information and what you can do to check its accuracy.	*8—After having been around for several years and encountering many different kinds of people and information, I'm pretty good at detecting BS. I can see through flimsy excuses by my peers and am skeptical about what anyone tells me.*	*Since BS is so prevalent and changes in different contexts, I will be on the lookout for it in courses and my other activities.*

total skill set ratings divided by number of skill sets in group

GINA'S ASSESSMENT OF CURRENT STATUS AND PLANS TO RAISE KHS

Know-How Group Score*	Skill Set	Minimum Skill Level (MSL)	Rate Yourself 1–10 and Comment on Current Status	Plans
9. Asking and Answering the Right Questions Score: 31/4 = 7.75	Pay Attention to Detail	You are able to "read between the lines" of documents you come across and determine the causes and implications of events.	8—I think I do a pretty good job of re-reading documents to find out what exactly they're trying to say or ask for. I also think that being older gives me an edge on analyzing experiences because I've had many, and I'm big on wanting to know why things happen and what the effects of events are.	There's always room for improvement in the skill, because you'll never catch everything in a document or figure out ALL of the causes and implications of events.
	Apply Knowledge	You are able to develop and test explanations and use them as a base for making forecasts in your own life.	8—I think there's always room for improvement with this, but I try to make objective judgments and explanations for things.	I need to practice developing and testing explanations to use for forecasting things in my own life. Courses in both my majors require the application of existing knowledge, so they should help me.
	Evaluate Actions and Policies	You set clear goals with specific measurements that will help you evaluate how well you performed your job search.	7—I'm able to set clear and measurable goals for things I do, but I honestly haven't started my job search yet.	I will practice my goal-setting skills when I start my job search.
10. Solving Problems Score: 20/3 = 6.67	Identify Problems	In at least three different group sessions in which an event is being planned or an action is under consideration, you are able to get the group to be clear about the problem and how to measure it.	8—In my student organizations, I've helped to plan several events, and so I've become accustomed to troubleshooting before problems arise. However, I need more practice because I sometimes don't see the problem immediately.	In courses and non-course activity, I will always ask, "What is the problem?" I take courses in which the underlying causes of problems in my field are explored.
	Develop Solutions	You have helped one student or administration organization implement a decision that deals with some clearly definable problem.	10—In the work cited above, I have come up with solutions. I am not sure I come up with the "best" solutions, but I definitely can create solutions.	
	Launch Solutions	You can write a chronological outline of how you developed and tried to implement a solution to a specific problem.	2—I have developed and launched solutions in student organizations, but I have never kept a record of it.	I will write a chronological outline of how I developed and tried to implement a solution to a specific problem.

GINA'S TOTAL KHS: 74.89

*total skill set ratings divided by number of skill sets in group

Note that for each Know-How Group, an average score for each group is determined by dividing the number of skill sets into the sum of points assigned. Only go to two decimal points, and add all ten scores. You will get a number that ranges between 0 (no MSL reached for each skill set) to 100 (reaching all MSLs on every skill set for each of the ten Know-How Groups). Gina's score of 74.89 shows excellent progress for a first-semester junior. If she completes her plan, her score will be over 90 by the time she graduates.

I suggest that you go to www.tenspeed.com (search for *10 things*) and complete this table as soon as possible and then revise it every three months. Revising on a regular basis will ensure that you continuously build your KHS.

One final point: even if you have achieved the MSL for a specific skill set, you have to continue to gain experience exercising those skill sets. You may have done an extensive data analysis with Excel or given a first rate PowerPoint presentation, but that was yesterday. You don't need to devote as much time to those skill sets in which you have achieved the MSL, but you need to make sure that you do not get rusty: use it or lose it!

DEVELOP A MODEL KHS LEARNING PLAN

College catalogues frequently give you a "model curriculum" for programs of study. These catalogues list the courses you should take so that you can complete the credit hours necessary to graduate in that program. Unfortunately, that will not work for developing your KHS, because the host of general skills you need to succeed in whatever career you undertake are not just a matter of completing 120 hours of college credit.

However, the notion of a year-by-year list of courses is not a bad one. To add to your KHS, you need to do two things. First, allow for course and non-course activities. Second, include what you do in the summers. The following table will be useful to you as you build your KHS strategy. The model is provided for a two-semester system, but you should be able to apply it to colleges that use a quarter system and also a winter intersession. Please note that a course requiring twenty pages of papers refers to turned-in assignments and does not mean in-class exams that add up to twenty pages. It can be one big paper, two ten-page papers, or four five-page papers. And remember, the model is for the general KHS skills and does not include specialized skills that you might need for a specific field.

MODEL KHS CURRICULUM

Year	Semester	Courses	Non-Course Activities
FRESHMAN	Fall	One course requiring at least 20 pages of papers.	Resident hall governance; campus job or sport activity.
	Spring	One course requiring at least 20 pages of papers; one class requiring applied statistics.	Volunteer position as campus tour guide; 20 hours off-campus community service.
	Summer		Office or retail job unless you can find something more educational.
SOPHOMORE	Fall	One course requiring at least 20 pages of papers.	Resident adviser *or* 20 hours in a student organization and 20 hours of community service; job in a university office.
	Spring	One course requiring at least 20 pages of papers; one course requiring a team project; one course requiring an oral presentation.	Resident adviser *or* 20 hours in a student organization and 20 hours of community service; job in a university office.
	Summer		Job or internship to develop sales, computer, and statistical or writing skills.
JUNIOR	Fall	One course requiring at least 20 pages of papers; one course requiring a team project; one course requiring application of basic statistics.	Leadership position at a student organization; management job position on or off campus.
	Spring	Off-campus semester.	Travel; immersion in another culture; community service.
	Summer		Competitive internship at a business, government, or nonprofit agency.
SENIOR	Fall	One course requiring at least 20 pages of papers; one course requiring a team project; one course requiring at least 20% fieldwork.	40 hours on job search *or* 20 hours on job search and 20 hours on graduate school search and test preparation.
	Spring	One course requiring at least 20 pages of papers; one course requiring an oral presentation.	Relaxation and implementation of career search plans; avoidance of senioritis.

This model curriculum will help you move to a KHS of 100. Note that the number of credit hours listed is half of the average 120 needed to graduate. The other 60 credit hours can be used to develop your other interests, to pick up more career-specific knowledge and skills, or to complete requirements that do not do much for a high KHS. It is always a good idea to pick up areas of knowledge and skill outside of the ten Know-How Groups, just as chapters 12 and 17 suggest. It may make you less boring, and it may even help you in your career.

USEFUL RESOURCES

College Rules! How to Study, Survive and Succeed in College by Sherrie Nist and Jodi Patrick Holschuh (Ten Speed Press, 2002). This book will help you think through how you can achieve your goals during college.

Instructions to the Cook: A Zen Master's Lessons on Living a Life That Matters by Bernard Glassman and Rick Fields (Harmony Books, 1997). This book is useful in thinking about choices you make in your life. A former engineer, turned Zen Buddhist, Glassman helps you set priorities in a meaningful way.

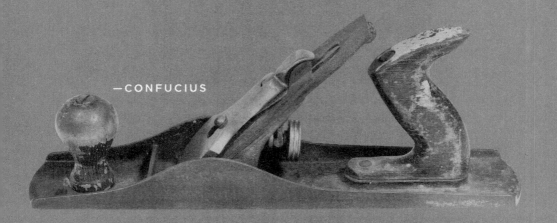

IF A TREE FALLS IN THE FOREST BUT NO ONE IS THERE TO HEAR IT, DOES IT MAKE A SOUND?

—CONFUCIUS

CHAPTER 19

MOVING TOWARD A PERFECT KHS RESUME, COVER LETTER, AND INTERVIEW

TOPICS

**SELECT THE SKILLS YOU WANT TO EMPHASIZE •
PRESENT EACH OF THE TEN KNOW-HOW GROUPS •
USE EXTRA CREDIT • CAPITALIZE ON WHAT YOU'VE LEARNED**

OK, nobody is perfect, and nobody reading this book is likely to earn a 100 KHS. But having a 100 KHS without making sure your potential future employers know it is like the proverbial tree falling in the forest. If you follow the guidelines in this chapter, you may not have a perfect KHS, but you will have a perfect resume, cover letter, and interview. Well, at least a near-perfect one!

The resume and cover letter need to clearly and powerfully demonstrate that you have a high KHS. Employers are looking for such resumes and cover letters, but they rarely find them. If you can create one that reflects even a decent KHS, you will be selected for an interview where you can close the deal.

Although this chapter focuses on communicating a high KHS, you will also need to communicate other things, including some knowledge of and experience with the field, and why you are interested in the job. However, your KHS is most important because, as discussed in the introduction and in chapter 16, employers like to train their new employees in the specifics of the field and job. Most companies see hiring "talented and hard-working people" as their top priority.

The importance of communicating a high KHS is also true for law, medical, and graduate school applications. Use your KHS as a base to write your advanced-degree applications.

This chapter is not a comprehensive primer on writing resumes and cover letters and performing well in interviews. Several outstanding books are available that will help you do that. My favorite resources appear at the end of this chapter. In addition, your college career service office will review and suggest revisions for your resume and cover letter, and provide practice interviewing.

Although you may be tempted to put off thinking about your resume, cover letter, and interview until you approach the end of your college career, think about it now. Hypothesizing what the end product will look like is a great way to figure out how to get there. Sure, the end product will change between now and when you finish college—it should!—but it will be much better than if you waited until your senior year to work on it. To illustrate, I tell my students to begin the process of writing a paper by writing the conclusion or summary first. It forces them to think about what they are trying to say and guides them to what they want to research and how they will organize their paper.

The same goes for developing a high KHS. If you construct a picture of the kind of resume, cover letter, and interview you want to provide when you graduate college, you will have a much better idea of what you are trying to do with your college education. You'll end up with an even better package than you initially planned to have. You've been working toward this all through college, so let those skills shine.

SELECT THE SKILLS YOU WANT TO EMPHASIZE

For any job sought by a college graduate, the standard is to meet the MSL for each of the thirty-eight skill sets. However, you cannot fit all thirty-eight into your resume, cover letter, and interview. Because you'll be competing against other job candidates for the very limited attention of those doing the hiring, be selective about which skill sets you present, and communicate your skills clearly *and* concisely. Think of yourself as a newspaper editor trying to entice the reader with what is both most important to the reader and true to the story.

In doing this, you will face tension between what you need to say to get the job and what you really want in your career beyond getting the job. To get the job, emphasize those skill sets that you think the employer is looking for. But what if you detest the idea of performing those skills for several years, if not a decade, until you are promoted? The job may be high paying, and you may have a good shot at it, but do not emphasize a skill set that will make you miserable.

If you have not attained the MSL for skill sets critical to the employer, should you still emphasize them anyway? You know the answer to that question. If not, check the second skill set in our chapter on Work Ethic. I raise the question here because job candidates do that all of the time. They lie about their skill levels. They make up bogus items on their resumes and even say they have college and graduate degrees they do not have. Don't do this, not because you will get caught in your interview and not because you will perform poorly in your job—don't do it because it is wrong.

So when you go after a job, be realistic about your options, especially if the economy is tanking, but think long and hard about what you are getting yourself into. Once you have decided to apply for a specific job opening or contact a group of organizations in a field of your choice, you're ready for the next phase of selecting the skills you want to emphasize.

You will need to do serious research. For a specific job, begin by carefully reading the job description and acquiring as much additional information as you can about the job. For a job search targeted at a group of employers, use the discussion in chapter 17 and especially an online service like eChoices to gain the information you need. If possible, conduct informational interviews about the general characteristics of the kind of position you are examining.

You should be in a position to conduct this research if you have met the MSL described in chapter 7 (Gathering Information). Don't ignore this phase in preparing your resume and cover letter. It will take time, but I find that those students who spend the time are rewarded with top-notch jobs.

Next, apply the information gained from your research to decide which skills you want to highlight. Sometimes the skill area will be obvious from the description. For example, for a sales position it might mention "working with people" or "problem-solving" for a consulting position.

At other times, the skill set might not be so obvious. The employer might be sensitive to recent events. After a series of high-profile cases of corporate corruption in 2002, the employer may be concerned about the integrity of whom they hire but not put it in the description. Or the employer might want someone for the short term who is proficient with Microsoft Excel or PowerPoint but would be afraid that emphasizing those skill areas might chase away potential applicants who eventually would develop into effective managers.

The following advice will help you think about what you want to put in your resume and cover letter and, even more important, how you want to present yourself if you get an interview. It provides a general overview. You will have to provide the specific words to show that you have a great KHS.

1. ESTABLISHING A WORK ETHIC

Every employer wants you to meet the MSL for this group, but you will have trouble directly demonstrating it in your cover letter and your resume. If you put it on paper, it might sound like you "protest too much." Your interview will be key because you will want to show both enthusiasm and focus.

On your resume or cover letter, there are a few ways you can convey your work ethic. For example, you can demonstrate that you have at least three of the four skill sets by writing on your resume "earned money to pay for (at least 50 percent) of my college education." Having paid a substantial part of your college costs yourself shows good self-motivation as well as time and money management. This suggestion puts students whose parents paid for their college at a disadvantage, but in this situation life is fair. Another way you can show you are a hard worker and good manager of time is to have a resume with a lot of academic and nonacademic activities. For example, your resume should show you worked or had an internship every summer and that you had two majors or at least a major and a minor. If you have a respectable GPA, the volume of activities will demonstrate that you can handle many tasks at once.

Finally, your GPA will be used to assess your work ethic. If you have above a 3.5, the employer will assume you do not have a problem with time management and self-motivation. Between a 3.0 and 3.5, the employer may have doubts. Below a 3.0 will raise major questions in the employer's mind. Therefore, mention your GPA if it is above a 3.0, but if below a 3.5 be prepared to present an explanation in the interview. For example, you might say, "I held two jobs" or "I decided my skills training was more important than my GPA." If you do not put your GPA on your resume, be ready for questions about it in the interview. These numbers apply to most majors except in engineering and the hard sciences. You can subtract .5 from the numbers cited above.

Honesty cannot be directly addressed in a resume or cover letter. Your interview is not likely to prove that you are an honest person, but it could raise fears about your being dishonest. If the interviewer smells something fishy when comparing what you wrote with what you say or catches you embellishing your skills too much in your resume, you can forget about the job.

2. DEVELOPING PHYSICAL SKILLS

Employers look for healthy people not only because they do not like absences but also because they want to keep their health-care costs down. These skill sets are so important but also so expected that they do not belong in the resume with the exception of typing. To suggest that you can type, you might say, "highly experienced at word processing" so that it would be assumed, or you could put your typing speed under the skill category if it is over 45 WPM. Your interview will take care of the skill sets "Stay Well" and "Look Good," assuming you are not hung over, do not have a cold, and pay attention to your clothes. Follow up your interview with a hand-written note if your handwriting is readable, and that will serve to convince the potential employer you take legible notes.

3. COMMUNICATE VERBALLY

Employers want their employees to be good communicators, which is frequently an unfulfilled desire. The most difficult of the three skill sets here is conversing one-on-one because it is easy to find training for the other two. Poor one-on-one communication can cost you the job more than anything else, and it depends on both your style of listening and speaking as well as that of the other person. Practice listening skills and follow the advice of Dale Carnegie in your interviews to minimize the chances that your interviewer will rate you as a poor communicator.

Your resume can take care of the use of visual displays by listing Microsoft PowerPoint as a skill and presenting a resume that is clear, concise, and attractive. The best way to illustrate that you are good at the first two on your resume and/or cover letter is to mention a significant team project or activity in your job, internship, or extracurricular activities. In your interview, bring up the project as an example of the value of good communications. You do not have to lie if the team did poorly because you can blame it on poor communications. If it did well, then there were obviously good communications. Either way, the interviewer will be happy to see that you understand that good communication is critical.

As far as presenting to groups goes, unless you have made formal presentations outside the classroom and gotten evidence of positive feedback, you will not be able to put it in your cover letter or resume. However, you may be asked to describe a successful presentation in your interview.

Overall, the interview itself will be most decisive for this Know-How group.

4. COMMUNICATING IN WRITING

Although not all jobs require writing reports or materials that will be broadly distributed, most require that you be able to put your thoughts onto paper or into email. With the growth of email (not only in one-on-one communications but also among groups of people), writing is more important than ever in the work world. A poorly written email on a company listserv could be catastrophic. For example, would you like to be the one who sent an email that the company is losing it credibility with the pubic when you meant "public?"

You can demonstrate solid writing ability by having a succinct cover letter and a clear resume. A single typo could cost you an interview, and two definitely will, so proof both several times. As far as the content of your cover letter and resume goes, highlight a job, internship, or a course in which you produced a written product. A report, newsletter, correspondence, or any other products of at least a full page in length will provide evidence of the first three skill sets. Having your resume online will be enough to convince your prospective employer you can use email beyond the norm.

5. WORKING DIRECTLY WITH PEOPLE

Every employer is very concerned about your ability to be a good coworker. The key here is to have several examples on your resume of your ability to work with others, which is also necessary to demonstrate solid verbal communication skills. They might include successful team projects, a part-time employer who kept you around for a long time, or being an elected officer in a student association (that includes Greek organizations). Being a resident adviser for a minimum of one full year is persuasive evidence because it means you made it through a rigorous selection process and stuck out a people-intensive experience. If you lasted only one semester, that may raise a red flag. Being a peer adviser or an undergraduate teaching assistant is also solid evidence of your people skills, including teaching.

6. INFLUENCING PEOPLE

Except for sales jobs, the skill sets in this group are not likely to be emphasized in job descriptions open to new college graduates. Politicking will actually be viewed as a negative unless you are going for a job in the political arena. However, all four skill sets will be in the back of the minds of most employers. If your cover letter and/or resume can cite a job you had in which you managed people or sold products, particularly over the telephone, you will convince employers not only that you can do well in those areas but also that you have leadership potential and political savvy. Having your resume describe some leadership position in student organizations would be good. Listing projects, either for credit or outside of class, in which you were the one responsible for initiating and completing the activity is also recommended. Winning awards for leadership within as well as outside the university will also help. A resident adviser's position will provide convincing evidence of your ability to influence people.

Your interview will also help. Frequently, questions are asked about your ability to lead or sell and sometimes manage. Your political sensitivity will be judged by how you answer questions. Take definitive positions on questions, but at the same time show sensitivity to different viewpoints. Good phrases to use in order to demonstrate good management and political skills during this phase of the interview are "finding compromises" and "building consensus." Use these phrases, if you can, to show that you have been able to help engineer a compromise or a consensus.

7. GATHERING INFORMATION

Different employers would value different skill sets in this group. Your resume and cover letter might be able to present the last three if you have completed a research project or worked on a job or internship in which surveys were used, interviews were conducted, or data was collected. You could list commercial databases you have worked with in the same line as you list computer software. As far as library holdings and searching the Web goes, showing that you have completed a major research project and produced a paper that has been recognized in some way could help. Talk about your information-gathering skills in your interview if you can discuss a project that you completed while in college.

8. USING QUANTITATIVE TOOLS

Every job requires some basic computational skills. As you move into management positions you will be faced with operating budgets, which require not only simple math but also spreadsheet capabilities. Most employers will assume that if you are a management, economics, or math major that you can perform these three skill sets. For most other majors, the subject may come up in the form of an arithmetic test or a question about your number skills. Put Microsoft Excel in your list of software on your resume right after Microsoft Word, assuming you have met the MSL for both of these. If you have worked with other quantitatively based programs like SPSS, mention those also. Although not only a quantitative tool, Microsoft Access skills are in high demand, so they should be listed if you have experience.

9. ASKING AND ANSWERING THE RIGHT QUESTIONS

All employers want their college hires to be able to think critically or be smart, which I have defined as the four skill sets in this group plus the problem-solving groups. To some extent, they might see a high GPA as evidence, but with grade inflation and experience over the years, they will never be convinced by that alone. This Know-How Group will be at the forefront of the interviewer's mind, and different employers have different ways of testing for it. Having typos in your resume or your cover letter, or lacking knowledge about the company interviewing and the job description will raise questions about attention to detail. Understanding the benefits package and asking an intelligent question will help the employer think you do pay attention to detail. Knowledge of the field and making statements showing you have done your homework about the company or organization will show you can apply knowledge. If you want to demonstrate evaluation competence, you should ask about the performance evaluation procedure used by the corporation. If you want to be proactive in your interview, ask how the mission statement (which you should have memorized) is related to the current plans of the corporation.

You may be able to refer to an internship or job in which you worked on a project that investigated a problem, evaluated a program or policy, or developed a plan. If that is the case, include it in your cover letter and resume. The interviewer will probably bring it up, but if not, you should. These kinds of projects are rare for undergraduates to complete, so you want to make sure your potential employer knows about them.

10. SOLVING PROBLEMS

Employers also want their employees to be problem solvers, which is frequently included in their definition of thinking critically and being smart. You may be able to show in your resume or cover letter that you have experience solving problems through a job, internship, or course work. Also, having spent a couple of semesters off campus and at least one overseas will help convince future employers that you are a problem solver. Off-campus semester experiences should be prominent in your resume and cover letter.

The interview will be important in helping the employer evaluate your capacity to identify and solve specific problems that you may confront in your job. Employers may give "tests" or set up situations to test your problem-solving ability. To prepare for this, think about the major problems that you might face in your job. You might also discuss the major problems that your organization might face. Typical problems are how to reduce costs, how to increase sales, membership, or number of clients, how to retain workers, how to improve the organization's public image, how to promote honesty, and how to increase cooperation among employees.

USE EXTRA CREDIT

Part One introduced the idea of extra credit that goes beyond the basic ten Know-How Groups. Deciding which of these, if any, to emphasize on your resume and cover letter and in your interview requires that you go through the same research and selection process as you do for the basic ten. It will depend on the kind of job you are seeking. In most cases, you do not want to use a lot of space in your resume and cover letter or time in your interview for any of these. For that reason, I will discuss them very briefly.

GAIN SOFTWARE EXPERTISE BEYOND MICROSOFT WORD AND EXCEL

List under the software experience section on your resume specific software programs and programming language you can use. If you have some real expertise demonstrated by a job or project you completed, insert the name of the software into the description. "Real expertise" means that you have had experience beyond course work. You may get questions and if you cannot demonstrate competence and experience, the interview will crash.

MASTER IN-DEPTH KNOWLEDGE OF ANY FIELD

If you have in-depth knowledge in a field like management or communications, it should be prominently shown on your resume and mentioned in your cover letter. If you are in a liberal arts program, the major is not important in most cases. Most companies that hire liberal arts graduates will say they do not care about the field. However, companies in some fields favor certain majors. Pharmaceutical companies will tilt toward science majors, while publishing companies will tilt toward English majors. It should be pretty easy to figure out. If there is a tilt and you have the right major, emphasize it. If not, a simple mention of your major will suffice. If asked why you selected that major, it's OK to say you selected it because you have always been interested in it or that you had a stimulating introductory course. If it makes sense, show how your major also helped you develop some of the essential skills.

ACCENT FOREIGN LANGUAGE SKILLS

Unless you are very proficient in a foreign language, this skill area requires only a mention as a major or minor. It will help make you look open-minded and cultured. However, if you can translate and/or speak a foreign language fluently, this could be a big selling point. Knowing Spanish fluently is an important selling point in areas that have a large Spanish-speaking population. Show you have lived in the country where the language is spoken and, if possible, present a project in which you used your language skills.

EMPHASIZE ARTISTIC AND MUSIC KNOWLEDGE AND/OR SKILL

Unless you are going into an artistic or musical field directly related to the job, mention this under the hobbies or personal information section of your resume. Definitely put it in if you can demonstrate your interest or skills persuasively and quickly, because you never know if the interviewer will decide to start a conversation about it.

STRESS SPORTS SKILLS

This area can be mentioned like the one above, but you may want to be careful. If it is golf or tennis, and you are good at it, put it in. If it is any other sport, mention it if you played it at the intercollegiate level, even as a walk-on or for one year. Going to sports bars does not count. Being a crazy fan of your college team may help if an alumnus interviews you.

PURSUE PLEASURE ACTIVITIES

Unless directly related to the field, this belongs under hobbies or personal information. Like the previous two extra-credit categories, your interviewer may find it interesting. Taking a wine-tasting course or being a microbrewery expert should not be included. Alcoholism is a big problem in the world of work as it is throughout the rest of society. Remember, employers are worried about both your work ethic and their health-care costs.

CAPITALIZE ON WHAT YOU'VE LEARNED

Two very important lessons can be learned from the previous discussion about how you can guarantee a high KHS by the time you graduate. The first is that the interview is critical to ensuring that potential employers will understand that you have a high KHS. The resume and cover letter are like the headline and opening paragraph of a newspaper article, while the interview process is like the rest of the story. It provides information on the skill sets that cannot be easily mentioned in the resume and cover letter. It also provides added depth to those that can be mentioned.

The following table provides a list of those skill sets that should be placed in your resume and cover letter and those that you will have to cover in your interview.

USING YOUR RESUME AND YOUR INTERVIEW TO SHOW OFF YOUR HIGH KHS		
Know-How Group	**Skill Sets to Show on Resume**	**Skill Sets to Demonstrate in Interview**
1. Establishing a Work Ethic	Kick Yourself in the Butt (list high GPA and quantity of activities), Manage Your Time (same as above)	Be Honest
2. Developing Physical Skills	Type 35 WPM Error Free (list only if you type at least 45 WPM)	Stay Well, Look Good
3. Communicating Verbally	Use Visual Displays (list PowerPoint as a skill; create a visually appealing resume)	Converse One-On-One, Present to Groups
4. Communicating in Writing	Write Well (list internship or job in which you wrote a lot), Edit and Proof (make sure there are no mistakes in resume or cover letter)	
5. Working Directly with People	Teach Others (list positions as teaching assistant or substitute teacher in a high school)	
6. Influencing People	Manage Efficiently (list job or internship), Sell Successfully (list sales job), Lead Effectively (list leadership awards and positions with student organizations)	Politick Wisely
7. Gathering Information	Use Commercial Databases (list as a skill), Conduct Interviews (list a research project), Use Surveys (same as above), Keep and Use Records (same as above)	
8. Using Quantitative Tools	Use Spreadsheet Programs (list specific programs)	
9. Asking and Answering the Right Questions	Pay Attention to Detail (make sure there are no mistakes in resume or cover letter)	Apply Knowledge, Evaluate Actions and Policies
10. Solving Problems		Identify Problems, Develop Solutions, Launch Solutions

As the table indicates, your resume and cover letter play a major role in less than half of the thirty-eight skill sets. Some aspects of work ethic, verbal communications, working with and influencing people as well as quantitative tools, asking and answering the right questions, and problem solving will have to be demonstrated in the interview. This means that you need to have genuine experiences to talk about in the interview, which leads to our second and related lesson from the previous discussion.

Your non-course activities are more important than your course work for landing a good job. You will notice that mentioning majors and course work is not emphasized while presenting your experiences outside of the classroom is. This is not because the course work is unimportant. Rather, it is because employers want to see that you have applied what you have learned in class to what you can do. Technical majors like accounting or graphic design in professional schools or the physical sciences in liberal arts can be critical, but for the majority of fields and jobs, the degree and the courses are not as important as demonstrating your skills.

Usually those jobs requiring technical majors clearly indicate that in the advertisements. For the majority of jobs, employers want the skills that are part of the Know-How Groups. If you use a lot of space in your resume and your cover letter or time in your interview to describe your major, you will reduce your chances of success. In your interview, however, you may be able to talk about how some great courses and your major specifically prepared you for this job.

Having warned you about overemphasizing your academic program and courses does not mean you cannot introduce some information. However, be strategic about it. For example, you could talk about taking a speech course because you know how important it is to speak to groups effectively, or you could discuss a conflict resolution course in which you picked up specific techniques on how to defuse a tense situation. You could talk about a course in writing in which you wrote grants for a nonprofit agency. You can indicate that your history classes were great because you really learned your way around the library, and you wrote long papers that your professor tore apart. This point is to show at least that the courses you took demonstrated your commitment to improving a specific skill set.

The two lessons say a lot about how you can graduate with a high KHS. Always think of the interconnections between what you do in your college years and what you will be saying in your resume, cover letter, and interview that you want to have when you enter the job market. Once you see these interconnections, you will realize that your KHS is more important than your GPA in getting a great first job and having a wonderful career. Pursue the strategies for boosting your KHS presented in chapters 12 through 16, and use the information about professions and the planning tools presented in chapters 17 and 18.

Whether you use the formal planning tools in chapter 18 or just keep your KHS in mind when you are making decisions about your future, you should have a clear picture of how your college years can be used to develop the skills you need for a successful career. Do not be overwhelmed by the size and complexity of the task. Once you get started, it will actually save you time and improve your performance during college. In any case, you will have a very bright career future if you are savvy about skills in your college education.

USEFUL RESOURCES

Dynamic Cover Letters for New Graduates by Katharine Hansen (Ten Speed Press, 2002). Provides sample cover letters for a variety of careers. The sections on emphasizing transferable skills and work experience will put your high KHS in the spotlight.

A Foot in the Door: Networking Your Way into the Hidden Job Market! by Katharine Hansen (Ten Speed Press, 2000). Important advice on informational interviewing and building contacts to find where the jobs are.

The Overnight Resume: The Fastest Way to Your Next Job! by Donald Asher (Ten Speed Press, 1999). Solid advice on creating resumes and how to use the Internet to send them.

Quintessential Careers (www.QuintCareers.com). Comprehensive place for you to train yourself in the various tasks required to mount a successful job search. The career test and quizzes section can help you evaluate such skills as preparing cover letters and resumes, and job-hunting etiquette. The site links to free and fee-based services.

What Color Is Your Parachute? A Practical Manual for Job-Hunters & Career-Changers by Richard N. Bolles (Ten Speed Press, most recent edition). Covers the entire range of topics on landing a job suited to you.

ENDNOTES

INTRODUCTION

1. Estimated full-time year-round work for 1997 to 1999 according to the U.S. Census Bureau, *Current Population Surveys,* March 1998, March 1999, and March 2000.

2. U.S. Department of Education, *Descriptive Summary of 1995–1996 Beginning Postsecondary Students: Six Years Later,* 2002.

3. U.S. Department of Education, National Center for Education Statistics, *1999–2000 National Postsecondary Student Aid Study,* 2000.

4. Peg Tyre, Karen Springen, and Julie Scelfo, "Bringing Up Adultolescents," *Newsweek* (March 15, 2002): 34.

5. Reprinted from *Job Outlook 2002,* by permission of the National Association of Colleges and Employers.

6. Kate Zernike, "Tests Are Not Just for Kids: Accountability Hits Higher Education, Education Life," *New York Times* (August 4, 2002): A4.

CHAPTER 1

1. D. P. Beach, "A Training Program to Improve Work Habits, Attitudes and Values." *Journal of Epsilon Pi Tau* (August 2, 1982): 69.

2. David Glenn, "Procrastination in College Students Is a Marker for Unhealthy Behaviors, Study Indicates," *The Chronicle of High Education* (August 26, 2002), available at http://chronicle.com/daily/2002/08/2002082602n.htm.

CHAPTER 2

1. Bejamin Franklin, "Silence Dogood, No. 4 on Higher Learning," *Benjamin Franklin on Education,* edited by John Hardin Best (New York: Columbia University Teachers College, 1961), 34.

CHAPTER 4

1. William Strunk, Jr., and E. B. White, *The Elements of Style* (Boston: Allyn & Bacon, 1999), 23.

CHAPTER 5

1. Dale Carnegie, *How to Win Friends and Influence People* (New York: Pocket Books, 1982), xiv.

2. David A. Goldsmith, *The MetaManagement Communicator Issue* (September 2002), available at http://metamatrixconsulting.com/newsletters/newsS36_Sep_2002a.htm.

CHAPTER 7

1. Richard N. Bolles, *What Color Is Your Parachute? 2002: A Practical Manual for Job-Hunters and Career-Changers* (Berkeley: Ten Speed Press, 2002), 27.

2. Frank Bettger, *How I Raised Myself from Failure to Success in Selling* (New York: Simon & Schuster, 1977), 18.

CHAPTER 9

1. Catherine Smith, email to author (June 23, 2002).

CHAPTER 11

1. Edward B. Fiske and Bruce Hammond, *The Fiske Guide to Getting into the Right College 2002,* (Naperville, IL: Sourcebooks, 2002), 7.

CHAPTER 12   1. Dave Moniz, "In Quest for Workers, Firms Search Ranks of U.S. Military," *Christian Science Monitor* (August 26, 1999), available at www.csmonitor.com/durable/1999/08/26/fp2s2-csm.shtml.

CHAPTER 14   1. Megan Rooney, "Keeping the Study in Study Abroad," *The Chronicle of Higher Education* (November 22, 2002), A63–64).

CHAPTER 15   1. William D. Coplin, *How You Can Help: An Easy Guide to Doing Good Deeds in Your Every Day Life* (New York: Routledge, 2000), 83.

CHAPTER 16   1. Randall Collins, "The Dirty Little Secrets of Credential Inflation!" *Chronicle of Higher Education* (September 27, 2002): sec. 2, B20.

2. Jeffrey Pfeffer and Christina T. Fong, "The End of Business Schools? Less Success than Meets the Eye," *Academy of Management Learning and Education*, vol. 1, issue 1 (September 2002).

CHAPTER 17   1. Reproduced by permission of Bridges.com—North America's leading provider of career and educational planning solutions. Copyright © 2003 Bridges.com Inc. All rights reserved.

2. Ibid.

3. Ibid.

4. Ibid.

CHAPTER 18   1. Jeffrey Young, "Homework? What Homework?" *Chronicle of Higher Education* (December 6, 2002): A35.

Adams, Henry, 58
adaptability, 97, 100–101
alcohol, 22, 23, 249
Alpha Phi Omega, 135
America's Best Colleges (USN&WR), 137–38
AmeriCorps, 201
analytical skills. *See* questions,
   asking/answering the right
appearance, 24–26
apprentice-based experience
   importance to employers, 153–55
   opportunities for, 155–57
   See also internships
Aristotle, 153, 154
artistic knowledge/skill, 121, 249
AT&T Finance Summer Internship
   Program, 158

Bacon, Francis, 99
Beach, D. P., 9
Bettger, Frank, 11, 82
Blair, Louis, 102–3, 171
Blake, William, 97
Bolles, Richard N., 78
BS detection, 94–96, 107
budgets, 18

Campus Compact, 134
career decisions, 207–19
   finding skills for, 215–17
   identifying interests, 208–9
   KHS and, 207, 217–18
   resources for, 219
   scanning professions, 212–15
   self-reflection process, 209–12
   volunteering and, 191–92
Career Triangle/Career Field
   Explorer, 209–12
Carleton University, 15
Carnegie, Dale, 53
Cervantes, Miguel de, 13
cheating, 14
Christian Science Monitor, 136
Chronicle of Higher Education, 196
CIA Internship Program, 158
Cleaver, Eldridge, 113
clothing, 25–26

college
   advantages/disadvantages of, 1–2
   career services at, 132–33, 166
   choosing, 129–38
   class attendance in, 16
   committee membership in, 57, 68
   computer facilities at, 133–34
   connections made at, 147–50
   course selection in, 142–47
   nontraditional options for, 137
   program choice in, 139–42
   rankings of, 137–38
   resources for, 123–24, 132, 150–51
   ROTC programs at, 135, 201
   service programs at, 134–35
   taking advantage of, 2–4
Collins, Randall, 196
communication skills, 31–39, 56, 107
   courses for, 33, 36, 38
   importance to employers, 2–3
   minimum skill level (MSL) for, 34, 36, 38
   non-course activities for, 33, 36, 38
   off-campus programs and, 176
   one-on-one conversations, 32–34, 119
   presentations, 34–36
   resources for, 38–39
   in resume/cover letter/interview, 243–44
   and teaching skills, 58
   visual displays, 37–38
   See also interpersonal skills; writing skills
computer skills
   and college choice, 133–34
   electronic information delivery, 48–50
   software expertise, 118–19, 248
   spreadsheet skills, 4, 89–91
   web design skills, 48–49, 118
   web-search skills, 77–79
   word-processing skills, 4, 26, 46–47
conflict, 54
connections
   at college, 147–50
   during internships, 170–71
   during volunteer work, 191
consulting companies, jobs at, 197
continuous improvement, 103–4, 107, 195
continuous learning, 99, 100–101
conversations, one-on-one, 32–34, 119
corporate jobs, 199–200
corruption, 67

courses
   time spent on KHS in, 223–26
   See also specific skill group
cover letters. *See* resumes/cover letters
creative process, 112
credit
   extra, 117
   for off-campus programs, 135, 181–83
credit cards, 18
critical thinking. *See* questions,
   asking/answering the right

Dale Carnegie Institute, 35, 137
databases, 76–77
deadlines, missing, 16
debt, 1–2, 18
decision-making, 127–28
DeLancey, Blaine, 95
DeRosa, Gina
   plan for raising KHS, 228–35
   time spent on KHS in courses, 223–26
   time spent on KHS in non-course
     activities, 226–28
destructive behavior, 23–24
detail, paying attention to, 97–98, 107
Dialog@Carl, 77
diet, 23
Don Quixote (Cervantes), 13

eChoices, 212, 215–17
editing, of writing, 44–45, 56
electronic information delivery, 48–50
email, 48, 49–50, 56
energy/passion/self-confidence.
   See self-motivation
enthusiasm. *See* self-motivation
evaluation skills, 102–4, 107
exercise, 23

faculty
   connections with, 147–49
   KHS-friendly, 144–47
fieldwork, 33, 55
FirstSearch, 77
Fong, Christina, 196
foreign language skills, 120, 178, 248
Franklin, Benjamin, 24–25, 154
fraternities, 57
   service, 135

Gates, Bill, 46
General Electric Financial Management
   Program (FMP), 196, 199
General Motors Intern Program, 158
Goldsmith, David, 56

golf, 121
GPA
   importance to employers, 2–4, 242
   and scholarships, 199
grade inflation, 117
graduate school, 196–99
graduation requirements, 143–44
graphs, using, 88
group presentations. *See* presentations

Habitat for Humanity, 135
health, 22–24
honesty, 13–14, 56
   importance to employers, 2–3, 243
*How I Raised Myself from Failure to
   Success in Selling* (Bettger), 11

Iacocca, Lee, 111
influencing people, 61–71
   courses for, 63, 65, 68, 70
   leadership skills, 69–70
   management skills, 62–63
   minimum skill level (MSL) for, 63, 65,
     68, 70
   non-course activities for, 63, 65, 68, 70
   political skills, 66–68
   resources for, 70–71
   in resume/cover letter/interview, 245
   sales skills, 63–65
information gathering, 73–83, 107
   courses for, 75, 76, 78, 80, 81, 83
   databases, 76–77
   importance to employers, 73–74
   interviews, 79–80
   libraries, 74–75
   minimum skill level (MSL) for, 75, 77, 79,
     80, 82, 83
   non-course activities for, 75, 77, 78–79,
     80, 81, 83
   record keeping, 82–83
   resources for, 83
   in resume/cover letter/interview, 245–46
   surveys, 81–82
   web-search skills, 77–79
Instant Messaging, 48, 49–50
Institute for International Education, 178
integrity, cultivating, 193
Internet, 48
   internship opportunities on, 165–66
   searching skills on, 77–79
internships, 17, 43, 68, 79
   advantages of, 156
   building experience base for, 157–63
   and college choice, 134
   landing, 164–69

at nonprofit organizations, 190, 191–92
opportunities for, 158
resources for, 172–73
taking advantage of, 169–71
interpersonal skills, 53–59, 107
courses for, 55, 57, 59
importance to employers, 2–3, 53
minimum skill level (MSL) for, 55, 57, 59
non-course activities for, 55, 57, 59
off-campus programs and, 176
relationship building, 54–55, 56
resources for, 59
in resume/cover letter/interview, 244–45
teaching skills, 58–59
teamwork, 55–57
See also influencing people
interviews
and alcohol, 22, 249
asking right questions during, 246–47
conducting, 79–80
informational, 217
and management skills, 62
and problem-solving skills, 113
and teamwork skills, 57
introductory skill courses, 144

job-hunting, on Internet, 78
Johnson and Johnson, 199

Know-How Groups, 5
in resume/cover letter/interview, 242–47
See also specific skill group
Know-How Score (KHS)
apprentice-based experience and, 153–55
blank forms for, 6, 223, 235
career decisions and, 207, 217–18
choices and boosting, 127–29
college choice and, 129–38
connections and, 147–50
course selection and, 142–47
extra credit for, 117–24, 247–49
importance to employers, 5–6
model curriculum for, 235–37
off-campus programs and, 175–77
plan for raising, 228–35
postgraduate, 201–2
program choice and, 139–42
resources for, 237, 252
in resume/cover letter/interview, 249–52
time spent on building, 222–28
volunteering and, 189–90
knowledge
applying, 99–102, 107
artistic/musical, 121, 249
in-depth, 119–20, 248

law school, 197–98
leadership skills, 69–70
Lexis-Nexis, 76, 77
liberal arts vs. professional programs,
139–42
libraries, 74–75
Lincoln Financial Group, 199
Lockheed Martin, 199
lying, 13, 14

management skills, 62–63
See also money management;
time management
Master's of Business Administration (MBA),
196, 198
Master's of Public Administration (MPA), 198
McLuhan, Marshall, 48
Mencken, H. L., 94–95
Microsoft
internship program at, 158
Microsoft Access, 76, 89
Microsoft Excel, 89–90
Microsoft FrontPage, 118
Microsoft Office User Specialization
certificate program, 137
Microsoft Outlook, 50
Microsoft Word, 46–47
military, as postgraduate alternative, 201
misspellings, 45
money management, 17–19
Moniz, Dave, 136
Mother Teresa, 189
multi-tasking, 15
music knowledge/skill, 121, 249

National Association of Colleges and
Employers (NACE), 2–3
National Survey of Student Engagement, 138
networking. See connections
New York Times, 4
Niebuhr, Reinhold, 53
non-course activities
time spent on KHS in, 226–28
See also specific skill group
nonprofit organizations, 190, 191–92
nontraditional learning, 137
Northeastern University, 134
note taking, 28–29
numbers, using, 86–87

observations, 33
off-campus programs
credit for, 135, 181–83
disadvantages of, 183–84
importance to employers, 175–77

off-campus programs, *cont'd*
  overseas vs. North American, 177–81
  resources for, 187
  searching for, 185–86
overcommitment, 159
overseas experiences, value of, 179–80

part-time jobs, 17, 43, 59, 157
passion. *See* self-motivation
Peace Corps, 201
people skills. *See* interpersonal skills
performance reviews, 103–4
Pfeffer, Jeffrey, 196
physical skills, 21–29
  appearance, 24–26
  courses for, 23, 25, 27, 29
  health, 22–24
  minimum skill level (MSL) for, 24, 26,
    27, 29
  non-course activities for, 23–24, 25–26,
    27, 29
  note taking, 28–29
  off-campus programs and, 176
  resources for, 29
  in resume/cover letter/interview, 243
  typing skills, 26–27, 29
planners, 16
Plato, 66
pleasure activities, 122–23, 249
political skills, 66–68
postgraduation alternatives, 195–203
  corporate jobs, 199–200
  graduate school, 196–99
  resources for, 202–3
  and skill development, 195, 201–2
PowerPoint, 37–38
presentations, 34–36
  PowerPoint, 37–38
  video playback of, 33
problem-solving skills, 107–15
  courses for, 109, 111, 114
  importance to employers, 107–8
  minimum skill level (MSL) for, 110,
    111, 114
  non-course activities for, 110, 111, 114
  off-campus programs and, 176
  resources for, 70–71, 114–15
  in resume/cover letter/interview, 247
  See also leadership skills
procrastination, 15
professional development, 201–2
professional programs vs. liberal arts,
  139–42

professions
  identifying interests, 208–9
  scanning, 212–15
  See also career decisions
proofreading, 44–45, 56
ProQuest, 76, 77
public-speaking habits, 35–36

quantitative skills, 85–91
  courses for, 87, 88, 90
  graphs/tables, 88
  minimum skill level (MSL) for, 87, 88, 91
  non-course activities for, 87, 88, 90
  numbers, 86–87
  off-campus programs and, 176
  resources for, 91
  in resume/cover letter/interview, 246
  spreadsheet skills, 4, 89–91
questions, asking/answering the right,
  93–105, 107
  attention to detail, 97–98
  BS detection, 94–96
  courses for, 96, 98, 101, 104
  evaluation skills, 102–4
  importance to employers, 93–94
  knowledge, applying, 99–102
  minimum skill level (MSL) for, 96, 99,
    102, 104
  non-course activities for, 96, 99, 101–2,
    104
  off-campus programs and, 176
  resources for, 105
  in resume/cover letter/interview, 246–47
  teaching skills and, 58

reading around/between the lines, 98
record keeping, 82–83
relationship building, 54–55, 56
research skills. *See* information gathering
Reserve Officer Training Corps (ROTC),
  136, 201
residence halls
  communication skills in, 34
  political skills in, 68
  wellness floors in, 23
resumes/cover letters
  electronic delivery of, 50
  for internships/summer jobs, 167–69
  KHS extra credit in, 247–49
  skills emphasized in, 240–47, 249–52
Rochester Institute of Technology, 134
Rockefeller, John D., 53
role playing, 55

sales skills, 63–65
scholarships, 199
scientific method, 100
Seinfeld, Jerry, 26
self-confidence. *See* self-motivation
self-motivation, 10–12, 170
self-reflection process, 209–12
Semester at Sea Program (University
   of Pittsburgh), 179–80
service programs, 134–35
skills
   importance to employers, 2–4
   See also Know-How Groups; Know-How
   Score (KHS); specific skill group
smoking, 24
social interaction, 25–26
software expertise, 118–19, 248
sororities, 57
sport skills, 121–22, 249
spreadsheet skills, 4, 89–91
study skills, 16
summer jobs, 164–69
surveys, using, 81–82

tables, using, 88
Teach for America, 201
teaching assistantships, 59
teaching skills, 58–59
teamwork, 55–57
   and communication skills, 33
   importance to employers, 2–3
teleconferencing, 48
temp firms, 26–27, 89
   for internships/summer jobs, 169
   as postgraduate alternative, 199–200
tennis, 121
time management, 15–16, 17, 44, 56
tracking (word-processing skill), 46, 47
tutoring, 59
typing skills, 26–27, 29

universities vs. colleges, 131
University of Virginia, 14
U.S. News & World Report, 137–38

verbal communication
   See communication skills
visual displays, 37–38
volunteer work, 189–93, 201

Washington, George, 10
web design skills, 48–49, 118
web-search skills, 77–79
What Color Is Your Parachute? (Bolles), 78
word-processing skills, 4, 26, 46–47
work ethic, 9–19
   courses for, 12, 14, 16, 18
   honesty, 13–14
   importance to employers, 2–3
   minimum skill level (MSL) for, 12, 14,
      16, 19
   money management, 17–19
   non-course activities for, 12, 14, 16, 18–19
   off-campus programs and, 176
   resources for, 19
   in resume/cover letter/interview, 242–43
   self-motivation, 10–12
   time management, 15–16, 17, 44
writer's block/diarrhea, 42
writing skills, 41–51
   courses for, 43, 45, 47, 49
   developing, 42–44
   editing/proofreading, 44–45, 56
   electronic information delivery, 48–50
   minimum skill level (MSL) for, 44, 45,
      47, 50
   non-course activities for, 43, 45, 47, 49–50
   resources for, 50–51
   in resume/cover letter/interview, 244
   word-processing skills, 46–47

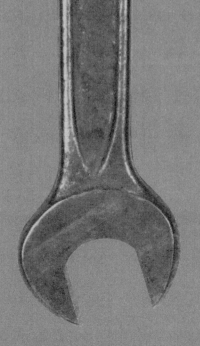

FOR TOOLS AND FORMS TO HELP BUILD YOUR OWN KNOW-HOW SCORE, VISIT WWW.TENSPEED.COM AND SEARCH FOR "10 THINGS."